Atop the Urban Hierarchy

Atop the Urban Hierarchy

Edited by

Robert A. Beauregard

Rowman & Littlefield Publishers, Inc.

ROWMAN & LITTLEFIELD PUBLISHERS, INC.

Published in the United States of America in 1989.
by Rowman & Littlefield Publishers, Inc.
81 Adams Drive, Totowa, New Jersey 07512

Library of Congress Cataloging-in-Publication Data

Atop the urban hierarchy / edited by Robert A. Beauregard.
  p.   cm.
  Bibliography: p.
  Includes index.
  1. Cities and towns- –United States- –Growth- –Case studies.
2. United States- –Economic conditions- –1945-   3. United States-
–Industries- –Location- –Case studies. I. Beauregard, Robert A.
HT384.U5A88   1988   88–18467 CIP
330.973'092'0917- –dc19
ISBN 0–8476–7554–8

5   4   3   2   1

Printed in the United States of America

Contents

Tables   vii

Figures   ix

Acknowledgments   xi

Preface   xiii

Chapter 1   Postwar Spatial Transformations   1
Robert A. Beauregard

Chapter 2   Economic Shifts and Land Use in the Global City: New York, 1940–1987   45
Norman I. Fainstein, Susan S. Fainstein, and Alex Schwartz

Chapter 3   Urban Restructuring: An Analysis of Social and Spatial Change in Los Angeles   87
Edward Soja, Rebecca Morales, and Goetz Wolff

Chapter 4   Planning for Chicago: The Changing Politics of Metropolitan Growth and Neighborhood Development   123
Marc A. Weiss and John T. Metzger

Chapter 5   Houston: Hyperdevelopment in the Sunbelt   153
Joe R. Feagin and Robert A. Beauregard

Chapter 6   The Spatial Transformation of Postwar Philadelphia   195
Robert A. Beauregard

Chapter 7   Urban Restructuring in Comparative Perspective   239
Robert A. Beauregard

CONTENTS

Bibliography   275

Index   295

Contributors   303

Tables

1.1 Top Ten Manufacturing Industries by Value-Added, 1921–1985   13

1.2 Employment Shares in Nonagricultural Industries for the United States, 1950–1984   31

2.1 New York City Population (in thousands), 1940–1984   47

2.2 New Dwelling Units Completed, 1921–1983   49

3.1 Employment Change in the Aerospace/Electronics Industries   98

4.1 Population and Manufacturing Employment in the Chicago SMSA, 1940–1982   132

4.2 Employment Shares by Industry in the Chicago SMSA, 1950–1980   133

4.3 Completed Commercial and Residential Projects and Annual Investment in Downtown Chicago, 1979–1984   136

4.4 Location of Manufacturing Employment in Cook County, 1972–1983   141

5.1 Selected Characteristics: City and Metropolitan Area, 1940–1980   162

5.2 Top Manufacturing Industries, 1947, 1967, and 1982   165

5.3 Resident Occupational Distributions, City of Houston, 1940–1980   168

5.4 Resident Employment Shares by Nonagricultural Industry, City of Houston, 1940–1980   170

6.1 Employment Shares by Industry, City of Philadelphia, 1940–1980   202

viii

6.2 Employment Shares by Occupation, City of Philadelphia, 1940–1980   203

6.3 Selected Characteristics for Three Periods in Philadelphia's Postwar Development   218

7.1 Absolute Change in Nonagricultural Resident Employment, 1950–1980   246

7.2 Selected Development Characteristics for the Five Cities and Metropolitan Areas   260

Figures

1.1 Value of New Construction in Place, United States, 1915–1985   6

1.2 Population Trends for the Five Cities, 1790–1984   17

1.3 Total New Housing Units, United States, 1920–1985   37

2.1 Map of the City of New York   46

2.2 Annual Office Space Construction, Manhattan, 1947–1986   48

2.3 New York City Employment by Industry, 1950–1985   50

2.4 Occupation of Employed Residents by Borough, 1950 and 1980   70

2.5 Total Assessed Valuation of Taxable Real Property: New York City, Manhattan and Outer Boroughs, 1963–1986 ($ 1983)   71

3.1 Changes in Sectoral Employment, 1960–1979   95

3.2 Location of Electronics Component Plants, 1981   101

3.3 Plant Closings and Major Layoffs, 1978–1982   105

3.4 Distribution of Major Ethnic Groups, 1980   109

3.5 Corporate and Banking Headquarters in the Los Angeles Region   113

4.1 Geographic Districts of Cook County   130

4.2 Chicago Standard Metropolitan Statistical Area (SMSA)   149

5.1 Map of the Houston Region   156

5.2 Major Existing and Developing Office Activity Centers   176

6.1 City Hall and the Statue of William Penn   196

6.2 Map of the City of Philadelphia   201

6.3   Postwar Development Projects, Gentrifying
      Neighborhoods, and Selected Places of Significance   206
7.1   Zone of Transition to Zone of Reinvestment   255

Acknowledgments

The roots of this volume can be traced to a panel on industrial and spatial restructuring held at the 1985 annual meetings of the Association of Collegiate Schools of Planning in Atlanta. Through Susan Fainstein's efforts, papers were presented on New York, Los Angeles, Chicago, and Philadelphia. The panel was enthusiastically received and many people commented to me about the possibility of reproducing the papers in a single work. Eugenie Birch of Hunter College, however, made the suggestion at the most propitious moment, inciting me to pursue the idea of publication with Susan Fainstein who then graciously granted to me her 'rights' over the panel. Paul Lee at Rowman & Littlefield provided support at another important juncture. Mary Simmons and Janet S. Johnston assisted patiently with the editorial process. Brenda Leonard cheerfully retyped Chapter 3, and the Department of Urban Planning and Policy Development at Rutgers University provided a range of useful and essential services. Finally, of course, there is the general support given by both valued colleagues and personal loves. Naming them would only embarass us all.

Preface

At the turn of the century, New York and Chicago were experiencing unprecedented growth and Philadelphia was a robust industrial center. Los Angeles and Houston were barely visible on the urban landscape. In the cities of the Northeast and Midwest, manufacturing, trade, and finance fueled the expansion of population and the investment in factories, tenements, railroad stations and infrastructure. Prosperity was the norm, and the problems with working-class slums, contagious diseases, and labor unrest promised to be soluble in the context of an ever-expanding economy.

By the 1970s, prosperity had been spatially rearranged. While Los Angeles and Houston enjoyed a rapid expansion of population and industry and benefited from major investments in new construction, New York, Chicago, and Philadelphia faced population loss, continued erosion of their manufacturing, and local governmental fiscal crises. No longer were machinery, automobile assembly, and steel the industries driving the national economy. Aerospace, oil exploration, computers, and defense had become the growth sectors, and the West and South became thriving regional economies. As migrants rushed to these regions in search of employment and the "good life," the cities underwent extraordinary physical expansions. The cities of the Northeast and Midwest, on the other hand, faced decline, disinvestment, the spread of slums, and political and economic isolation from surrounding municipalities.

Any historical analysis of the uneven development of cities within the United States must recognize these links between national and regional economies and the speed and direction of population change, physical expansion, and transformation of the built environment. Textile factories were established in the early 1800s, and around them row after row of worker housing was arrayed. As the factories began to close in the 1940s, adjacent housing deteriorated

xiii

and the neighborhoods eventually became blighted and spotted with abandoned structures. Airplane assembly plants were established on the West Coast during World War II, and suburban tract housing spread as developers responded to workers' demands for residences close to, yet separate from, the workplace.

Even though such examples of the spatiality of the economy are innumerable, they can easily become simplifications. Histories of company towns such as Gary, Indiana, frequently demonstrate a strong connection between the local industry and the structuring of the surrounding environment (Beauregard and Holcomb 1979). For large cities on the order of New York and Los Angeles, however, not to mention smaller places such as Pawtucket, Rhode Island, the spatial consequences of economic growth and change are not so easily traced to the built environment. Economic forces are intertwined with social relations, political activities, cultural dispositions, environmental constraints, and symbolic sensitivities. The particularities of place, moreover, are all-important. Articulating the paths along which these forces travel is not so easily accomplished. What seems to be contextual, and thus structural—that is, the growth and sectoral restructuring of the economy—plays itself out on a field of contingencies.

Consequently, one overgeneralizes if one characterizes the period following World War II as a period in which large, older manufacturing cities declined as their manufacturing base eroded, and cities positioned to take advantage of high-technology, service, energy, and administrative functions grew. Neither is allusion to a manufacturing-service shift, a central city-suburban reversal, or a Snowbelt-Sunbelt migration an accurate explanation of the historical diversity of economic restructuring and spatial transformations. One should not glide blithely across such multifaceted and deeply entrenched changes in the structure and composition of American society.

The purpose of this book is to describe the complexity of the spatial rearrangements of five postwar cities—New York, Los Angeles, Chicago, Houston and Philadelphia—and their relation to the economic changes that have been underway since the mid-1940s. Major emphasis is placed upon local financial institutions, entrepreneurs and developers, governments and elected officials, neighborhood and community groups, individual households, and other "agents" and how they *mediate* the relation between economic restructuring and spatial transformations. These mediating agents transmit shifts in production and exchange to rearrangements of the built environment and, in turn, transmit the constraints and opportunities inherent in that environment back to the economic sphere. Such dynamics can only be understood historically. The goal of this volume is to enrich empirically and situate historically this broad theme in the actual experiences of cities.

Background. An expanding body of scholarly literature considers economic restructuring and its attendant causes and consequences, particularly as the latter are expressed geographically. One group of scholars has explored the extent to which specific industrial sectors have acted as driving forces that lead to major spatial transformations at city and regional levels. Among the city studies are investigations of the relation between oil and gas exploration and the growth of Denver (Judd 1983), of petrochemicals and the intra-metropolitan development of New Orleans (Smith and Keller 1983), of the oil industry and the boom and bust of Houston (Feagin 1984b), and of the automotive industry and the decline of Detroit (Hill 1983). Regional analyses include Saxenian's (1984) fine work on the semiconductor industry and the development and despoiling of Santa Clara county, California. These locality studies have intellectual origins in the early work of Sawers (1975), on urban form and the mode of production, and Gordon (1984), on the relation between commercial, industrial and corporate stages of capitalist accumulation and the built form of the city. Also behind the scenes is a host of historical analyses (such as Walker 1978; Zunz 1982) and the many city biographies produced by urban historians (see Schnore 1975).

Other researchers have focused on the complex rearrangements of manufacturing and service activities within central cities to explain particular forms of urban restructuring (often emphasizing urban redevelopment projects) and neighborhood change. Edward Soja and his coauthors (1983, 1985, 1986) have interpreted in spatial terms the economic and social transformations of the Los Angeles region, while Joe R. Feagin (1987) has drawn linkages between the vitality of the oil industry and property development in Houston. Norman I. Fainstein and Susan S. Fainstein (1983) on New Haven, Fainstein and Fainstein (1987) on New York City, and Susan S. Fainstein, Norman I. Fainstein and P. J. Armistead (1983) on San Francisco are good examples of works concerned with governmentally aided redevelopment in response to sectoral shifts. Neighborhood-focused investigations are almost wholly concerned with gentrification (see Smith and Williams, 1986).

A number of studies take a more pronounced national perspective. Mollenkopf (1981) has identified the implications of the manufacturing-service shift for the varying growth rates of cities within different regional contexts and, more specifically, has probed the relation among sectoral shifts, national and local political forces, and the prospects for urban redevelopment in San Francisco and Boston (1983). Noyelle (1983) and his associates at the Conservation of Human Resources Project at Columbia University have described empirically the emergence of "advanced services" and the concomitant redifferentiation of metropolitan hierarchies in the United States. They characterize metropolises as having different spatial realms (for example, international, national, regional) related to their specialization in certain types of economic activity (such as, industrial-military). Scott (1982, 1986) has taken what was assumed in the work of Noyelle and associates—the interdependencies that create spatial linkages among firms—and formulated theoretical and empirical perspectives on these relations at the metropolitan and intrametropolitan scales.

More general analyses geared to economic and industrial restructuring draw spatial implications in less specifically defined geographical contexts. Peet (1987) places the action on an international plane with advanced capitalist countries undergoing industrial devolution while peripheral countries suffer "disorganic development" that brings massive immiseration, cultural imperialism, and repressive political regimes. The regional adjustment theory of Clark, Gertler, and Whiteman (1986) provides a broad national overview of the spatial manifestations of temporal changes in labor, prices, and capital investment for the postwar United States. Markusen (1985a) examines the relationships among the movement of various industries through profit (or product) cycles, the development of oligopolies in those industries, and the resultant regional distribution of production sites. Massey and Meegan probe the sectoral composition of the uneven pattern of city unemployment (1982a) and also explore in depth the various mechanisms that generate uneven regional rates of employment within declining industrial sectors (1982b).

Important to the latter two approaches has been the work of Bluestone and Harrison (1982) who addressed plant closings in mainly economic terms but also considered their political and spatial implications. Harrison (1984) later elaborated their perspective in his case study of the decline of the textile and the footwear industries and the socioeconomic status of New England. Of central theoretical and political importance is the attention paid to the impacts of massive industrial disinvestment on specific communities and regions. See, for example, Webber (1986) on the impacts of a declining steel industry on Hamilton, Ontario, and Clark's (1986) portrayal of the regional consequences of major changes in the U.S. automobile industry in the Midwest.

The theoretical perspective that predominates in this book thus has strong roots in economic and urban geography and in urban and regional planning, with more tenuous roots in local histories. In all but the latter, the spatial has been central. Space as a theoretical construct is no longer nonproblematic; it has become an object for intellectual debate rather than a passive background subject to simple specification (see Gregory and Urry 1985). The contributors also avoid a direct tracing of spatial transformations from the outlines of sectoral shifts. Instead they follow two paths. One scrutinizes the production process, investment decisions, the social relations of production, and technological innovation and adoption. The other attempts to discover mediating agents who link changes in the sphere of production to transformations of the built environment. Causal powers and liabilties are not simply imputed to economic activities; the objective is to understand the spatial reverberations of economic forces and how social, political, cultural, and physical forms shape, and are shaped by, the enterprises of production, distribution, and investment.

This new understanding has not stemmed merely from theoretical musings, but has been compelled by historical events. The recession of the mid-1970s and its attendant social dislocations; the community trauma caused by plant closings in steel, automotive assembly, and electronics industries; the shock of OPEC price rises; the stagflation of the late 1970s; and the invasion of Japanese goods all were unmistakable signs that the power and composition of the U.S. economy were in flux. The nation's political debacles in Vietnam, Beirut, and Iran, the promulgation of explicit and at times strident pro-market and nationalistic ideology linked to a reinvigoration of the Cold War, the massive federal deficit, and the incidences of local fiscal crises hint at a connection between economic restructuring and political turbulence.

Against this background, the precipitous postwar decline of industrial cities, the regional shifts apparent in the 1970s, and the off-shore spatial strategies of U.S. and multinational corporations, coupled with heightened international economic competition, helped to place the economic and political turmoil in a spatial context. Phoenix and Dallas boomed, while Detroit and Newark bordered on financial insolvency and social disintegration. The Sunbelt and the Rustbelt became appropriate metaphors for present and future prospects. Numerous assembly plants were relocated south of the border in Mexico, while Korean and Taiwanese manufacturing undercut domestic production. Yet by the mid-1980s, New England's economy was once again robust, and cities such as Boston and Pittsburgh were proclaiming a renascence. Many cities in the Sunbelt, Houston and Dallas in particular, were overbuilt and employment was short. Only international competition seemed still to threaten, ultimately to be exorcised by renewed American competitiveness.

In this context, social commentators were compelled to explore the international and national forces impinging on urban and regional development, and to focus more tightly on the "particularities of place" (Massey 1984). Economic transformations did not always materialize in the built environment in similar ways. The postwar spatial changes in Providence and Portland, Oregon, could not be equated, despite their participation in a common national political economy and culture. The contingencies of place frequently eluded the sweep of abstract and generalizing theory. Theory often became, in the word of critics, "totalizing," locking us into bold and rigid explanations insensitive to the contradictions and heterogeneity of history (Cooke 1987). Locality studies were offered as antidote (Murgatroyd 1985). They would capture the specificity of local responses and refract the restructuring of the political economy at various spatial scales. Whereas grand theory ignores, at its peril, the uniqueness of place and the overdetermination of events, locality studies must avoid degenerating into isolated stories of ostensibly unique places and events bereft of any sense of the historical structure of social change (Beauregard 1988a; Smith 1987; Warner 1968b).

Five Cities. Within this perspective, we present five case studies of the forces mediating between political economic restructuring and the physical, social and political transformation of space. As of 1988, New York, Los Angeles, Chicago, Houston and Philadelphia were the five largest cities in the country. They occupied the top of the urban hierarchy. The country's historically dominant city, New York, along with its long-time rival, Philadelphia, owe their great size and influence to the consolidation of industrial capitalism before the turn of the century upon a solid base of commercial and financial activity. Chicago, which was virtually non-existent, while New York and Philadelphia were thriving cities, was a boom-town from 1870 to 1930, its growth spurred not only by shoes and boots, clothing, and furniture but also by newer industries such as electrical machinery, refrigerated dressed meat, and railroad transport. By the 1970s, all three were characterized by population and employment loss, physical deterioration, and fiscal difficulties.

When New York, Philadelphia, and Chicago were climbing to national and even international prominence, Los Angeles and Houston were small towns on the economic and political periphery. Their growth spurts came in a different era, and the economic forces driving that growth were of a dissimilar sectoral nature. Los Angeles began its ascendancy about 1920. Automotive assembly and, later, war-based expansion in aerospace, petroleum refining, international trade, and textiles were the primary sectors. Houston did not "take off" until the regional dominance of its port was secured and oil was discovered. Those industries were subsequently supported by oil drilling firms and refineries, and refineries made profitable by the demand generated by the proliferation of the automobile. Houston's greatest population growth occurred in the 1950s. Federal intervention established the National Aeronautics and Space Administration complex in the 1960s and had earlier subsidized the construction of the ship channel. In the 1960s and 1970s, both Los Angeles and Houston, unlike the other three cities, enjoyed strong economic performance and robust real estate development.

Not only do these five cities present variations in economic and demographic development in the postwar period, but they also present different spatial patterns. Philadelphia's core, with its single central business district, historic areas and block upon block of low-rise, working-class row housing contrasts with Houston's multinucleated commercial development and garden apartment complexes spread across a low-density landscape. Los Angeles represents the quintessential automobile city, and New York, particularly Manhattan, the hindrances and opportunities of congestion. Houston and Los Angeles cover vast land areas compared to the more circumscribed geopolitical boundaries of Chicago and Philadelphia.

Since New York and Los Angeles are commonly considered to be global cities, these five largest U.S. cities are likely to experience and encapsulate international as well as national forces in their clearest and most amplified form. Houston's specialization in oil makes it susceptible to international geopolitics, Chicago's reliance on steel and machine tools ties it closely to industrial change, New York's dominance of financial markets offers direct ties to the sources of global, national, and regional investment patterns, and the diversification of Los Angeles and Philadelphia offers opportunities for a variety of spatial manifestations. As large, dynamic, and complex cities, these five enable us to explore the spatial mediation of political economic restructuring in its richest form.

Each of the case studies, in its own way, addresses this general theme. To establish an historical background, the first chapter describes the economic and geographic changes throughout the United States in the postwar period. The final chapter, to integrate these case studies into a coherent sense of the nature of economic restructuring and spatial transformations of U.S. cities, provides a comparative analysis. While our attention is directed solely to cities atop the urban hierarchy, our conclusions extend beyond these five cities and demonstrate, we believe, the connections between economy, polity, and space in postwar United States.

Robert A. Beauregard

CHAPTER 1

Postwar Spatial Transformations

Robert A. Beauregard

The story of postwar spatial restructuring in the United States has been told frequently, and in numerous versions. Most observers can describe the decline of large central cities, massive suburbanization, and the growth of the West and the South. The outlines are obvious, the understanding common. The more knowledgeable can extend such general statements to include the rise of new cities in the South, the resurgence in the 1980s of inner-city neighborhoods and central business districts within cities once characterized as hopeless, the decline of rural America, the development of nonmetropolitan areas, the relentless urbanization of inner-ring suburbs, and the increasing integration of national space. Fewer are sufficiently knowledgeable to expound on the shifting urban hierarchy and the functional integration of cities into regional, national, and global networks, or trace these spatial transformations to forces stemming from, and influencing, a variety of spatial scales.

Yet because the story has been repeated many times, and the plot has become so recognizable, one begins to wonder whether the received wisdom is, in fact, a matter of definitive assessment or unchallenged consensus. Our understanding of the past is altered so often by some new revelation or interpretation that one cannot hold uncritically to any history. Certainly this is the case with postwar spatial development and, more specifically, the dynamics of urban hierarchies. We are faced not simply with the accumulation of facts and the subsequent decay of explanations, but with the possibility of new interpretations emanating from theoretical advances.

This is the position in which we find ourselves; theoretical advances compel a reassessment of previous knowledge. Economic influences over communities are now cast in a more complex framework, space

1

has lost its passive nature and taken an active role in urban and regional development, and the intricacies of civil society have become part of a holistic approach to the alteration of social formations. As a result, the purpose of this chapter is not simply to position the postwar transformation of the five cities in a larger national and international context of spatial restructuring, but also to re-tell the story of this country's postwar spatial transformations from a new vantage point.

The argument unfolds as follows: economic forces, mediated by State action at the international and national spatial scales, establish the broad outlines of regional development within the United States. These forces impinge on major industrial sectors and industries, which are clustered across space in highly uneven patterns. The fate of sectors and industries thereby contributes to the general fate of regions, a fate that can be rapidly or slowly reversed by state intervention, but never fully overcome. The industrial and community response to these international and national forces influences the fortunes of cities and metropolitan areas. Activities might emerge to take advantage of a new national position in the international economy, or major plants close and skilled labor migrate to more prosperous places. Growth and decline, however, will exist simultaneously as the particularities of place mediate overall regional trends. Within cities, forces lower on the spatial scale will take over, while community groups, municipal governments, property investors, and local booster groups respond to and attempt to manipulate their place within the urban, metropolitan, and regional hierarchies. The result is a rearrangement of the national urban hierarchy as some cities become tied to international capital, others become prominent within the region, and still others establish metropolitan dominance.

The practical consequences of this argument are reflected in the organization of this chapter, which begins with a brief overview of the spatial transformations that characterized the United States just prior to World War II. The discourse then turns to the postwar era, focusing on the pervasiveness of economic restructuring across a variety of spatial scales. In the immediate postwar period the United States dominated international, particularly European, trade, and the national issue was the transition from a wartime to a peacetime economy. Providing an avenue for this transition and further bolstering production was a massive suburbanization coupled with military incursions in Korea and Vietnam, the topics of the next section. Still, certain sectors of the economy remained problematic—agriculture in particular—and the ensuing black internal migration introduces the decline of the central cities. Urban decline was exacerbated by a loss of hegemony in international markets, increased foreign competition, and a subsequent, traumatic sectoral restructuring in the 1970s. Stabilization and recovery followed in the next decade; while earlier spatial trends continued, others reemerged as central cities became sites for office investment and gentrification. By the middle of the 1980s, the consequences for the urban hierarchy had been profound, and our five cities had been repositioned within this everchanging landscape.

Prelude to Postwar Transformations

World War II did not obliterate previous patterns of urban development and allow postwar society to create new processes and spatial arrangements on a *tabula rasa*. The war was a major and devastating event, but it did not reverse the momentum of earlier forces. The country's postwar spatial development was clearly conditioned by what had occurred in previous decades.

The postwar period was preceded by six years of international conflict and by a worldwide depression throughout the 1930s. That depression, moreover, was a child of prosperity and a massive building boom. The latter had a tremendous effect upon the built environment, while the depression and the war were instrumental in the spatial rearrangement of population and investment and in the disinvestment that fell heavily on many cities. These events established a base upon which postwar urban development was built. Richard A. Walker (1978:172), for example, in commenting upon suburbanization, argues that "The greater part of the postwar pattern of city building was fully worked out by the 1920s." Nonetheless, significant qualitative changes followed the end of World War I, many of which were crucially important for postwar cities (Jackson 1975:141). A brief review of these trends will set the context for a more intensive investigation of postwar spatial transformations.

The Census of 1920 marked the official emergence in the United States of an "urban" society: more than 50 percent of the population was found to reside in incorporated places of 2500 or more inhabitants, and more than 20 percent of the country's 105.7 million people lived in cities with populations exceeding a quarter of a million people. By 1950, that proportion had grown to more than 34 percent, and 64 percent of the population lived in urban areas. Ten cities were added to the one-quarter- to one-half-million category, four to the one-half- to one-million category, and two joined three others as having more than a million people residing within their boundaries.[1] The 1920s, 1930s, and 1940s witnessed a spatial concentration of people and an concomitant expansion in our demographically defined urban character.

With the exception of St. Louis (6th) and Los Angeles (10th), the top ten cities by population in 1920 were all located in the northeastern and the northcentral regions of the country. New York, Chicago, Philadelphia, Detroit, and Cleveland headed the list, while Boston, Baltimore, and Pittsburgh were wedged between St. Louis and Los Angeles. Houston was 45th. By 1950, a few changes were evident. Los Angeles had moved to 4th, St. Louis had fallen to 8th, and Pittsburgh had dropped out of the top ten. Washington, D.C. was now 9th, and Houston, surprisingly, was 14th. Even those cities which had slipped in rank over the three decades had experienced population growth: 86 percent in Detroit, and 15 percent in Cleveland. What change ensued in the urban hierarchy involved relative growth; no absolute declines in population occurred at the top.

To characterize this three-decade period simply as one of spatial concentration of population in cities is to simplify a time of very complex spatial transformations. Most often mentioned is the "metropolitanization" of the United States as suburban development accelerated, abetted by automobile and highway development. The period also encompassed regional migrations of both people and capital, along with a significant withdrawal of capital from the central cities.

For the United States, World War I was an economic boon. Before the U.S. entry into the war, domestic manufacturers of war material and food producers provided supplies to the combatants in Europe, thus tripling exports to Europe between 1914 and 1917 (Puth 1982:342–44). Involvement in the war fueled the U.S. economy, but also brought inflation when supply failed to keep pace with demand. At the end of the war, the United States had suffered no physical damage to its factories and landscape and had had fewer deaths and casualties than any of its allies. The economy continued to expand after the war, bolstered by a robust construction industry, growing export markets, and an inflationary psychology. From 1920 to 1921 a brief postwar recession occurred, but the economy then turned prosperous and consumer demand, spurred by productivity gains and rising personal incomes, reached unprecedented heights. Consumer spending on nondurable goods increased, and durable goods, particularly the automobile, were also in great demand. Mass production made the automobile financially accessible to more and more consumers, and with the development of highway systems across the United States, the automobile became an increasingly convenient form of personal transportation. Moreover, it helped to extend the spatial decentralization of land development that had heretofore been a function of the street railways (Warner, 1962). Los Angeles, in particular, grew in this fashion, even before the establishment of the freeway system (Warner 1972:137–38).

One component of this prosperity was a massive building boom. Between a trough in 1917 and a peak in 1927, the yearly value of new construction in place expanded from $10.2 billion to $24.1 billion, in constant dollars (see Figure 1.1). Between 1920 and 1929, more than 7 million new dwelling units were added to the housing stock, with production jumping from 247,000 in 1920 to 937,000 in 1925.[2] The national wealth embedded in structures increased by nearly 38 percent, in 1929 prices, between 1922 and 1929 (U.S. Bureau of the Census, 1975:256). The skyscraper became an increasingly common building type, and cities expanded rapidly with the growth of industrial, commercial, and residential districts. The tremendous amount of building activity convinced many city governments of the need to hire city planners, specifically to unravel the traffic congestion on roads and highways built for horse and buggy and streetcars, but not suited to the movement and storage of the automobile (Scott 1969:183–92).

Cities were expanding not just within, but also outside their boundaries. Suburbs now became places of work, not just residential communities, when factories and retail establishments were located beyond city boundaries. Between 1910 and 1940, the proportion of the population residing in metropolitan areas increased from 31 percent to 48 percent, with the expansion occurring in all regions of the country (Fox 1986:35). Suburban development was certainly not new (see Jackson 1975), but now the process and its pattern changed as suburbanites' attachment to the streetcar and the rail line for commuting was replaced by the greater spatial flexibility of the automobile (Jackson 1985:157–89; Warner 1962). The automobile enabled suburban land conversion to accelerate as wages rose, the labor force had its largest ever absolute expansion, and housing prices fell.[3]

Despite overall prosperity, many areas of the country were in dire economic straits (Puth 1982:359–62). The shipbuilding industry had

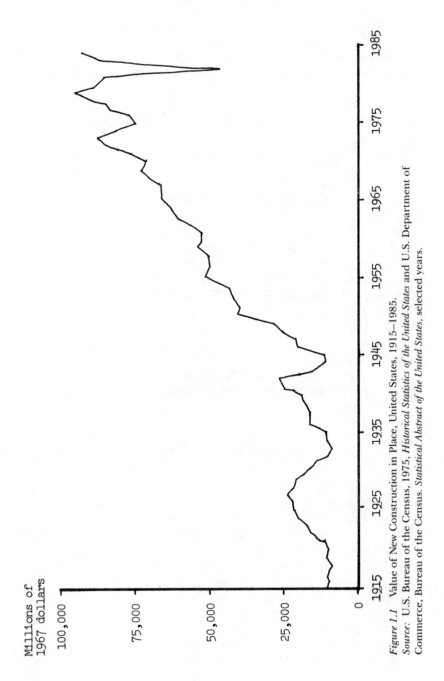

Figure 1.1 Value of New Construction in Place, United States, 1915–1985.
Source: U.S. Bureau of the Census, 1975, *Historical Statistics of the United States* and U.S. Department of Commerce, Bureau of the Census. *Statistical Abstract of the United States,* selected years.

overproduced during the war, as had such industries in other countries, and the end of the conflict left it oversupplied and facing a shrinking market. Major shipbuilding areas such as the Delaware River, with operations in Camden, Philadelphia, Wilmington, and Chester, were forced to lay off workers and cut back on the purchase of supplies. Areas of the northeastern and northcentral states suffered from the decline in the demand for coal. Agriculture was in particularly bad shape. Demand fell off sharply after the war, and the farming community never recovered; even the heightened consumer spending of the Roaring Twenties was no help. Consumption of food did not increase in proportion to rising household incomes, and overproduction drove down prices even more. A series of droughts caused further havoc; the northern Great Lakes, the Ozarks, and the Appalachias were hard-hit. On the other hand, California, Florida and other states which grew citrus fruits and out-of-season vegetables had higher-than-average farm incomes.

The depressed state of agriculture exacerbated migration from marginal farm areas into more urban ones and helped to maintain the movement of blacks from the South to the North, even after the need to fill wartime industrial jobs in the northern cities had ceased. In fact, the collapse of southern agriculture continued throughout the 1930s and 1940s (Fusfeld and Bates 1984:52–66). This shifting of population within the country coincided with a steep decline in immigration. Immigration had peaked just prior to World War I and would arrive at its lowest point as World War II was just under way (U.S. Department of Labor 1976:378).

Depression

While the stock market crash in October 1929 brought a virtual halt to capital investment and factory production, it did not stifle the spatial transformations characteristic of the 1920s. In terms of interregional migration, in fact, it exacerbated them. Factories closed, banks closed, and household income plummeted. The crisis in the economy spread beyond manufacturing to retail and services, then back to wholesale and into real estate. Unemployment was extraordinarily high, and consumer spending fell off drastically. When private capital for investment in buildings disappeared, the construction industry became virtually stagnant. From 1927's $24.1 billion national peak of building activity, construction fell to $7.3 billion in 1933. New housing starts, traditionally sensitive to economic conditions, declined to their lowest point in the 20th century (U.S. Department of Commerce 1966). These conditions produced massive disinvestment in the built environment, because money for maintenance, repairs, and renovations was no longer available. Mortgage foreclosures, rent delinquency, and overcrowding were characteristic of the residential market. "In 1933, about 60 percent of Philadelphia's landlords were pursuing eviction proceedings against one or more tenants" (Fusfeld and Bates 1984:390). In addition, since local governments experienced a fall-off in tax revenues, the maintenance of public infrastructure also suffered.

On the one hand, such dire economic conditions stifled population movements. The suburbanization of the 1920s slowed considerably without the capital for new housing or the incomes to purchase or rent it. The migration of blacks from the South to the North also diminished; few parts of the country had jobs available. Cities in particular suffered. Joblessness in the poorer black districts of Chicago was estimated to have reached 90 percent (ibid.:38). On the other hand, cities generally maintained their population base. Philadelphia had a slight population loss, although Houston increased by more than 30 percent during the 1930s. Few cities moved into higher size categories, and the urban hierarchy generally changed little. Of the top ten, only St. Louis shifted position, dropping from 7th to 8th. In addition, interregional migration of a particular sort appeared. The impoverishment of agricultural areas in the South and Southwest, coupled with a series of droughts creating the Dust Bowl in Oklahoma and Texas and a mythology about the richly abundant farmland in California, instigated a movement toward that state. People migrated in search of jobs and ahead of creditors, but for the most part the population stayed in place, often moving in with relatives in order to save the cost of rent or mortgage payments.

The implementation of numerous New Deal programs had little immediate effect on these larger spatial trends, but within communities the impact on the build environment was significant. Most important were the public works, employment programs designed to construct numerous public facilities. The Roosevelt administration attempted to do with governmental funds what private funds were unable to do: provide jobs for the unemployed. While the private portion of the built environment continued to deteriorate, the public portion was renewed and expanded. In large cities and small towns across the nation, parks, playgrounds, hospitals, schools, housing, roads, sewer lines and a multitude of other public works were constructed. Houston, a major recepient of such federal aid, received substantial infrastructure that would later facilitate its postwar prosperity (Feagin 1984a). In rural areas, the Civilian Conservation Corps planted trees and developed state and national parks, doing for the countryside what the Public Works Administration was doing for the cities. As private investment in new construction declined from the $8 billion range in the late 1920s to $3.1 billion in 1938, work relief expenditures (mainly involving public works) expanded from $0.1 billion in 1933 to $1.2 billion in 1938 (National Resources Planning Board 1940:16–23).

Nonetheless, this unprecedented infusion of governmental funds did little to re-ignite suburbanization, stem the overall erosion of the built environment, or redirect migration. The Rural Resettlement Administration attempted to relocate population out of overpopulated cities in the Great Lakes and Great Plains regions and into newly established "greenbelt" communities outside major metropolitan areas. Blighted areas of cities thereby would be emptied for subsequent renewal (Scott 1969:335–42). Only three, small communities were built: Greenbelt, Maryland, Greenhills, Ohio, and Greendale, Wisconsin. Moreover, the New Deal's endeavor to protect farmland and reinvigorate agriculture had only minimal short-term economic effects, although its long-term importance for better land management cannot be denied. By the late 1930s the economy was beginning to display some vigor, but the clouds of impending military conflict had already formed.

World War II

The war in Europe first produced a demand for American manufactured goods, agricultural products, and shipping, and a boost to the U.S. economy that reopened factories and reduced unemployment. With the U.S. entrance into the war in late 1941, the economic impact of war mobilization changed dramatically. Investment in new construction increased, and manufacturing employment nearly doubled, increasing 86 percent between 1938 and 1943. In 1944 unemployment dropped to 1.2 percent, equivalent to a full-employment economy, largely caused by the need for military personnel. The labor shortage, moreover, drew many more women into the labor force. Military spending rose from $1.8 billion in 1940 to $80.5 billion in 1945, in current dollars (Puth 1982:408), with a corresponding expansion in the federal deficit.

War mobilization had dramatic spatial consequences. Shipbuilding became essential, with the result that numerous coastal cities—such as Houston, Tacoma, and Newport News—experienced rapid employment jumps and population increases. Military bases expanded, and warplanes were built; the San Diego economy boomed, and its population expanded by two-thirds. The need for tanks, jeeps, and trucks caused the Detroit area to blossom with factory after factory. Airplanes were a necessity, and the West Coast, particularly Los Angeles and Seattle, enjoyed an economic surge. While many war suppliers were located along the fringes of the country, a fear of attack induced the federal government to encourage numerous wartime factories in the interior. Major manufacturing plants were established in Charlestown, Indiana, Wichita, and Louisville, Kentucky, (Scott 1969:368–96). Mobilization seemed to be spread evenly across the country, but a closer look shows that new plants were concentrated in the South and West, while existing capacity was being utilized in the Northeast and Midwest.

Population shifts followed. Small towns became medium-size cities virtually overnight, while many large cities underwent population increases previously equaled only by the waves of immigration prior to World War I. One consequence was a massive housing shortage. The federal government was compelled to subsidize worker housing around defense plants, but still overcrowding persisted. New roads and infrastructure were needed in greenfield areas. In a number of defense plant communities, such as Willow Grove outside Detroit, elaborate plans were drawn but never implemented, and the construction of housing and infrastructure was shoddy and expedient (ibid.:394–96). Despite all the new investment, the existing built environment of the cities continued to deteriorate, because municipal governments could not raise taxes to maintain their infrastructure. Money was diverted to defense, and roads, bridges, sewers, and schools had to wait. Simultaneously, little capital was available for new private construction, renovation, or maintenance. In Philadelphia, the value of real estate had fallen from a 1932 high of $3.5 billion to just under $2.5 billion in 1941 (Tinkcom 1982:646). The seeds of postwar urban decline were being sown.

At war's end, a massive migration occurred. Millions of military personnel returned home, and more than 10 million individuals became civilians. Defense factories closed down; their workers left to find other employment, and many women moved back into the household. As the postwar period began, most cities in the Northeast and Midwest were virtually stagnant. In the West and South, on the other hand, war mobilization had spurred development in such places as Los Angeles, Houston, and Seattle. The older cities were burdened with undermaintained public and private property; the newer cities faced a gap between the supply and demand for infrastructure. Suburban areas, other than those which had received defense factories, had changed little since the 1920s. Rural areas blessed with agriculture or natural resources had prospered during the war, but were confronted with a great deal of uncertainty as the Allies started to reconstruct their agricultural sectors. Overall, the trend of population movement was away from the older, larger industrial cities, away from the Northeast and Midwest, away from agricultural regions, and to the suburbs. The United States, moreover, was only just becoming an economic and military world power, and its spatial transformations were still relatively driven by internal forces.

International Dominance and Domestic Conversion

As 1945 came to an end, the United States was faced with the need to dismantle the wartime military, close or retool defense-oriented factories, absorb returning military personnel into the labor market and the community, and generally convert a war economy to a peacetime one. Prior to the armistice, numerous experts had forecasted a postwar recession and proposed state-directed employment and investment policies to counteract the inevitable economic downturn. A combination of the desperate need for manufactured goods in Europe and Japan, astute foreign policy, and a boom in domestic consumption—subsumed under the rubric of suburbanization—dispelled the impending recession and established the conditions for one of the longest periods of prosperity in the nation's history. The spatial consequences were dramatic.

As the war ended, the national government began to reduce federal expenditures, which fell from $84.6 billion in 1945 to $34.9 billion in 1948, with much of this drop due to the fall in military expenditures (Puth 1982:453). Tanks, fighter planes, uniforms, warships, hand grenades and all the paraphrenalia of military conflict were no longer needed in such large quantities or in such steady flows. As orders for such goods decreased, private firms faced the prospects of either closure or retooling. Naval bases, airfields, and army camps also became redundant. For military installations, the options were different: shrinkage or abandonment. Government investments in aluminum plants, aircraft factories, and machine tool facilities were sold to the private sector, which provided businesses in these industries with a start on conversion and recovery (Chafe 1986:113).

The automotive complex centered on Detroit and the airplane complexes on the West Coast (from Los Angeles to San Diego and around Seattle) and on Long Island made the transition to domestic production. The former switched to trucks and automobiles, the latter to airplanes for a rapidly expanding commercial airline industry. Other industries and areas were not as fortunate and found themselves facing closure or drastic shrinkage. Shipbuilding continued in places like Camden, New Jersey, and Houston for a few years, but eventually succumbed to international competition from Sweden and Japan. By 1987 the industry was relatively small and almost wholly dependent on governmental contracts. Often linked spatially with naval bases, such local economies were doubly burdened by a decline in demand for ships and ship repair and by a reduction in the military presence. Army and air force bases across the country were closed or faced drastic curtailment. For example, Camp Kilmer in Piscataway, New Jersey, an embarkation site for personnel being sent overseas, was almost wholly dismantled. Localities that suffered recession after the withdrawal of war production were either relatively small or primarily East Coast port cities. Where large population agglomerations had concentrated during the war to support major defense production, such as in Los Angeles and Houston, the conversion of production to domestic demand proceeded smoothly and with little disruption of the economy.

Since the end of World War I, however, the economy had undergone significant restructuring. Manufacturing remained the dominant employment sector, but within manufacturing some important shifts had occurred by 1950 (see Table 1.1). Textile mill products, wearing apparel, and printing and publishing had declined in importance. Lumber and wood, petroleum and coal, stone, clay and glass, and leather products had dropped out of the top ten manufacturing industries. New to the top ten were primary and fabricated metals, nonelectrical machinery and transportation equipment, mostly automobiles. The commodities mined or manufactured in the Northeast, South and Northwest were being replaced by commodities produced in the Midwest and, to a lesser extent, the West. Fabricated metals and nonelectrical machinery were also northeastern products, but transportation equipment and primary metals were midwestern. The New

Table 1.1 Top Ten Manufacturing Industries by Value Added,
1921–1985

		Value Added (in millions of 1958 dollars)
1921:	1. Food and kindred products	2,120
	2. Textile mill products	1,824
	3. Apparel and other textiles	1,408
	4. Printing and publishing	1,306
	5. Lumber and wood products	853
	6. Chemicals	834
	7. Leather and leather products	610
	8. Stone, clay and glass	605
	9. Electrical equipment and supplies	547
	10. Petroleum and coal products	430
1937:	1. Food and kindred products	3,485
	2. Primary metal products	2,169
	3. Nonelectrical machinery	2,037
	4. Chemicals	1,819
	5. Textile mill products	1,818
	6. Transportation equipment	1,773
	7. Printing and publishing	1,765
	8. Fabricated metal products	1,401
	9. Apparel and other textiles	1,386
	10. Electrical equipment and supplies	941
1950:	1. Food and kindred products	10,104
	2. Nonelectrical machinery	8,765
	3. Transportation equipment	8,547
	4. Primary metal products	7,951
	5. Chemicals	7,237
	6. Fabricated metal products	6,211
	7. Textile mill products	5,642
	8. Printing and publishing	4,907
	9. Electrical equipment and supplies	4,815
	10. Apparel and textile products	4,176

1985:	1. Transportation equipment	120,953
	2. Nonelectrical machinery	110,224
	3. Electrical equipment and supplies	109,862
	4. Food and kindred products	104,146
	5. Chemicals	95,258
	6. Printing and publishing	73,054
	7. Fabricated metals	69,162
	8. Paper and allied products	40,387
	9. Instruments and related products	40,278
	10. Primary metal products	38,082

Source: U.S. Department of Commerce, *Annual Survey of Manufactures,* selected years.

England textile towns, unable to substitute new industries for declining ones, suffered the most. Decline, however, was not widespread in the immediate postwar years.

One factor facilitating the transition to a peacetime economy was international demand, which prevented over-capacity, labor surpluses, and capital shortages from creating a recession. After the war, U.S. industries received an abundance of orders for capital and noncapital goods from Europe and Japan, whose productive capacity in both manufacturing and agriculture had been ravaged. Bombings had devastated many cities, whose highest priorities were thus to rehouse the population and retool the factories. Machinery and food were desperately needed, as well as a variety of consumer goods. Such purchases required capital, and capital was also in short supply after the war effort.

George C. Marshall, secretary of state under President Truman, helped to create a program that, once started in 1947, provided capital and enabled the U.S. economy to weather an almost inevitable postwar recession (Chafe 1986:67–70; Donovan 1977:287–91). The Marshall Plan, in the form of humanitarian aid for the rebuilding of Europe, created a circuit of capital extending from the Treasury of the United States, to the governments of Europe, to European purchasers, and back to producers in the United States. The plan thus boosted American exports, infused capital circuitously into the American economy, and generated demand for labor in this country. The movement of exports also helped to bolster the shipping industry at a time when war-related shipping was drastically curtailed. Capital goods, industrial supplies, and food led the list of postwar exports. Agricultural areas and areas with concentrations of manufacturing plants benefited. Between 1940 and 1946, the total value of exports more than doubled, and then increased by more than 50 percent between 1946 and 1947 (U.S. Bureau of the Census 1975:895). The Marshall Plan provided a boost to international trade that made the United States a creditor nation until the 1970s. The excess of exports over imports, in turn, sustained domestic production, which expanded employment and income and generally served as a key prop for postwar prosperity.

Another factor that might have contributed to a recession was the sudden and massive infusion of military personnel into the labor market. Between May 1945 and December 1946, the armed forces declined from 12.1 million to 1.9 million members (Brownlee 1979:475). Some ex-service personnel were absorbed into the expanding economy; others opted for college aided by the G.I. Bill, which deferred their entry into the labor market and raised the educational and skill level of the workforce (Chafe 1986:112). In 1945, more than 5 million people abandoned the labor market, followed by another 2 million in 1946 (Brownlee 1979:475). While some were male retirees, many were young married women returning to the household. This combination of international trade, educational-employment policy, and family formation helped to control the interaction of labor supply and demand, and contributed to the prevention of postwar recession and thus to postwar prosperity. Of crucial importance, however, is that economic growth was also being abetted and sustained by a massive binge of domestic consumption implicated in a major spatial transformation: suburbanization.

Suburbanization

The movement of residences from the central cities into contiguous, peripheral areas began during the 19th century, but always represented only a small-scale migration of relatively affluent families (Walker 1978). Postwar prosperity, combined with the saturation of central-city land and two decades of disinvestment in the central-city built environment, produced a qualitative change in the nature of suburbanization (Fox 1986:50–78; Jackson 1985:190–218, 231–45). Beginning in the later 1940s, suburban migration became an option not only for the upper middle class, but also for all segments of the middle class and for the more affluent of the working class. The percentage of the country's population living in the suburban fringe went from 15.3 in 1940 to 30.6 in 1960, an increase of 34.7 million people (Fox 1986:51). In addition, it was not a simple residential phenomenon but involved as well the subsequent out-migration of factories and retail establishments from the cities.

Throughout the depression and World War II, individuals had faced an uncertain future and a precarious economic present, one consequence of which was the postponement by a large portion of the population of marriage and child-rearing. The war, which absorbed men into the military, exacerbated such behavior. Pent-up reproductive demand characterized the early postwar period. Servicemen and servicewomen returned to marry and start families, as did many women who left the labor force at the end of the war. As one means to prevent a possible postwar recession, the federal government provided these new households, through FHA and VA mortgage insurance, the opportunity to own homes. This encouraged the construction of housing, which stimulated the construction industry and all its suppliers and linked activities such as real estate marketing. The demand for new homes, moreover, had a decided spatial bias.

The central city was not to become the residence of these new households. A variety of factors combined to direct their investments to "bedroom" suburbs, the towns adjacent to central cities but without the employment base to occupy the male earners. One factor was the bias built into the FHA mortgage insurance program, toward new construction rather than rehabilitation (Gelfand 1975:216–22). New construction supposedly would have a greater stimulative, economic effect, since it not only involved larger sums of capital per dwelling unit but also required the purchase of land and the construction of infrastructure and public and private support facilities. Second, the urban built environment was generally not that attractive, and city housing was viewed as a more risky investment. Thus, the new households were faced with a choice between new housing at lower densities in "sylvan" settings or existing housing requiring costly maintenance in higher density surroundings. As a result, population growth in the older, central cities declined, although cities such as Los Angeles and Houston, with open space and an ability to annex, continued to grow (see Figure 1.2).

These broad background factors were later enhanced by the construction of interstate highways, by the movement of commercial and industrial establishments to the suburbs, and by the increasing presence of minorities—mainly Negroes—in the central cities. The federal government's program of highway construction had been planned to provide for nationwide trade via truck transportation and for the military capability of moving personnel and equipment quickly to

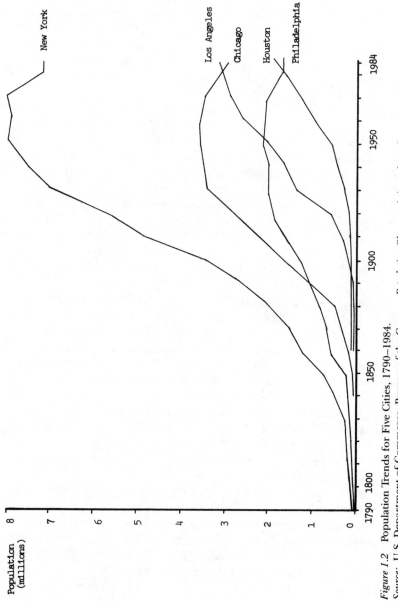

Figure 1.2 Population Trends for Five Cities, 1790–1984.

Source: U.S. Department of Commerce, Bureau of the Census, *Population Characteristics,* selected years.

points of attack (ibid.:222–34).[4] The resultant system of limited-access highways, in their connections to inner-city road networks, facilitated suburbanites' commuting to jobs in the central city and made suburban residence a more viable option. In turn, the highways enabled commercial establishments to locate outside the city and still have access to a transportation network. The reliance on railroads lessened as trucks and interstate highways combined to create a spatially more flexible form of transportation.

This decentralization of industry further drew households from the central city. The federal government became involved in the outward movement of some industries, such as steel. Concerned about possible invasion, the government encouraged decentralization into "priority areas" outside cities, and favored large-scale housing developers, such as Leavitt (Checkoway 1984), with the assurance of FHA mortgages so they would provide the residences for workers in these decentralized plants. One of the best examples of such a development is just north of Philadelphia in Bucks County; U.S. Steel's Fairless complex and Levittown, Pennsylvania, grew in tandem. Retail development soon followed to serve the suburban population (Jackson 1985:257–61).

Simultaneously, as one might expect in such a large-scale movement supported by the federal government and central to the prosperity of the economy, an ideology of suburban desirability and central-city avoidance emerged. The suburbs came to represent the postwar American dream of homeownership, closeness to nature, freedom of mobility (via the automobile), upward class mobility, and opportunities for passing that mobility along to the offspring. Suburbs were believed to be the best places for bringing up children: open space, isolation from traffic-clogged streets, access to good schools operating under the watchfulness of Parent-Teacher Associations, and neighbors equally concerned with education. The class escalator was to be driven by education.

The central city was viewed as blighted, congested, and dangerous: housing of poor quality, property extremely expensive, nature nonexistent, parking scarce, roadways clogged, and schools below average. At the core of this ideological pronouncement were minorities. The increasing presence of low-income blacks from the rural South, concentrated in slum neighborhoods, gave central cities an aura of poverty, unemployment, and crime, and blacks thereby became the fulcrum around which the negative urban ideology pivoted. Suburbanization had a definite racial dimension.

This ideology justified the movement of the white population away from the central cities and the development of the suburbs. Simultaneously the robust economy, low unemployment and expanding wages provided the material underpinnings for suburbanization. The relationship was dialectic, for suburbanization also provided a massive consumer demand that further fueled the economy. In addition to the tremendous infusion of capital into homebuilding and related construction fields, the movement required the purchase of a variety of goods and services to support suburban existence. Foremost was the automobile, which enabled commuting and the many trips to scattered suburban facilities, from schools to supermarkets. Suburban living encompassed large labor-saving appliances, new furniture, lawn-care equipment, and chaise lounges and a barbecue grill for the patio. A crucial vector of life in the postwar suburbs was the personal consumption that attended it. The affluence derived from the workplace was directed back into the economy.

While suburbanization was integrated into the larger flow of capital and helped to create and enhance numerous industries (from automobiles to electrical appliances to furniture to baby products), it also reintegrated the central city in a new form of spatial organization. Capital and people were decentralized. The phenomenon was not simply city growth by accretion, but lower density development beyond city boundaries, a pattern which soon came to be known as sprawl.

The older industrial cities were the primary sites for this form of suburbanization. In the newer cities of the South and West where land was still available, suburbanization enabled the cities themselves to expand. Some older industrial cities also had unimproved land that attracted a small portion of suburban out-migration: Philadelphia's northeast area went from farmland to residential-commercial development, and Staten Island served to retain some of New York City's decentralizing population. In cities where development had saturated the available space, contiguous communities became the option of choice, such as Schaumberg and Northfield outside Chicago. Long Island beyond Brooklyn, given great prominence by the Levittown development, became the epitome of the suburban frontier. The area of New Jersey just across the Delaware River from Philadelphia experienced rapid growth. All cities were affected. From 1940 to 1970 the suburban fringes of metropolitan areas grew by 275 percent, while the population in central cities rose by 50 percent. New suburban communities, such as Scarsdale, New York, Greenwich,

Connecticut, Cherry Hill, New Jersey, and Evanston, Illinois, gained national prominence. By 1970, 37.2 percent of the country's population resided in suburban areas and 31.4 percent in central cities, with the remainder in nonmetropolitan areas, in contrast with 1940 percentages of 15.3 and 32.5, respectively (Fox 1986:51)

Metropolis

For some, as we have seen, suburbanization represented the rejection of the city as the site for investment, consumption, and reproduction. For others, the city was simply being extended into another spatial form, the metropolis (Hawley 1971). Whereas the central city had been the dominant spatial form of the industrial period, the metropolitan area was the dominant spatial form of the postwar period. The metropolis was an amalgam of central city and suburbs, integrated by employment and consumption and by the commuting that made possible the separation of work from residence. Such diverse social phenomena as neighborhood ties, church affiliations, and professional sports teams also helped to create a metropolitan image. In the early years of the postwar period, this perception was credible and convincing; but as factories and malls located in the suburbs and the central city became a place to avoid, that integration no longer seemed viable. Spatial differentiation was more pronounced, and now the suburbs were not simply bedroom communities, but relatively self-contained communities. The notion of an integrated metropolis disintegrated, as the center faded beyond the perception of suburbanites.

So important had the metropolitan area become economically and politically that the Bureau of the Census derived a new category of "space" and of data collection: the Standard Metropolitan Statistical Area (SMSA).[5] In 1950, the census recorded 168 SMSAs, each with a central city of at least 50,000 persons and with its contiguous counties integrated by functional activities and work-related commuting. By 1960 there were 212 SMSAs, 243 by 1970, and 318 by 1980. In 1950, 56.1 percent of the national population resided within their midst, and in 1980 the corresponding figure had grown to 74.8 percent. The ranking of cities and the ranking of metropolitan areas coincided in the early years of the postwar period, but increasingly diverged as central cities lost their prominence in the 1960s and 1970s when suburbs gained in economic and political importance. While Milwaukee, Houston, and Buffalo ranked 13th through 15th in the urban hierarchy along the population dimension in 1950, they ranked 16th, 17th, and 14th, respectively, in the metropolitan hierarchy. By 1980, the discrepancy had become more pronounced. San Francisco, Memphis, and Washington, D.C., ranked 13th, 14th, and 15th in the urban hierarchy, but ranked 6th, 42nd, and 7th along the metropolitan hierarchy. New York, Los Angeles, Chicago, and Philadelphia maintained equivalent positions on both scales in 1980, but Houston with its ability to annex was higher on the city scale than on the metropolitan one. Without doubt, by 1960 the metropolis had become the dominant postwar spatial form.

Urban Redevelopment and Decline

The migration of capital and people to the suburbs was a major component of postwar economic growth and corresponded with a flow of governmental funds into the central cities. Unlike suburban investment, urban reinvestment was not embedded in a wide array of consumer purchases. Nonetheless, it is important both for its attempt to transform urban space and the counterforces it experienced. Obviously, urban redevelopment alone did not have to support economic expansion. Suburban development took the lead, abetted by favorable international trade and later by major military actions—the Korean conflict (1950–1953) and the Vietnam war (1961–1973).

Central-city redevelopment was premised on the belief that the deterioration of the older, industrial central cities was caused by a combination of temporary disinvestment, precipitated by the depression and World War II, and by real estate practices, including speculation, which failed to recognize the true value of central-city properties (Colean 1953; Gelfand 1975). From this perspective the elimination of blight (that is, property which has lost its value) and the enhancement of property values with new investment seemed feasible. Held mainly by downtown property interests (Weiss 1981), that position was reinforced further by recognition that extensive capital investment had already been made in the central cities and could not easily, from a financial standpoint, be abandoned, and also by a belief that suburbanization was not a direct threat to core cities. Rather, suburbanization was a restructuring of the urban region in which the central city would emerge as still dominant, but within a metropolis in which the hinterlands (now suburbs) were more extensive, more developed, and more economically competitive.

Blight was not the only rationale for urban redevelopment. Federal support of redevelopment, through the 1949 and 1954 housing acts, was also a result of pressure from "housers" interested in providing public housing for low-income families. Both groups favored slum clearance, an activity virtually unopposed by experts in the late 1940s and early 1950s. Title I of the housing acts focused on redevelopment: establishing public agencies to coordinate the process, providing monies for slum clearance and site preparation, and subsidizing developers. Title II dealt with public housing. The first was meant to reduce the risk prevailing in the central city property market, particularly in the central business district (CBD) by removing the barriers (that is, slums and blighted property) to new development and increasing developers' profit margins through land write-downs. The second would clear slums and replace dilapidated housing with new housing projects for the low-income population, thereby removing the blight of slum neighborhoods from areas adjacent to CBDs.

For some, the two types of projects were mutually supportive: Title I would clear sites, and portions of those sites would be set aside for public housing. For others, particularly those favoring redevelopment, they were antagonistic. Public housing, with its low-income and increasingly minority residents, would discourage further investment and, moreover, not constitute the "highest and best use" for sites within or adjacent to the CBD. The latter advocates, having control over the power of slum clearance and developer selection, prevailed, and most of the housing built subsequently on CBD redevelopment sites was for the middle and upper classes.

New York City, Pittsburgh, Philadelphia, and New Haven were leaders in developing urban renewal plans and drawing down federal aid for property acquisition, demolition and clearance, and site improvements (Lowe 1967). San Francisco, Washington, D.C., Boston, Chicago, Baltimore, and Oakland were also some of the many cities which took advantage of this opportunity to remove blight and attract new capital investment. Los Angeles, on the other hand, was less aggressive early on, and Houston never participated in the Urban Renewal program. In New York City, Robert Moses was a major force and became so astute at renewal that directors from across the country flocked to New York to learn from him. Philadelphia engaged in massive slum clearance in North Philadelphia, recaptured a lower class neighborhood (now Society Hill) for the middle class, and facilitated the expansion of its universities, among other projects. Chicago concentrated on downtown redevelopment in the Loop, public housing on the South Side, and institutional expansion, including the universities of Chicago and Illinois and the medical complex southwest of the Loop.

The spatial impacts of urban renewal were often profound at the scale of neighborhoods and commercial strips, but contrary to the hopes of many supporters, the spatial consequences of redevelopment were confined primarily to the city itself, with little effect on the overwhelming metropolitan pattern of decentralization. Central business districts generally experienced a transformation from relatively low-rise office and commercial development, characterized by congested streets and lack of parking, to large-scale developments, often amalgamating blocks, of high-rise structures with new open space consisting of plazas and retail space turned away from the street (Beauregard 1986a). Parking lots and garages emerged as a dominant land use, and streets continued to be congested with vehicular traffic. New buildings, such as the Gallery shopping mall in Philadelphia, seemed to be distanced from the sidewalks toward which earlier commercial activity had been focused. Cultural facilities were often placed as islands within the existing city, a design exemplified by New York's Lincoln Center. The new economic activities of the CBD—administration, finance, business—reflected their orientation to the suburbs from whence many of their workers came, as well as the fear with which developers confronted the prevailing urban fabric. In many ways, with redevelopment the CBD became less vibrant, and many CBDs became ghost towns at night after the workers had returned to the suburbs. The nighttime and weekend retail activity moved to the suburbs when central-city department stores established branches in shopping malls, or simply ended operations altogether.

The effects of redevelopment were not confined to the CBD. The zone of transition adjacent to these centers often was absorbed into the new CBD or became the location for slum clearance, followed by residential, usually middle-class, developments. The latter resulted in spread effects as the residents of slum dwellings were forced to relocate in neighborhoods farther from the center; overcrowding in the new locations often contributed to the reestablishment of the slums from which they had recently been displaced (Gans 1968). The decentralization of the poor also played a role in the geographical decentralization of the white middle class, who fled minorities who had been displaced by governmental actions. Moreover, the public housing projects designed to eradicate slums became, in a perverse way, centers for slum formation in the inner cities. Low-income minorities were concentrated in high-rise buildings, which became centers of unemployment, family disorganization, and teen-age rebelliousness. While the CBD was being recaptured by capital, adjacent neighborhoods and residential areas even more distant were becoming the dumping grounds for the poor and the oppressed. In Philadelphia, for example, minorities had once been concentrated just south of Center City. With their increasing numbers and the spread of public housing, they soon moved farther south into Italian South Philadelphia and into North Philadelphia, ranging as far as five to seven miles from the CBD.

The redevelopment of central cities, nonetheless, did not change the overall trend toward the movement of capital, along with middle- and upper-class households, to the suburbs. Despite massive federal investments in places such as New Haven, New York, and Philadelphia, these cities continued to lose population and jobs. The central cities increasingly suffered from a deteriorating image and, more important, a relative loss of investment as the centroid of economic and political activity migrated farther and farther from the CBD. The forces of development were definitely directed toward suburban communities. The central cities were being abandoned to a select group of administrative, financial and cultural activities, on the one hand, and on the other to the poor and the elderly and to isolated clusters of middle- and upper-class families in affluent neighborhoods within the core or on the periphery of the central city itself. Prosperity for individuals, business establishments, and governments, although clearly uneven in its spatial manifestation, was objectively and symbolically a suburban phenomenon. The central cities were stagnating at best and were simply a coda to the larger economic score.

Regional Decline and Race

The glow of consumer spending and international hegemony blinded most observers to the uneven economic and spatial development of the early postwar period. Economic growth was not rampant across all sectors, and central-city decline was not simply an unfortunate side effect of suburbanization.

Various regions of the country experienced population out-migration and job loss. The expanded use of electrical power for residential, commercial, and industrial use, coupled with an increase in the use of oil for fuel, drove down the demand for coal in the 1950s. Areas of Appalachia—northeastern Pennsylvania, western Kentucky, West

Virginia—became depressed. Unemployment rose, household incomes fell, and the young began to migrate to other parts of the country. The Chicago, Indianapolis, and Detroit areas attracted many of these people to the automotive industry. The decline was felt not only in rural areas, but in the cities of these regions as well. The populations of Scranton and Wheeling declined by 17 percent and 18 percent, respectively. Rural poverty, no less harsh than its urban counterpart, was more spatially diffused and less easy to measure, much less to ameliorate. Regional policy was implemented by the federal government, but no infusion of capital for infrastructure or planning could reverse the economic shifts that had made this region's natural resource an unwanted commodity.

The mining industry was not the only one in dire straits and contributing to regional decline. The agricultural sector, despite its massive exports and increasing productivity, also had a dark side. The trend toward corporate, capital-intensive farming forced small farms out of the market. Between 1950 and 1975 the number of farms declined from 5.4 million to 2.8 million (Puth 1982:427). The transformation was particularly important in the South, where many blacks had been share-croppers or tenant farmers. Coupled with the mechanization of cotton harvesting and the lack of manufacturing growth in southern cities during this early postwar period, not to mention white southern racial discrimination, the migration of blacks from the rural South to northern and southern cities was exacerbated. In 1940, more than 48 percent of the black population resided in the rural South. That figure had dropped to just under 25 percent by 1960, and the proportion in the urban North and West had increased from 20.5 percent to 38.1 percent (Fusfeld and Bates 1984:64–66).

The presence of large and spatially concentrated numbers of rural, low-income blacks in the central cities was a pivotal element in the postwar, anti-urban ideology. While a certain optimism might have accompanied early attempts at urban renewal, an optimism buoyed by a belief in the temporality of disinvestment, the formation of black ghettos and the seemingly intractable problems of crime and poverty linked to the minority population engendered an even stronger pessimism. As blacks entered the central cities, the manufacturing jobs in which they hoped to make their fortunes were leaving. At the same time they faced the de facto discrimination of northern real estate and labor markets, school systems, and public services. The result was that their location in marginal neighborhoods that in years past had served as the first residences of upward mobile foreign immigrants, became for American blacks the final resting place for their aspirations (Fusfeld and Bates 1984:82–102). Black ghettos emerged in most of the larger cities: Bedford Stuyvesant in Brooklyn, North Philadelphia, Watts in Los Angeles, and the South Side of Chicago. For many, future residential mobility would be only a matter of displacement caused by urban renewal and interstate highways, rather than upward economic and social advancement.

So daunted were the media by the presence of blacks in the central cities that, during the late 1950s and early 1960s, alarmist articles portending that many larger cities were becoming dominated by a black majority were common. One article stated: "Unless something occurs to check the current trends, some of the most important cities of this country are going to wind up under Negro control."[6] The fears perpetuated white flight and represented not just latent racist tendencies, but a general ignorance as to how to prevent, much less eliminate, the growing prevalence of black poverty, crime, and under-education. Urban decline, the loss of population and employment, and the flight of capital, in general, were strongly tied to the existence of black ghettos and the problems they, and white society, spawned. Abandonment of parts or all of these cities was contemplated, with commentators proclaiming that they would eventually become mere "reservations" for the unwanted of society (Sternlieb 1971). Amid prosperity existed the unavoidable presence of cities in decline, increasingly the space for the poor. The new metaphors for metropolitan development became the ring and the doughnut. Each conjured up images of a hole surrounded by something of value, the poor central cities encased in suburban wealth. The only solution was to accept the inevitable and abandon the central cities to the old, the poor, and the minorities. The urban riots of the mid-1960s made this solution seem even more logical and defensible.

War

The overall prosperity at home and the fortunes enjoyed in international markets were paralleled by an international political influence that was frequently exercised. The airlift to Berlin (1948), the Cuban Missile Crisis (1962), the occupation of the Dominican Republic in 1965, and the Marshall Plan, among other U.S. actions, fed into and reinforced a vision of the United States as a world power with global interests and responsibilities. The government's foreign policy provided an essential justification for domestic production of defense facilities and military products and for research and development of new systems of offensive and'defensive weapons. Binding that policy into a dense core was the threat of communism and the fear not only that it would spread, but that the Soviet Union, the agent of this movement, would develop the military capability to encroach upon the free world itself. The key element in this scenario was the atom bomb, a device that rose to prominence as a deterrent against a third world war (Halliday 1983).

The military-industrial complex that the Cold War foreign policy spawned helped to fuel the suburbanization movement through its expansion of plant and provision of high wage employment, and thus to abet the decline of the central cities. In the 1950s, that sector was further expanded with the instigation of the Korean conflict. Never officially declared a war by the United States executive or legislature, it still served as an opportunity for massive capital investment in manufacturing and a mobilization of a portion of the population into the military. Spatially it reinforced the trend of new development to the West Coast as military facilities and aircraft factories were expanded. San Diego and Los Angeles, along with Seattle, benefited from this war-based economic expansion. The scale of the Korean conflict, however, was not great enough to create nationwide spatial restructuring, as had occurred during World War II. Nonetheless, the conflict played an important role in invigorating certain industries, directing investment to the West Coast, and further fueling suburbanization in that region and less so in the Northeast—for example, in Long Island with its aircraft and defense plants.

Prosperity reigned in this early postwar period between 1945 and the beginning of the 1970s. International dominance in trade, suburbanization, and foreign military policy combined to create an unprecedented economic boom. Capital followed the flows of population, and the spatial consequences were profound. Metropolitan areas emerged with clearly defined and robust suburbs, central cities declined, certain regions became depressed, and the West Coast moved out of the periphery. During such an upward trajectory, it was difficult to foresee the impending international restructuring of manufacturing and trade and the concomitant industrial transformation of the national economy.

Domestic Crisis and International Competition

While the middle class was awash in economic prosperity, corporations were heady with expansion, and the State imbibed with its military incursions—Korea, Vietnam—and its battle against the communist threat; developed, war-ravaged nations were rebuilding their industrial capacity and expanding food production, and less-developed countries in Africa and the Far East were acquiring the capability to produce goods, not just to export raw materials. A series of economic shocks in the 1970s brutally clarified this transition, and public attention quickly turned to deindustrialization, plant closings, manufacturing decline, trade deficits, and debtor-nation status. The crisis was reflected in a regional restructuring that drove some cities upward along a trajectory of growth and others further along the path of decline.

For all its international hegemony in the 1950s and 1960s, U.S. industry was unprepared for the emergence of strong and, in certain sectors, overwhelming competition in both international trade and domestic production. In retrospect the signs were there, but only in the 1970s did the consequences become apparent. Trade relations were shifting. While the United States had once been dominant both in agriculture and manufacturing, the latter eroded with the emergence of highly productive manufacturing centers in Western Europe and Japan along with low-wage assembly operations in developing countries. Agriculture remained strong, however, and increased its share of exports from 12.1 percent in 1970 to 16.4 percent in 1975 and 19.0 percent in 1980. The most perceptible shift involved the Organization of Petroleum Exporting Countries (OPEC). This cartel was formed to control the flow of crude oil to developed countries, mainly from the Middle East and thus to regulate its price. From 1947 to 1975 the import share of crude material and fuels doubled, and the value of imports from OPEC members increased ninefold from 1971 to 1976 (Puth 1982:448). OPEC's policies had major effects on the domestic price of oil, and the change in price of this essential commodity reverberated throughout the economy. The shifting of the composition of exports and imports would result a few years later in a massive trade deficit in the late 1970s and 1980s, and debtor status for the first time in U.S. history.

The domestic implications of this restructuring of international capitalism were profound and widespread. Japan and various European nations (particularly West Germany) began to compete aggressively with the United States in the domestic and foreign markets for steel, automobiles, and electronic consumer goods. American steel mills were generally of an older vintage, less productive, and unable to compete on a price basis with the newer and more technologically advanced mills in Japan, West Germany, and later South Korea. American automobile manufacturers were unprepared for the movement away from heavy fuel-inefficient automobiles, had persisted in out-moded production techniques, and were top-heavy with middle management as well as unable to compete in the low end of the market. Volkswagon, Honda, Datsun, and Toyota captured a larger and larger share of the U.S. market. The American motorcycle was almost completely eliminated by Japanese competition, and the major U.S. firm (Harley-Davidson) managed to survive only with governmental protection. A similar scenario applied to electronic goods. American televisions became increasingly rare, and American stereos even more difficult to find on retail shelves. New electronic components—personal stereos, laser disk players, videocassette recorders, telephone answering machines—flowed into the country. American industries in these sectors had lost competitiveness and were much less innovative (Bluestone and Harrison 1982:111–90; Castells 1985; Lawrence 1984; Markusen 1985a).

Textiles, apparels, furniture, and various other domestic industries were also suffering from international competition (see Table 1.1). Many were relatively labor-intensive and found themselves competing both with foreign-owned firms and with U.S. firms that were shipping assembly operations off-shore to low-wage countries, such as Puerto Rico, Korea, Mexico, and Taiwan, or selling technology to foreign firms. Years of class struggle and economic prosperity to boost the wages of American labor had left it vulnerable now to the ability of multinational corporations to shift production sites to countries where labor was cheap. Production was increasingly a matter of spatial linkages, not simply across regions, but across national boundaries.

International competition and the devastating effects it was having on domestic production became intertwined in the 1970s with a series of economic events that further weakened capital markets with inflation and caused a real depreciation in the value of the dollar in international monetary markets (Harrington 1980:40–79). An ill-advised grain deal with the Soviet Union in 1972 caused domestic food prices to soar, and the Vietnam War inflated wages and profits in the defense sector. The greatest shock came from OPEC. In 1973 OPEC instituted an oil embargo that led to an unprecedented increase in gasoline prices for the consumer. The price per gallon, in only a few months, jumped from an average of 30 cents to close to two dollars. Moreover, gasoline was in short supply. Lines formed at gasoline stations, rationing was discussed and briefly instituted in rudimentary form, and an energy crisis was proclaimed. The economy went into an inflationary spiral. Prices rose, not only for gasoline, but for all commodities whose production required or directly included petroleum products. Inflation became the central element in governmental economic policy, and for a short moment a Republican president tinkered with wage and price controls. The repercussions were felt internationally as the value of dollar sank in relation, most important, to countries competing directly with the United States.

Stagflation and shifting international economic relations echoed throughout the national economy. While the manufacturing-service shift had been underway for some years, the recession of 1973–1975 made it patently obvious. The consequences were important for labor. A new occupational structure confronted current workers and new entrants into the civilian labor force (Ginzberg and Vojta 1981). While jobs in manufacturing had increased in number, they had become a smaller and smaller proportion of employment opportunities (see Table 1.2). The growth sectors of the economy were services (personal and business), retail trade, and government. Between 1950 and 1980, the number of manufacturing jobs increased by 5.4 million but the number of service, retail, and governmental jobs increased by 17.3, 10.0, and 10.2 million respectively. Nonagricultural employment had expanded by approximately 120 percent across the three decades, although manufacturing had expanded only by 35.6 percent. Moreover, from the mid-1970s onward, manufacturing employment, the historic fulcrum of American industry, was virtually stagnant. In 1974 and 1975, the country experienced its worst postwar recession. Unemployment and inflation reached double digits, and the U.S. economy seemed to be losing its international dominance.

The federal government could not be counted on to intervene in the economy, to reinvigorate national industries, or to right international trade relations. The war in Vietnam had bolstered the defense industry and in some sense had inflated demand for goods and labor, but the war had become a political and military liability. The federal government, particularly in the Johnson administration (1963–1968), had undertaken major domestic programs. War mobilization, even with a less than national commitment, combined with a domestic binge of reform legislation, had worked its burden on the federal budget and laid the groundwork for rapidly expanding deficits, which by the mid-1980s would be so high as to attract blame for a sluggish national economy and relatively high interest rates. The political

Table 1.2 Employment Shares in Nonagricultural Industries for the United States, 1950–1984

	1950	1960	1970	1980	1985
Mining	2.0	1.3	0.7	0.7	0.6
Construction	5.2	5.3	5.5	5.9	5.7
Manufacturing	33.7	30.9	24.8	20.7	19.1
Transportation, communications and public utilities	8.9	7.4	6.0	5.5	5.3
Wholesale Trade	5.6	5.5	5.4	5.6	5.7
Retail trade	15.2	15.5	16.2	16.9	17.8
Finance, insurance and real estate	4.2	4.9	5.0	5.7	6.1
Services[a]	11.9	13.5	20.6	22.7	24.3
Government	13.3	15.7	15.8	16.3	15.4
Total	100.0	100.0	100.0	100.0	100.0
Absolute value[b]	45,222	54,347	79,219	99,843	103,548

a. Includes private household services.
b. In millions.

Source: U. S. Department of Commerce, Bureau of the Census, *Statistical Abstract of the United States,* selected years.

response was a decline in national defense expenditures as a proportion of federal outlays (26.0 percent to 22.7 percent) and as a proportion of GNP (8.2 percent to 5.7 percent) between 1975 and 1980.[7]

The federal government had also been politically weakened by the Vietnam War. Antiwar protests in the late 1960s and early 1970s had eroded its legitimacy and, specifically, had weakened its ability to intervene on the side of capital or to undertake aggressive foreign policy that might result in domestic benefits for the economy. Inflation, a growing deficit, and an erosion of ideological support for government restricted domestic policy targeted to specific industries, even while rampant inflation and high unemployment—stagflation—brought pressures for assertive fiscal and monetary policy. Raising taxes, in fact, was no longer a political option in a period of deep economic recession. Both the Carter (1976–1980) and Reagan (1980–1988) administrations espoused an antigovernment, self-help ideology. Although intermittently involved in firm and industry bail-outs, they were opposed to any distortion of the free market. The national economic shake-out would not be prevented through government action.

The spatial consequences of this economic restructuring took the dramatic form of plant closings (Bluestone and Harrison 1982). Steel mills in Youngstown, Ohio, Chicago, and Pittsburgh; automotive assembly plants in Mahwah, New Jersey, Detroit, and Los Angeles; and numerous other manufacturing plants in communities throughout the Northeast and Midwest were emptied. Textiles and shoe manufacturing virtually disappeared in New England. Production ceased, and the workers were abruptly handed their notices with no hope of a subsequent rehiring. In those communities where the factories had dominated local employment, and thus local economic activity, the effects were devastating. Massive unemployment led to mortgage foreclosures, out-migration, family problems, declining retail sales and, coupled with the withdrawal of corporate activity, severe blows to local tax revenues and thus governmental services. Communities in the Pittsburgh region became virtual ghost towns and survived mainly on short-lived severance pay, informal labor and governmental retirement, unemployment, and welfare benefits (Clark 1988). Few cities in the manufacturing belt escaped.

National development was being held hostage by the hypermobility of capital across regional and national boundaries (Bluestone and Harrison 1982:15–19). Coupled with international competition and all the other factors creating the deepest recession since before World War II, the struggle between capital and labor took a qualitative turn. The period of labor peace that had been ensured by economic growth was ended. The hardest-hit industries—steel and automotive assembly—were unionized industries. Organized labor found itself confronting either widespread unemployment or give-backs, the reduction of wages and benefits. The choice was structured by capital, and capital's interests were bluntly stated. If the former were selected, unions would continue to decline in importance, and union members would have to accept lower-wage jobs in other industries. If the latter, the advances gained by years of class struggle would be abolished. Capital had the option of choosing both. In the face of a highly touted shift from manufacturing to services, labor was at a distinct disadvantaged.

Regional Shifts

The decline of manufacturing served to focus attention on regional realignments. No longer were the Northeast and the Midwest the centers of productive activity and economic growth. The Manufacturing Belt became the Rustbelt and, in another metaphor, the Snowbelt. The perception was not of a temporary decline in their fortunes, but of a permanent shift of investment and people from these areas to the South and the West, the Sunbelt. The new regions of growth would be built upon new industries—services, oil exploration, aerospace—and certain old industries—defense (Sale 1977). The resultant shifts in capital and population, moreover, were not motivated merely by economic considerations. The Sunbelt was virtually that, an area of yearround recreation, a consumption-based lifestyle, low-density development, and dynamic and clean cities such as Phoenix, Houston, San Antonio, Los Angeles, and San Diego (Bernard and Rice 1983). The Snowbelt was the opposite: dreary winters, congestion, a declining economy of limited opportunities, and dirty, dense, and dangerous cities.

National growth clustered around the new growth poles—metropolitan areas—of the South and West (see Sternlieb and Hughes 1978; Tabb 1984). Between 1960 and 1975, population growth in the West was more than double that in the Northeast and North Central regions, while that in the South exceeded 50 percent of that in the Snowbelt regions. Total employment change in the Sunbelt was almost threefold that in the Northeast and North Central regions, with the

Northeast having an absolute decline. The South and the West were even adding to their manufacturing sectors at high rates, and outpacing their rival regions in nonmanufacturing employment growth. Job growth paralleled migration. The Snowbelt experienced absolute out-migration between 1960 and 1975. The flows of population to the South and the West produced a construction boom with residential and commercial leading the way. The result was to equalize the existing disparities of income, capital investment, and population between the manufacturing-based regions and the South and West with their newer industries.

These regional shifts exacerbated prevailing urban decline and slowed suburbanization in the metropolises of the Snowbelt, and heightened urban growth and sprawl in the Sunbelt. The cities of the North and Midwest—New York, Philadelphia, and Chicago—were now faced with regional shifts to accompany the negative consequences of the suburban migration of capital and population. The demise of manufacturing, high unemployment rates, the weakening of the tax base, and inflation combined to produce fiscal chaos. The demand for city services was unabated, even with population loss, but the ability to provide those services was diminishing. A number of cities were so burdened that they faced fiscal crises with the potential for bankruptcy. Cleveland, Philadelphia, Detroit, and Pittsburgh were in dire straits, but the most dramatic instance was New York City (Alcaly and Mermelstein 1977; Tabb 1982). In the summer of 1975, New York City declared virtual bankruptcy and was taken over by quasi-public corporations, whose task was to purge the government of its fiscal profligacy by cutting back services, raising taxes, and restructuring the city's debt, all in a way that would justify the bail-out provided by the federal and state governments. With a resident population comprised of a larger and larger portion of minorities, and with no sign of the cessation of suburbanization, many were willing to accept the existence of the claim that the city was dead and that the only response was to make its death as painless as possible (Baer 1976).

Although Snowbelt central cities were facing the prospects of long-term poverty, Sunbelt cities were booming. Houston, with its shipping and oil industry, Phoenix, with electronics and aerospace plants, Los Angeles, with aerospace, and Tampa, with tourism, shipping, and financial activities, were enjoying unprecedented development. Capital and people were flocking to them. Residential and office construction contributed to massive physical expansion. Unemployment was low, and incomes were rising. Migration helped to boost these cities up the urban hierarchy. Houston went from 7th in 1960 to 5th in 1980, Phoenix from 29th to 9th, and San Diego from 18th to 8th. Los Angeles solidified its hold over second place. Boston went from 13th to 20th, Cleveland from 8th to 18th, and Pittsburgh from 16th to 30th. The Sunbelt cities were new and vibrant, riding the wave of the new economic growth in services, technology, and energy.

Recovery, Resurgence, and Revitalization

The middle and the late 1970s were thus a time of national economic restructuring and slow economic growth. Consumer spending was eroded as real wages fell, and unprecedented postwar levels of unemployment, inflation, and plant deaths were reached. Simultaneously, prosperity reigned in the Sunbelt and, for their cities, an urban future was not in doubt. Nonetheless, this regional growth did not dispel political clamor for a national industrial policy, reindustrialization, and other governmental interventions that would reassert the economic growth that had previously characterized the postwar period (Wachter and Wachter 1981). Recognizing the technological and trade challenges posed by Japan, policymakers at the federal, state, and local levels and many economic elites called for greater attention to the high-tech revolution and to U.S. competitiveness (Castells 1985). The country would have to make a transition to a post-industrial society, one centered around advanced services and sophisticated technologies, and abandon the gritty manufacturing of the out-moded industrial era. Within this political and economic context, the uneven development of space became even more apparent: regional shifts in the 1980s favored the Northeast and not the South; the older industrial central cities seemingly prospered with new commercial and residential development; and even suburban growth accelerated and took on a new quality. The 1980s were a time of national economic recovery, regional resurgence, and urban revitalization.

Economic Recovery

Starting in the early 1980s, unemployment began a steady decline, inflation waned and soon returned to normal levels, and a steady but slow growth in Gross National Product characterized the economy.

The drop in inflation spurred consumer spending, particularly in the housing industry, as interest rates dropped by nearly half over a few years (see Figure 1.3). The lower cost of capital, coupled with the tax reform of the 1981 Economic Recovery and Tax Act, encouraged new commercial development based upon tax syndicates and historic tax credits (Downs 1985: 93–96).[8] Because such development was fueled mainly by tax advantages, office buildings, adaptive reuse of historic structures, and retail malls could proceed with their developers and investors almost unmindful of any tight relation between supply and demand. The property market was further fueled by the flow of foreign capital from OPEC and other countries reaping the benefits of this country's trade deficit and political stability.

Demand for producer and consumer goods and services was also robust. Although manufacturing continued to decline—plant closings were less frequent and ostensibly smaller in scale—the service and high-tech sectors were booming ("Strange Recovery" 1985). Retail trade, microcomputers, communications, and finance were strong. Numerous jobs opened up in these sectors, and areas where they were concentrated, such as Boston, New York, and suburban Philadelphia, found unemployment rates dropping, consumer spending increasing, and property development strong. Not just the cities of the West and Southwest prospered. The economies of Los Angeles and Tampa were doing fine, as were those in Chicago and Washington, D.C. On the other hand, Houston by 1983 was suffering a severe recession. In the aggregate, the national economy showed all the signs, with few exceptions, of having weathered a period of restructuring. It emerged stronger—minus its uncompetitive industries—and poised for a long period of growth.

The federal government, under the label of the Reagan Revolution, took a great deal of credit for this recovery. The tax reform act had not only reduced levies on various forms of new investment and channeled capital into property development, but by doing so had created a national "good business climate." The federal government also took a passive stance in terms of profiteering from the hypermobility of capital. Leveraged buy-outs, take-overs, mergers, and foreign investments became a preferred path for profit maximization. Such activities did little to increase productive capacity nor add to the Gross National Product. Rather, capital was simply shifted from one investor to another. Despite criticism ranging across the ideological spectrum from both capital and labor, the federal government ignored what seemed to be a major drain on productive potential and job creation.

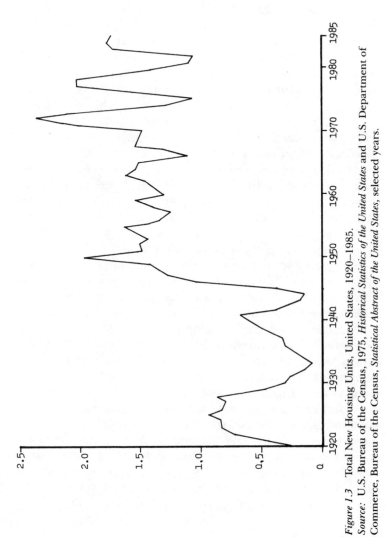

Figure 1.3 Total New Housing Units, United States, 1920–1985.
Source: U.S. Bureau of the Census, 1975, *Historical Statistics of the United States* and U.S. Department of Commerce, Bureau of the Census, *Statistical Abstract of the United States*, selected years.

The economy was also bolstered by the Reagan administration's expressed goal to expand the military establishment. The military budget increased from $164.0 billion to $226.7 billion in constant dollars between 1980 and 1985. The military-industrial complex was rich with defense contracts, and this also helped spur the high-tech sector (Markusen and Bloch 1985). The whole military build-up was supported ideologically by an aggressive and interventionist foreign policy represented by the debacle in Lebanon, where the Marines were attacked (1983), the invasion of Grenada (1984), and the protection of shipping lanes in the Persian Gulf (1987). Overlaid on this policy was the Strategic Defense Initiative (Star Wars), another in a long line of defense systems that would end war, in this case by making a nuclear attack a preordained failure. The downside of this military-led economic growth, however, was both serious cuts in the nonmilitary budget (such as social services, housing, economic development) and a rapidly rising federal deficit that, many believed, weakened the economy by siphoning off capital and raising its cost.

Thus all was not well in this period of recovery. The antitax and promilitary bias of the Reagan administration made it extremely difficult to reduce the deficit. Military spending produced no useful goods and services, and also had the effect of inflating the costs of production. A rising trade deficit was exacerbated by an overly strong dollar which discouraged purchases of American goods and encouraged domestic buyers to rummage in foreign markets. In turn, American manufacturing productivity was being questioned, the comparison between the Japanese and American automobile industry being a prime example (Lawrence 1984). Confusion as to management and investment practices added to the inability to compete on international markets. While services, an increasing portion of U.S. economic activity, are not as mobile internationally as manufacturing activities, by the mid-1980s they were also facing foreign competition in construction, computer software, and banking. With overproduction, a strong dollar, and falling prices in crude oil markets, the country's international posture was put at odds with domestic economic growth.

Regional Resurgence

The economic recovery had a decidedly regional bias. The Northeast became the quintessential success story of how a region could shake-out its older manufacturing sector and adapt to a new service economy. The South, on the other hand, was stagnating and suffering all the downside consequences of a boom-bust economy.

In the Northeast, textiles, shoes and many older manufacturing industries had closed (Harrison 1984). The fulcrums of economic development were now services and high technology. Med-tech, education and advanced business services constituted the former, while microcomputers, biotechnology, and robotics composed the latter. In addition, the area enjoyed a property development boom. The regions of Boston, New York, Philadelphia, and Hartford, to name just four, had robust construction industries and "hot" residential markets. While on a regional basis the areas excluded from economic growth (such as the mill towns outside Pittsburgh and in western Massachusetts) were often overlooked, there was a recognized and debatable underside of this resurgence: low wage, dead-end jobs (Bluestone and Harrison 1986). The diminution of manufacturing production had eliminated well-paid skilled jobs and the replacement of that broad sector with service firms had substituted low-paid, minimally skilled employment. Thus while unemployment rates approached their lowest theoretical limit, many critics argued that the overall implication was not economic development, but growth with inequity.

In the South, national economic recovery was not widely shared. Many areas whose economies specialized in or were dependent on oil exploration, refining, and importing faced oversupplies and falling crude oil prices. Houston, New Orleans, and Dallas went from boom to bust, their oil-based industries went into decline, and unemployment rose. Their rampant property markets went suddenly moribund; office buildings remained empty, vacancy rates increased, apartment owners went begging for renters, and housing lost market value. To the west, however, economic recovery reappeared. California basked in the glow created by military expenditures and technological developments, as did the whole West Coast from San Diego to Portland and Seattle. On the other hand, Denver, another region strongly tied to oil exploration, did not fare well.

Energy development, nonetheless, seemed the only weak sector in the economy. Automotive assembly in the mid-1980s was recovering, while the steel industry had been down-sized, and a few experts projected a return to former levels of output and employment. Overriding all thoughts of national economic disaster was the romance with high-technology. Not only was it, along with advanced services, given credit for the recovery, but it was christened the economic growth pole of the future (Hall 1985). Computer chips, micro- and supercomputers, biotechnology, computer software, robotics, and other machine-based, highly technical products and processes constituted the high-tech sector. High-tech meant entry of the United States once again in the early stages of a complex and robust product cycle. The country could, in turn, build on its supposed advantages in research and development (R & D), university education, and innovation. The result would be a filling of the void left by the restructuring of traditional, industrial manufacturing, the emergence of high-skilled, high-paid job opportunities, and investments with long-term profitability and international significance.

Economic development agencies at the state and local levels—the federal government had withdrawn from such subnational economic assistance—pursued high-tech with great fanfare. They touted their educated workforce, reputable universities, opportunities for research and development and quality of life. Silicon Valley, centered on Stanford University in California, and the Route 128 complex, to the west of Harvard, M.I.T. and other Boston universities, became the models to emulate. The Research Triangle in North Carolina followed, and throughout the country numerous states and cities proclaimed high-tech development. Even Pittsburgh boasted that, although the steel industry had left, high technology was firmly implanted in the city and growing. Yet there was a dark side. High-tech includes both manufacturing and research and development operations, and the assembly functions of the former are "foot-loose," low-waged, and unlikely to generate the spin-off economic growth upon which part of the hope of high-tech development is based. Moreover, even high-tech industries can decline, as witnessed by Japanese advances over U.S. firms in computer chips and shake-outs in the microcomputer field.

Urban Revitalization

While states and regions placed their hopes on high-tech, many cities across the country were blessed with a surge in property development. City government, and economic development agencies did not ignore high-tech, but if it came to the region it most likely located in the suburban ring. This was the case in Philadelphia and even Boston. Directly transforming the urban landscape was the growth in advanced producer and business services: finance, insurance, real estate, legal services, administration, and a variety of business services. This sectoral growth generated and was bolstered by particular forms of property development, namely office building construction and gentrification. The older industrial cities, like New York, Baltimore, Philadelphia, and Chicago, experienced both (Holcomb and Beauregard 1981).

Between 1980 and 1987, office development boomed in numerous cities, driven by earlier tax reforms and the lowered cost of capital, and supported by the expansion of service industries. Millions of square feet of office space were added to New York City, Chicago, Philadelphia, and Los Angeles. Houston added 40 percent (66.1 million square feet) of its office space between 1980 and 1983 in 232 new, large office buildings, but the recession in the mid-1980s resulted in a sharp drop in office construction (Feagin 1987:175). Major additions characterized a host of cities: Boston, San Francisco, Portland, Phoenix, and Tampa Bay. Office development was seen as encouraging the transition to a service economy, drawing jobs to the cities, bolstering the tax base, and generally establishing the city on a trajectory of long-term growth.

The service economy was also given credit for the redevelopment of older working-class, low-income, and mixed-use areas by more affluent households (Beauregard 1986b). Gentrification came to inner-city neighborhoods as young professionals purchased and rehabilitated housing or moved into developer-created, up-scale condominiums and apartments. The elderly, the low-income, and many long-term residents of these areas were displaced, but the attitude of the city government was sanguine. No longer were the young simply moving to the suburbs; they were staying in the city, improving the housing stock, raising housing values, fostering commercial development, and contributing to the tax base. For the older industrial cities which a few years back had faced fiscal crises, gentrification, whose roots extended to those times, seemed heaven-sent and sure to have numerous multiplier effects in the attraction of more and more office development (Beauregard 1985).

Gentrified and gentrifying neighborhoods became the stuff of city magazines and newspaper articles, each touting the renascence of formerly abandoned or run-down neighborhoods (Laska and Spain 1980; Smith and Williams 1986). Queen Village, Fairmount, and Old City in Philadelphia; South End in Boston; SoHo, the Lower East Side, Chelsea, and Cobble Hill in New York City; Fells Point in Baltimore; Capital Hill and Adams-Morgan in Washington; and much of the North Side of Chicago along the lake became widely recognized, gentrified areas. The rate of population loss previously experienced by these cities abated, and decline became an historical phenomenon. People and capital seemed to be rediscovering the city.

Reinforcing the office and residential development were a host of commercial projects involving retail trade and restaurants, marinas, and various personal services (such as health clubs). Major commercial malls were erected or expanded in Philadelphia, New York City, Kansas City, and Chicago. Waterfront development became a central element in the redevelopment plans of numerous cities which explored ways to recapture these scenic areas and to replace the shipping, warehousing and factories that had once been located there. Such projects were pervasive: South Street Seaport in New York City, Harborplace in Baltimore, Penn's Landing in Philadelphia, Fanueil Hall in Boston, Laclede's Landing in St. Louis, and Riverwalk in New Orleans.

Investment in the built environment, however, was not confined to the central cities. Suburban areas across the country also found themselves with new commercial and residential developments. Along New Jersey's central corridor and in Westchester County (on the borders of New York City), in the King of Prussia area to the northwest of Philadelphia, outside Chicago beyond O'Hare Airport, south of San Francisco, and throughout the Los Angeles region (particularly Orange County), employment and population growth were pronounced. Suburbanization was on an upswing, but with a different twist (Nelson 1986). Office development, not residential development, was driving investment. Along and at the intersection of major and sometimes minor highways, office parks proliferated. Moreover, they were not just back offices, but independent service establishments and subsidiaries of larger firms. The increase in employment brought with it heightened demands for housing, a subsequent inflation of property values, and a surge of new residential construction. This rapid decentralization produced land-use conflicts as offices and condominia invaded once-bucolic places and eliminated farmland. The stresses were visually apparent on the streets, where traffic congestion—traffic jams on rural roads—became of overriding concern. The problems, however, were overlooked in the euphoria of economic growth.

In the 1980s, then, the country rebounded from the severe recession and economic restructuring of the previous decade. Regional shifts took another turn as the South lost sectoral favor. Once-distressed central cities experienced major commercial and residential investment in their cores, and suburban areas returned to the path of rapid expansion. Fostering this spatial change was a national economy riding the waves of advanced services, high-tech, and property development. The unevenness in the processes of spatial development was reflected in the unevenness of economic development. Behind the recovery lay slow growth in GNP, weak productivity increases, a massive trade imbalance to the detriment of the United States, and an historic federal treasury deficit.

Conclusions

Ths postwar period is not a cloth of simple weave and monochrome threads, but a patchwork quilt of economic growth and decline, innovation and stagnation, uneven spatial development, and shifting, often erratic state policies. Each of the five cities in this study experienced and contributed to these overarching trends in different ways. They are situated in each of the four regions, serve as sites for a variety of industrial activities, and compete with cities within their regions for regional growth or, in the case of New York and Los Angeles, for global status (Stanback and Noyelle 1982). They emerged from the postwar period in different positions than they had entered it. New York, of course, retained the number-one ranking that it had had in 1945; the other four cities did not. Chicago fell from 2nd to 3rd, and Philadelphia from 3rd to 5th. Los Angeles went from 4th to 2nd, while Houston traveled the greatest distance: 14th just after the war, it was 4th by the mid-1980s.

Explaining and understanding these shifts requires the historical background just sketched, but that background is insufficient for complete comprehension. We need to look more closely at the particularities of place in order to learn how and why the agents of development within these large cities helped to create and responded to the forces at wider spatial scales. What enabled groups to take advantage of international realignments, national restructuring, and regional shifts? When did they fail to do so, and why? What were the forces that shaped the spatial form and the built environment in these five cities?

Notes

1. Unless otherwise noted, data have been taken from Department of Commerce, Bureau of the Census decennial publications, and Department of Commerce, *Statistical Abstract of the United States* for various years.

2. Data on dollar value of new construction in place and new housing units were taken from U.S. Bureau of the Census, *Historical Statistics of the United States*, Washington, D.C.: Government Printing Office, 1975; and U.S. Department of Commerce, *Statistical Abstract of the United States* for various years. The values were deflated using the GNP implicit price deflator, with 1958 as the base year.

3. From 1920 to 1930 the civilian labor force expanded by 7.2 million workers, the largest absolute decade change since 1800, when the first statistics became available. See U.S. Department of Labor 1976:380.

4. One must remember that the late 1940s and 1950s were a period of international tension around the ideological conflict between the free world and the communist one—the first Cold War (Halliday 1983).

5. For 1940, Bureau of the Census data do exist for the metropolitan district for selected cities, and SMSA data have been projected back to 1940, but 1950 was the first full use of the SMSA in the decennial census.

6. See "Negro Cities, White Suburbs—It's the Prospect for the Year 2000," *U.S. News and World Report* 60, no. 8 (February 21, 1960): pp. 72–73; and "Can the Big Cities Come Back?" *U.S. News and World Report* 63, no. 10 (September 4, 1967): pp. 28–31.

7. These trends would be reversed during the Reagan administration by its aggressive military policy and overall support of a resurrection of the Cold War (Halliday 1983).

8. Philadelphia claimed to be one of the major beneficiaries of this tax-driven development, particularly in the adaptive reuse of historic structures, many of which became rental apartments.

CHAPTER 2

Economic Shifts and Land Use in the Global City: New York, 1940–1987

Norman I. Fainstein, Susan S. Fainstein, and Alex Schwartz

Throughout the 20th century, New York has held its place as the nation's largest and wealthiest city. Its cosmopolitan culture, polyglot population, and extraordinarily dense core make it atypical among American cities; its size and economic dominance have placed it at the top of the American urban hierarchy. The image of the Manhattan business district symbolizes money and power around the world. During the nadir of the city's fiscal crisis in the mid-1970s, New York briefly seemed threatened with loss of its ascendant position, but a remarkable resurgence has reversed that trend. The city has regained or even enhanced its status as cultural leader and financial center. Renewed activity reveals itself through growth in population, investment, employment, and new construction. A magnet for global migration, it attracts multitudes of new immigrants who have invigorated many dying neighborhoods; it heads the itinerary of millions of visitors, stimulating a hotel and restaurant boom. Still, the city's renascence obscures ongoing negative factors: the concentration of growth in Manhattan rather than throughout the five boroughs; very high levels of minority unemployment; increasing disparities of income; a severe housing shortage; sharp losses of manufacturing employment, and heavy dependence on the health of the financial industry.

To speak of the growth of New York City apart from a discussion of the entire metropolitan region tends to overemphasize the city's independence. New York's performance is part of the region's expansion; in fact, while growing absolutely, its relative position within the

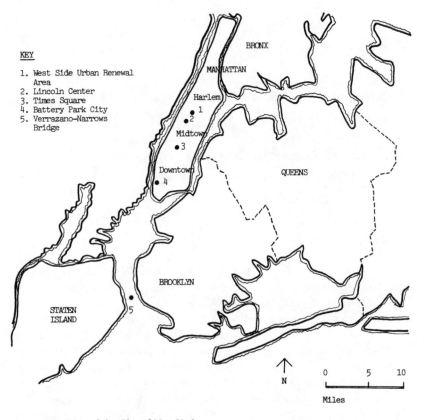

KEY

1. West Side Urban Renewal
   Area
2. Lincoln Center
3. Times Square
4. Battery Park City
5. Verrazano–Narrows
   Bridge

Figure 2.1   Map of the City of New York.

metropolitan area has declined with respect to both population and employment. Whether the striking recent prosperity of the region can be attributed to spin-offs from the city's powerful core, or vice versa, the fate of the city is clearly tied to that of the tri-state area. Nonetheless, certain New York City functions have not decentralized within the region and mark it as a global city. Primary are its central role in the world financial system, and its concentration of media, advertising, public relations, law, and accounting firms. Less auspicious is its function as home to the great majority of the region's low-income and minority population who, as a consequence of suburban exclusion and, perhaps, the superiority of New York's social services, remain encapsulated within the city.

New York's changing fortunes are partially revealed through trends in population and employment. Postwar population peaked in 1970 at 7.9 million, dropped by more than 10 percent during the following decade, but rose again by an estimated 2.6 percent in the next five years (Table 2.1). Aggregate employment also shows a pattern of postwar rise, decline, and resurgence; between 1969 and 1977 payroll employment fell by 16 percent, from 3.8 million to 3.2 million, but turned around sharply in that year (U.S. Bureau of Labor Statistics 1979: 423–35; 1982: 189–92; 1986: Table B-8). Although the addition of 218,000 jobs between 1977 and 1984 was insufficient to restore employment to its previous benchmark, it nevertheless represented the largest increase of the postwar period and surpassed by far the employment increments of the next-largest older cities (Ehrenhalt 1985: 26).

Data on construction provide another indicator of postwar economic activity. New office space in the Manhattan CBD expanded dramatically in the 1957–73 period; an astonishing 52 million square feet were added in just the four years 1970–73 (Figure 2.2). For the next eight years, which comprised the trough of the city's decline, new construction was minimal, but in 1982 there was a sudden jump. In 1986 office construction reached 11 million square feet, a number exceeded only in the peak years of 1971 and 1972. Construction of new dwelling units similarly declined drastically during the 1970s, the

Table 2.1 New York City Population (in thousands), 1940–1984

	1940	1950	1960	1970	1980	1984
Manhattan	1,890	1,960	1,698	1,539	1,428	1,456
Percent white	83	79	74	54	50	NA
Brooklyn	2,698	2,738	2,627	2,602	2,231	2,254
Percent white	95	92	85	60	48	NA
Bronx	1,395	1,451	1,425	1,472	1,169	1,173
Percent white	98	93	88	50	34	NA
Queens	1,298	1,551	1,810	1,986	1,891	1,911
Percent white	97	96	91	78	62	NA
Staten Island	174	192	222	295	352	371
Percent white	98	96	95	90	85	NA
New York City	7,455	7,892	7,782	7,895	7,072	7,165
Percent white[a]	94	90	85	62	51	NA

[a]Prior to 1970, "white" includes individuals of Hispanic origin who are defined as Puerto Ricans.

Source: US Bureau of the Census (1986: Table A, 202); NYC Council on Economic Education (1985): 1; Rosenwaike (1972): 121, 133, 136, 141, 197.

Millions of Rentable
Square Feet

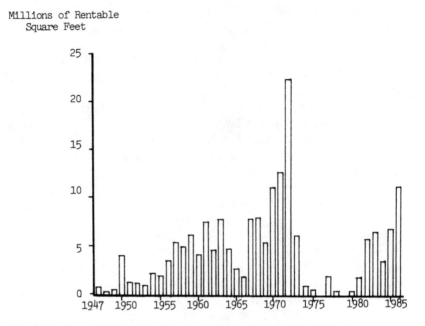

Figure 2.2   Annual Office Space Construction, Manhattan, 1947–1986.
Source: Real Estate Board of New York (1985a: Table 1).

increment constituting less than half of the amount constructed during the previous decade (Table 2.2). But recovery did not occur in this sector, and the pace for the 1980s was even slower than in the preceding years.

Aggregate data, however, mask the transformation that was occurring in the population and economy. Thus, even during the years of total population increase, white population dropped; this decline accelerated in the 1970s. Consequently the city shifted from being 13 percent minority in 1950 to being nearly half non-white in 1980 (Table 2.1). Reliable ethnic breakdowns are not available after 1980, but no evidence suggests that the trend has reversed. Along with the change in racial composition came a decline in median family income, which fell continuously after 1949 in relation to the nation and suburban ring and dropped absolutely, measured in constant dollars, between 1969 and 1982 (Tobier 1984: 40).

While the resident population was becoming poorer and less skilled, the employment structure was providing fewer blue-collar jobs. A steady contraction in manufacturing employment throughout

Table 2.2   New Dwelling Units Completed, 1921–1983

	Total	Public[a]	Publicly assisted	Private
1921–30	762	0	01	761
1931–40	207	10	05	192
1941–50	166	26	12	128
1951–60	323	72	17	234
1961–70	348	41	75	232
1971–80	165	. . . . 111		54[b]
1981–83	25	NA		NA
Total	1,996			

[a]As of 1982, about 169,000 public units in 247 projects housed a population of about 491,000. The racial breakdown of occupants was about 10 percent white, 58 percent black, 28 percent Puerto Rican, and 4 percent "other."
[b]Of these, 14,000 received partial tax abatements.

Source: Elizabeth Roistacher and Emanuel Tobier, "Housing Policy," in Brecher and Horton, eds., (1981): Table 6.1; New York City Housing Authority, *Project Data,* January 1, 1982, p. 43; New York City Housing Authority, Research and Statistics Division, "Special Tabulation of Tenant Characteristics," January 1, 1983, p. 1.

the entire postwar period accelerated during the 1970s and continues to the present (Figure 2.3). Overall, 62 percent of the more than one and a half-million jobs that existed in 1948 in the manufacturing and transportation-utilities sectors were lost. Of blue-collar sectors, only construction has reflected the ups and downs of the entire economy, dropping during the 1970s by more than half from its 1962 peak, but recovering in 1985 to approach its 1948 level. In contrast, manufacturing continued to decline even in the context of national recovery. Altogether the blue-collar sectors composed about 47 percent of total private-sector employment in 1960, while in 1985 they had fallen to 25 percent (U.S. Bureau of Labor Statistics 1983, 1986).

New York's changing population and economy have led to a transformation of its built environment. But change in the physical environment did not occur automatically, nor was the direction of causality one-sided. Both investment and disinvestment have seriously strained the city's commercial areas, residential neighborhoods, and infrastructure. Reactions to the stimuli of economic growth and decline have been uneven and have frequently resulted in severe negative externalities. Private developers and public agencies have responded to and generated demand for additional office space, but

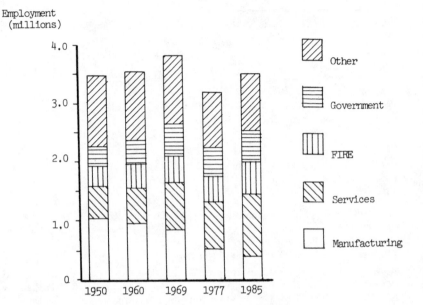

Employment
(millions)

Figure 2.3   New York City Employment by Industry, 1950–1985.
Other Includes construction, wholesale and retail trade, transportation, and utilities.
Source: U.S. Bureau of Labor Statistics (1986: Table B8; 1982: 189–92; 1979: 423–35).

often at the price of congestion, sunless streets, and overtaxed public
facilities in Manhattan. Residential development has not kept pace
with population movements and changes in household composition.
In desirable areas of Manhattan, as well as in enclaves within the
boroughs, housing demand has forced prices to the luxury level;
elsewhere large areas of the Bronx, Brooklyn, and Manhattan contain
the shells of abandoned residences. Fiscal stringency and bureaucratic
inertia have produced an inadequate transportation system as well as
serious deficiencies in other public facilities, including schools, parks,
sanitation depots, and police stations.

Development policy has been used to promote commercial construction, to change the character of residential habitation, and to
exploit economic prosperity so as to produce public amenities and
private benefits. Initiative has come from both the public and private
sectors, with the role of both varying over time. While physical
development cannot produce economic prosperity, it is nevertheless
the principal tool available to public officials in their efforts to
stimulate the local economy. Moreover, it can result in enormous

profits for those private developers and contractors who are major contributors to the campaign funds of elected officials.

In this chapter we explore the interaction between New York City's economy, society, and built environment. Our focus is the conscious actions directed at altering physical structure, either in response to economic and social change or in order to provoke such changes. We delineate the history of the city throughout three economic stages: (a) the dual-based economy (1940–69), when the work force was almost equally employed in manufacturing and services; (b) deindustrialization (1970–77), when manufacturing jobs plummeted; and (c) the global city (1978 to the present), when the surge in advanced services, particularly in the financial sector, has reinvigorated aggregate employment but has not halted the decline of manufacturing. Following our examination of the three periods, we analyze the role played by mediating forces in shaping New York's physical environment, seeking thereby to address the question of the relationship between economic change, social relations, and spatial transformation.

The Dual-Based Economy: 1940–1969

New York in 1940 appeared much as it had for more than a half-century: a great port, its piers lined with merchantmen and passenger liners, its harbor busy with ferries and lighters; a skyline dominated by Manhattan with its two clusters of skyscrapers, a more dense concentration still in the downtown financial district. European immigrants, most of them impoverished, lived under often terrible conditions in deteriorated tenements near factories, warehouses, and the harbor, and in somewhat newer, less-crowded quarters adjacent to transit lines in northern Manhattan and the other boroughs; wealthy neighborhoods of brownstones and apartments were primarily in Manhattan, but also in comfortable sections elsewhere, such as Brooklyn Heights, Park Slope, and Flatbush in Brooklyn, the Grand Concourse in the Bronx, and Forest Hills, Queens. Transportation depended on the electric motors that drove the subways, elevated trains (in 1940 two still obscured the Manhattan sky), trolley cars, and commuter railroads that brought workers into the Manhattan central business district (CBD), where the great majority of jobs was located. The economy was rooted in diverse goods-producing and transport industries, yet with important strength in the service-producing sector.

Elected to office in 1934, the liberal Fiorello LaGuardia regime aimed to provide housing, playgrounds, parks, roads, and especially jobs to its mobilized, white, working-class constituency. New York still suffered from the effects of the depression, with its low wages and high unemployment. But preparation for war promised to put the unemployed back to work in the factories and on the docks. Planners, politicians, and business elites had little doubt that the city's economic hegemony would automatically produce local recovery, once national trends improved.

By 1969 New York could look back at three decades of steady growth. Manufacturing employment had declined steadily after 1953, as the city proved increasingly vulnerable to external competition, particularly from an internationalized garment industry (Temporary Commission 1976). But manufacturing losses of 240,000 jobs were more than compensated for by gains elsewhere (see Figure 2.2). In fact, total employment reached a historic high in 1969, a product of rapid expansion during the 1960s of finance, insurance, real estate, and service industries, as the city built upon its previous national strengths. Partly in response to minority group pressure, the public sector (primarily municipal government) expanded by close to 40 percent, adding 150,000 jobs in the decade (Figure 2.1). The unemployment rate of the city's resident population stood at 3.1 percent in 1968 and 3.6 percent in 1969, a little lower than the U.S. average at the time (Temporary Commission 1977: 19, 24).

In contrast to 1940, then, New York's economy appeared on firm ground, rooted in the dual bases of diversified manufacturing and office employment that had long been its foundation. The years since the war had made the office sector more dominant, but future change looked like it would be gradual. With suitable governmental intervention, New York could be redeveloped in an orderly fashion for the rising service industries of the 1970s, as long as its restive minority population did not destabilize the city (N.Y.C. Planning Commission 1969: 1). The central concern of government was not so much creating economic development as eliminating slums, providing public infrastructure, and assisting the disadvantaged to receive their share of its benefits.

Underneath the trajectory of economic growth lay a number of significant transformations. The first of these was demographic. The non-Hispanic white population declined by more than 800,000 during the 1950s and by about 1.2 million in the next decade (Table 2.1). Aggregate contraction of the white population, and particularly of middle-income families, was accompanied by a shift in its center of gravity to the more recently developed areas of Queens and Staten Island—New York City's internal suburbs. Black and Hispanic groups expanded by about a million each over these same years. By 1969 their ghettos occupied large expanses of previously white central Brooklyn and southern Queens. In Manhattan, however, the picture was significantly different. While low-income Hispanic neighbor-hoods (mainly Puerto Rican until the mid-1960s) grew first in East Harlem and later in Washington Heights, the borough's black popu-lation actually contracted slightly. In fact, as we will discuss below, small black neighborhoods outside Harlem were exorcised through urban renewal, and the geographical boundaries of the Harlem ghetto never crossed the invisible walls of 96th Street on the east side, 110th Street in the center, and 125th Street on the west side of Manhattan.

The altered demography of the city eventually provided the social basis for a transformed politics. As the 1960s closed, the class and ethnic alignments that dominated city politics through the 1940s and 1950s were overshadowed by the cleavage of race. Blacks, accompa-nied by a more passive Puerto Rican population, now struggled with whites for cultural recognition and political power. Their rallying cries were, first, integration and nondiscrimination, then black power and community control (Fainstein and Fainstein 1974). John Lindsay, a liberal mayor, with a very different constituency from LaGuardia's, sought to provide housing and services, grant the ghettos limited self-rule, and assure minority groups an equal economic opportunity.

Transformation of the Built Environment

The built environment of the city at the close of the 1960s looked strikingly different from two or three decades earlier. Much of the waterfront devoted to freight lay in decay, its activity having moved across the harbor to New Jersey, where the Port Authority (PA) had developed marine terminals for containerized cargo (Danielson and Doig 1982: 328–33). Similarly, the midtown West Side piers for passenger liners and their surrounding streets were increasingly underutilized, despite the presence of new city and Port Authority facilities (which quickly proved to be white elephants). In contrast, the great expansion of international air travel resulted in rapid development surrounding Kennedy Airport in south Queens. Super-highways crisscrossed the outer boroughs, since goods were now transported mainly by truck rather than rail, and as suburbanized commuters became increasingly dependent on cars and buses for trips into Manhattan. (Nonetheless, about 56 percent of Manhattan CBD workers arrived daily by subway, and weekday ridership was still 91 percent of its 1940 level. See Pushkarev 1980: Table 1.)

While some factory districts fell into decay, newly constructed office skyscrapers occupied an expanding area of midtown and lower Man-hattan. Most notably, extensive commercial development had re-placed townhouses and tenements with high-rise office buildings throughout the midtown East Side. Thus, the net stock of major office buildings increased by 40 percent in this area between 1946 and 1964 (Real Estate Board 1985a: Table IV). Similarly, booming private housing construction along with institutional expansion, es-pecially by hospitals, completely recast the residential character of East Side Manhattan between 14th and 86th Streets. What had previously been a tenement district, blighted by the Third Avenue elevated trains and the noxious East River waterfront, had become the site of some of the city's most luxurious housing, as well as the headquarters of the United Nations.

Although private investment had created most of these changes, local government had a significant role. For much of this period, a set of public and private elites—epitomized by the tremendous personal power of Robert Moses and the Rockefellers—played a directive role in reshaping the built environment of the city (Fainstein and Fainstein 1988). Even after the rise of powerful community and minority group opposition in the 1960s, government continued its planned interven-tion to mediate and channel forces created by a changing domestic base and the activities of private real estate developers.

Highways and Transportation

As early as 1930 Robert Moses, drawing freely from the 1929 Regional Plan, had outlined what would become the arterial system of the city (Caro 1974, chap. 40). During the 1930s and 1940s he implemented a number of major highway projects, including the notorious Cross-Bronx Expressway, which displaced thousands of households and probably hastened the destruction of the South Bronx. The Port Authority, for its part, had twice expanded the Lincoln Tunnel and its Manhattan approaches, destroying hundreds of West Side tenements in the process, constructed a Manhattan bus terminal, and made important improvements to the region's airports. The Joint Arterial Facilities Program, announced in 1955 by the Port Authority and the Triborough Bridge and Tunnel Authority (TBTA), resulted in the construction of three bridges and dozens of miles of expressways during the next decade.

Of all the projects, the Verrazano Narrows Bridge probably had the biggest impact on the city. Its Brooklyn access highways displaced thousands of people. Bay Ridge residents and Brooklyn's elected officials vehemently opposed the project, but Moses was backed by a constellation of construction industry interests that saw huge profits in the bridge, in its supporting highways, and in the opening of Staten Island to real estate development. Eventually Moses prevailed. The bridge greatly facilitated the growth of Staten Island as a home for white middle-income households. With its opening in 1964, the value of undeveloped land in Staten Island increased thirteenfold from its 1959 level (Danielson and Doig 1982: 203).

In restrospect, the Joint Program appears to have sought an efficient interconnection of the authorities present and proposed toll-producing facilities. Autos and trucks could circulate around and through the region without being bottled up in Manhattan. With no plans for strengthened mass-transit facilities, the Joint Program assumed commuters would increasingly drive into Manhattan. They would be provided with new means of access: Manhattan was to be trisected by elevated highways at 125th Street, 30th Street, and Grand Street (none of which was ever built). In effect, the PA-TBTA envisioned the New York core as a network of superhighways, interchanges, and parking garages. But community and liberal opposition in the mid-1960s to key elements of this highway plan—along with the razing in 1956 of the Third Avenue elevated line—stimulated development of the city's business district along different, and perhaps more profitable, lines.

Urban Renewal and Public Housing Under Robert Moses

The stage for top-down urban redevelopment was set well before the inception of the federal urban renewal program in 1949. During the depression, the LaGuardia administration sponsored slum clearance, public housing, and major public works. By 1940, the nascent City Planning Commission had laid out ambitious plans for rebuilding residential neighborhoods and transportation infrastructure. After the war, New York started urban renewal and highway programs years ahead of other big cities. Through his control of TBTA, the Committee on Slum Clearance Projects (CSC), the Department of Parks and Recreation, all federal construction funds, and (indirectly) the Public Housing Authority, Robert Moses was able to dominate development policy. His approach was to reject master planning (except for highways), cater to the automotive industries, and let private developers take the lead in determining the location and character of urban renewal projects.

Moses established the "New York" method for urban renewal, a public-private partnership that anticipated the unplanned, capital-driven development programs of the Edward Koch-Ronald Reagan era. He privatized uban renewal by giving developers immediate title to occupied parcels of land and then allowing them to undertake site clearance, relocate occupants, arrange financing, and erect new structures. As an added incentive, Moses used federal funds to guarantee developers a 10 percent return on pre-clearance assessed value. It was typical for sponsoring institutions, banking houses, private developers, or politicians in Moses's personal network to identify prospective sites that were then duly declared to be blighted and therefore to qualify legally for urban renewal. This system allowed Moses to implement projects rapidly and thereby acquire for New York a disproportionate share of federal funds.

It also produced Moses's downfall as urban renewal czar around 1960. Nationally urban renewal had come under increasing fire from liberal politicians and academics for its antidemocratic character and commitment to wholesale clearance, frequently of viable working-class neighborhoods. In New York, the Robert Wagner mayoralty was rocked by scandals involving corrupt practices of the CSC and threatened by a liberal reform movement in the Democratic party. Eventually, Moses became too costly to Wagner. By that time, however, Moses's renewal and highway projects had changed the face of the city. Altogether, urban renewal and highway building displaced at least half a million New Yorkers from their homes between 1945 and 1960 (Caro, 1974: 20). In contrast to the appearance of a recovering Europe, the combined forces of urban redevelopment and housing abandonment gave New York an increasingly bombed-out aspect as the war receded into the past.

The pattern of CSC's projects reflected the political and market rationality of the New York method. Three-quarters of the projects were in Manhattan, where powerful institutions wanted to expand or protect themselves, and where the greatest profits could be realized from redevelopment (Panuch 1960; U.S. Housing and Home Finance Agency 1962; U.S. Department of Housing and Urban Development 1974). Expansion-minded universities sponsored several urban renewal sites: New York University in Washington Square, NYU Medical School in Kips Bay (the East 20s), Fordham in Lincoln Square, and Pratt Institute in Bedford-Stuyvesant. In Morningside Heights, an organization backed by David Rockefeller joined with Columbia University to replace with middle-income housing a black tenement district that had grown south of 125th Street. Other sponsors included TBTA itself, which built the Coliseum in Columbus Circle, and Lincoln Center, Inc., another Rockefeller enterprise, which anchored the Lincoln Square housing project. The nonprofit United Housing Foundation (UHF) built middle-income units at Penn Station South and elsewhere in Manhattan. Private developers, often with Tammany connections, constructed middle- and upper-income housing at many sites. One of the more notorious for its "Negro removal" as well as corruption was Park West Village (Manhattantown), where urban renewal helped check the growth of a black concentration on the verge of extending the Harlem ghetto into the middle-class Upper West Side.

Although Robert Moses frequently proclaimed his opposition to planning, the phase of postwar urban redevelopment that he dominated revealed, at the least, a consistent pattern of operation. Areas selected for redevelopment were mainly working-class residential, with potential for private investment. While some were in poor condition, they certainly did not comprise the worst slums in the city (City-wide Council 1957; Abrams 1965). Reuse was mainly residential, although with universities and hospitals often sponsoring the housing. Friedland (1983, Table 4.1) found that during this period 19 percent of renewed land in larger cities was devoted to residential reuse. In contrast, the New York figure exceeded 25 percent in every instance, and usually was much higher (U.S. Housing and Home Finance Agency 1962).

Territorial redistribution was regressive. New housing in urban renewal areas was mainly occupied by middle- and upper-income, predominantly white populations. As of 1960, apartments on cleared land had rental levels about 2.5 times those of the original units (calculated from Panuch 1960); this was the national pattern as well. Lower income households were displaced in large numbers. According to Davies (1966), 15,000 people were removed to make way for

Park West Village alone. Spillover effects undoubtedly contributed to the deterioration of other areas. Blacks displaced from various sites in Manhattan were forced by a discriminatory housing market into extant ghettos. Overall, the impact of urban renewal was to increase racial segregation.

During the period when he directed the city's slum clearance program, Moses also controlled the Housing Authority, the nation's most active by far. He believed that new low-income housing should be contained in old working-class neighborhoods unattractive to private developers. He considered redevelopment of mainly commercial areas to be socialistic, but he thought government intervention to raze slums was appropriate. Accordingly, in Moses's hands, both the CSC and the Housing Authority cleared slums. The difference lay only in reuse: the Committee on Slum Clearance encouraged development of middle- and upper-income housing in desirable areas, while the Housing Authority constructed public housing in more peripheral locations. In the process of erecting about 135,000 new housing units through 1965, the Housing Authority eliminated a similar number of existing units (Roistacher and Tobier 1980).

Urban Renewal and Housing Programs in the 1960s

With Robert Moses no longer in control, the city's urban renewal program reflected a new philosophy of neighborhood preservation and rehabilitation, instead of wholesale clearance (N.Y.C. Planning Commission 1965: 6–8). The West Side urban renewal project, the city's most ambitious residential redevelopment effort of the 1960s, embodied the approach. The project covered a socially heterogeneous twenty blocks north of 86th Street in Manhattan. In its original formulation, the West Side plan called for rehabilitation of architecturally distinguished brownstones on the side streets, along with phased clearance of tenements on the avenues. It required relocation of almost 6000 households and proposed new construction of 7800 units—5 percent of them low income, 30 percent middle income, and 65 percent upper income (Davies 1966: 121).

The project was embroiled in controversy for years. During the 1960s the most pressing demands were for more low-income housing and community participation. Mayors Wagner and Lindsay both eventually made concessions that tripled the percentage of low-income units. By the 1970s, however, activists in the increasingly gentrified neighborhood resisted further expansion of low-income housing.

Although the West Side project was not finally completed until more than twenty years after its inception, it produced exactly its intended results: it reestablished a middle- and upper-income community on the West Side with moderate levels of class and racial integration, created spillover effects that contributed to the gentrification of surrounding areas, and formed a node of redevelopment on upper Columbus and Amsterdam Avenues that eventually linked up with the Lincoln Center urban renewal area.

When John Lindsay took office in 1966, he continued the "fine-grained" approach to urban renewal established under Wagner, but targeted efforts increasingly to the major black ghettos of the city. The greater availability of federal funds allowed urban renewal to be supplemented by an assortment of programs for code enforcement, neighborhood preservation, and social improvement. New York was one of the first municipalities to participate in the federal Model Cities Program (Fox 1974: 5–6). Begun in 1966, this program sought to coordinate physical redevelopment and social services within designated poverty areas. The administration concentrated most of its housing construction and rehabilitation funds in the three Model Cities neighborhoods and mounted ancillary programs for job training, day care, health services, and education.

Lindsay and his elite business allies also tried to foster community-based economic development as an alternative to welfare dependency. The most notable of these efforts was the Bedford-Stuyvesant Restoration, founded by Senator Robert Kennedy in 1967. While some of these efforts at development in poor neighborhoods produced significant successes, their aggregate effects were severely constrained by two factors: the gross inadequacy of new low-income housing construction in the face of accelerated abandonment, and the continued allocation of governmental resources to CBD projects.

Housing programs. Until 1950 public housing in New York was mainly a white program with some racial integration, a consequence of the link between public housing and slum clearance that was largely restricted to white lower Manhattan. During the 1950s, fast growth of the minority population, increased white prosperity, and government placement of welfare families in the housing projects changed the racial composition of tenants (Jackson 1976: Abrams, 1965: 273; Starr 1970: 355; see also note [a] of Table 2.2). Consequently, public housing lost much of its earlier electoral support. Whites equated public housing construction with minority-group penetration of their neighborhoods. The turn to smaller projects in response to earlier criticisms also meant more sites needed to be developed, multiplying the opportunities for veto. In 1964 and 1965 bond referenda were defeated for public housing sponsored by New York State. Combined with communal hostility—and curtailment of federal expenditures by President Nixon a few years later—the elimination of the state program brought new public housing construction for low-income residents to a virtual halt in the city. Only 41,000 units were built during the 1960s (Table 2.2), 27,000 of which were legacies of the Wagner administration (Roistacher and Tobier 1980: Table 6.1).

The decline of the public housing program meant that publicly supported housing became increasingly dependent on subsidized non-profit and private developers. This housing was targeted to moderate- and middle-income households. During the 1960s, the pace of subsidized housing construction increased markedly, in part because of the activity of the United Housing Foundation (created by a consortium of labor unions in 1951), and in part because of the leadership of Governor Nelson Rockefeller in revitalizing the New York State Mitchell-Lama program for middle-income housing. Many subsidized units were built on land in Manhattan previously cleared by Moses's urban renewal projects, thereby assuring upper-working-class and middle-class occupancy of central locations in the city. Overall, more than 75,000 units were constructed in the city after 1960 (see Table 2.2).

Redevelopment of the Manhattan business district. The Rockefellers, from the mid-1950s on, were the dominant figures in the redevelopment of lower Manhattan. They pursued a fourfold strategy, acting to (a) intervene directly in the real estate market of the financial district, (b) sponsor a growth-oriented coalition through a business planning group, (c) mobilize huge investment by a public agency, the Port Authority, and (d) encourage the city to undertake supportive projects.

Lower Manhattan went into decline after World War II. Since the area was primarily nonresidential, its problems, from the perspective of the businesses located there, did not stem from lower-class occupancy or potential minority influx. Rather, they resulted from antiquated structures inappropriate for modern business uses. More than 80 percent of the office space had been constructed prior to 1920, and no new buildings had gone up since the war (derived from Real Estate Board 1952: Table 4). Areas to the north and west were filled with manufacturing lofts and wholesale food markets, whose occupants were either going out of business or seeking more modern quarters elsewhere. Unless action was taken, the postwar movement of banks, insurance companies, and law firms to midtown would accelerate, with the eventual total decay of the Wall Street area, and possibly of all lower Manhattan. Although development capital was available, each potential investor viewed commitment to the area as too risky.

David Rockefeller and his Chase Bank promoted concerted action. Chase announced construction of its own new headquarters building and helped finance several other structures. William Zeckendorf, the developer, followed by arranging for the movement of five large banks into new quarters in a game of musical chairs that he termed his "Wall Street maneuver." Within a decade of Chase's decision, private capital had erected thirty buildings and added more than 11 million square feet downtown (calculated from Robinson 1976: Map 7).

While Zeckendorf maneuvered real estate, David Rockefeller created a vehicle that helped unite and define business interests. After experimenting with a subcommittee of the New York State Chamber of Commerce, he established in 1957 the more narrowly focused Downtown-Lower Manhattan Association (DLMA), which he dominated. Its objective, according to Rockefeller's aide Warren Lindquist, was to assure that downtown continued to be "the heart pump of the capital blood that sustains the free world" (Collier and Horowitz 1976: 315). Lindquist claimed DLMA was creating a physical environment that would permit downtown business institutions "to enjoy their share of the expanding commerce of the city—excuse me—of the country and of the world" (Robinson 1976: 37).

DLMA commissioned studies that culminated in a plan for lower Manhattan and proposals for government action. DLMA wanted urban renewal of the commercial slums along the East River, relocation of the west side markets, widening of streets, construction of the proposed Lower Manhattan Expressway at Grand Street (which it viewed as a barrier to the incursion of manufacturing uses from the north) development of a Second Avenue subway and, most important, the creation of a world trade center under the auspices of the Port Authority (see ibid.; 1976; Stein 1980).

The city began a series of projects around 1960 to implement the elements of the DLMA master plan. A wholesale food market was built at Hunts Point in the Bronx to house firms previously located in lower Manhattan (NYC Planning Commission 1960: 38). In a related move, the city established the Washington Street urban renewal project, through which it condemned the old markets and compensated their owners with federal funds (Robinson 1976: 197ff). The municipal government refashioned previous plans to build housing on the East River south of the Brooklyn Bridge. After a series of alterations, it eventually permitted private capital to redevelop part of this area, while it established additional urban renewal projects that resulted, over the ensuing decade, in the Civic Center, Pace University, and Beekman Hospital. The Port Authority, with the help and guidance of Governor Nelson Rockefeller, reshaped and expanded DLMA's proposal for a trade center; when the facility opened in the early 1970s it represented a public investment of more than $1 billion and added 10 million square feet of modern office space. The Lower-Manhattan Expressway was, as previously noted, never constructed, despite strong support from Mayor Wagner and initially from Mayor Lindsay; instead the neighborhood it would have destroyed—Soho—became gentrified during the 1970s and a site of luxury consumption in the 1980s (McClelland and Magdovitz 1981: 250).

When Mayor Lindsay took office in 1966, planning by the DLMA had established the character of the area's future. The administration's commitment to improving low-income residential areas did not preclude it from supporting these plans. In fact, other than the Lower Manhattan Expressway, all the original elements in the DLMA strategy were implemented, although construction of the very costly Second Avenue Subway was halted and then abandoned during the fiscal crisis of the mid-1970s. Moreover, even while municipal agencies concentrated their development resources in the poorest neighborhoods, Lindsay encouraged New York State agencies to invest heavily in the Manhattan core and to target benefits to upper-income residents. Thus, the New York State Urban Development Corporation (UDC) constructed more than 2000 housing units on Roosevelt Island opposite the midtown east side, 70 percent of which were rented to middle- and upper-income tenants (Brilliant 1975: 79); the Port Authority, as noted, proceeded with construction of the massive World Trade Center downtown; and the Battery Park City Authority issued bonds for construction of millions of square feet of office space and mainly luxury housing on the Hudson River landfill created from excavation for the World Trade Center. One of the reasons for the fiscal crisis of the mid-1970s was the strain on resources caused by Lindsay's attempt simultaneously to assist the lower classes and to establish the Manhattan infrastructure necessary for office-based production and managerial class consumption.

De-Industrialization: 1970–1977

The term "crisis" has been overused to characterize almost any current problem in government, economics, health, or environment. Yet it is hard to find a more apt term to describe the conditions of New York City during most of the 1970s. New York is, of course, famous for its fiscal crisis of 1975, but this dramatic event reflected, followed, and contributed to several other crises as well: a collapsing industrial base, a housing stock ravaged by abandonment; a tax base eroded by economic contraction, widespread real estate tax delinquency, massive population losses, social programs overwhelmed by increased poverty and joblessness, and crumbling infrastructure.

Many contemporary observers foresaw the giant city's immutable demise (for instance, Sternlieb and Hughes 1976). Yet, from the standpoint of the late 1980s, the 1970–77 period appears quite different. Rather than the beginning of the end, the period marks a time of political realignment and economic transformation. The climate of crisis enabled the city's political, business, and union leaders to form new alliances, create new institutions, and rearrange the terms and priorities of city government, thereby laying the path to global city status in the 1980s.

Economic Collapse and Social Crisis

At the time no one would have predicted that 1969 would be the peak employment year for a decade. In each of the following years, however, New York lost, on average, almost 80,000 jobs. The final toll for the 1970–77 period exceeded 600,000 jobs, roughly one-sixth of the city's 1969 employment total. Besides its scale, the 1970–77 employment downtown is also striking for the range of industries affected. All major sectors lost employment, public and private, manufacturing and services. Significantly government employment, rather than behaving countercyclically fell by more than 54,000 jobs (Figure 2.2).

In addition to aggregate employment declines, the 1970s sparked concern about the out-migration of corporate headquarters. In 1961 151 Fortune 500 industrial firms were headquartered in New York City. By 1971 the number had dwindled to 79, and to 72 by 1981 (Gerard 1972; Mollenkopf 1988). Overall, manufacturing office employment in New York City declined by one-third, from 85,000 to 57,400, between 1969 and 1978. Meanwhile administrative office employment in the suburbs grew by 25 percent to 23,200 (NYCCEE 1985: chart 47, p.44). Some analysts interpreted these trends as evidence of New York's diminishing stature as a national or global business center.

Both reflecting and precipitating the city's rampant employment losses, the demographic shifts of the earlier postwar period continued during the 1970s. The black and Hispanic population increased by 3 and 17 percent respectively, and "white flight" was greater than ever. As shown in Table 2.1, the 1970s saw New York lose more than 800,000 residents, almost all of whom were non-Hispanic whites. This was the first significant population decrease in more than 150 years.

Changing racial composition revealed itself in income characteristics. Median family income in constant 1967 dollars fell from $18,619 in 1969 to $16,818 in 1979, a decline of nearly 10 percent. Meanwhile median regional (SCA) family income posted a slight increase. Residents with household incomes below federal poverty standards increased by 25 percent from 1970 to 1980, while all other income groups diminished in number. Whereas the number of impoverished white residents decreased by 12 percent, the number of poor blacks increased by 40 percent, and poor Hispanics by 52 percent (Tobier and Stafford 1985: Table 2.5).

Fiscal Crisis

In the late 1960s during Lindsay's second administration, New York's government became increasingly reliant on short-term debt to meet the city's accelerating operating expenses. At first, these short term notes were fully retired by the end of each fiscal year. At the same time as expenditures were rising, however, the economic downturn, combined with rampant real estate tax delinquency and reductions in intergovernmental assistance, caused revenues to decline. The city was often unable to redeem its short-term debt, and borrowed to roll over existing debt and obtain additional funds for the operating budget. This short-term debt dependence lasted through the latter part of Lindsay's second term and continued to worsen under the subsequent administration of Mayor Abraham Beame. For several years the banks willingly refinanced New York's mounting debt at premium interest rates. But they drew back in February 1975, when the state's Urban Development Corporation, a principal backer and builder of subsidized New York City housing, defaulted on $100 million of short-term paper. Not only were underwriters and lenders wary of the soundness of their several billion dollars' worth of New York City securities, they also feared their own liability for promoting and selling bonds of dubious value (Morris 1980; Shefter 1985). Finally, on April 15, 1975, the financial community announced that it would no longer issue new New York City bonds or roll over any of the city's existing debt.[1]

With New York essentially bankrupt, the city government became subject to de facto receivership jointly administered by Albany, Washington, the major banks, and municipal unions. The city's budget was overseen by the Municipal Assistance Corporation (MAC), which issued state-guaranteed bonds for the city, the state-appointed Emergency Financial Control Board (EFCB), and the U.S. Treasury Department's Office of New York City Finance. Dominated by business interests, these agencies sought to bring expenditures in line with revenues by cutting social service and municipal employment allocations while increasing business incentives. Municipal employment was slashed by one-quarter, subway fares were raised, the century-long tradition of free tuition at the City University was abolished, as was the much more recent policy of open admission. Daycare and maternal assistance programs were reduced or eliminated.

Mitigation of racial and social inequality ceased to be a priority of the city government. Even while the number of people in poverty was increasing, the city's basic welfare grant remained unchanged; tightened eligibility standards caused the number of city residents on welfare to fall from 984,900 in 1975 to 879,000 in 1980 (Tobier and Stafford 1985: Table 27). The generation and retention of jobs and revenues became the foremost policy objective. In the immediate aftermath of the fiscal crisis, this renewed emphasis on economic development did not translate into city-financed projects or overt subsidy programs—these did not appear until the economic revivial of the 1980s. Instead, the economic development priority was expressed through off-budget measures, including tax abatements and elimination or reduction of various business, property, and income taxes, as well as through weakened land-use regulations.

Infrastructure, Office Construction, and Housing

The fiscal crisis wreaked havoc on the city's capital budget. During the late 1960s and early 1970s, the Lindsay and Beame administrations dipped into the capital budget to help meet pressing operating expenses. After the fiscal crisis the capital budget was virtually obliterated. In constant 1967 dollars, capital expenditures fell from $1.7 billion in 1975 to $422 million in 1978, a decline of 75 percent (Shefter 1985: 138). During this time the city halted most of its major construction projects, including a third water tunnel, the Second Avenue subway, and the expansion of the City University. Even more consequential, it ceased maintaining its already neglected and rapidly deteriorating capital facilities. The collapse of the West Side Highway dramatized the magnitude of neglect even before the fiscal crisis, yet the city did not start any major capital improvements until the 1980s (Boast and Keilin 1980; Hartman 1985).

The construction boom of the early 1970s (Figure 2.1) produced an office glut, with double-digit vacancy rates lasting from 1972 to 1976 (Schwartz 1979). By 1974 office construction essentially halted, and new housing production faltered as well. Private construction fell from 11,386 units in 1974 to 3,034 in 1975, and remained under 9,000 through 1978. The 1974 federal moratorium on new public housing construction, termination of the financially beleaguered Urban Development Corporation's subsidized housing programs, and the demise of the highly productive Mitchell-Lama program for middle-income housing, all culminated in a dramatic reduction of public and subsidized private housing. Publicly assisted (public and subsidized) housing construction fell from 4357 units in 1974 to 786 in 1975. From 1970 to 1974, more than 74,000 publicly assisted units were built, 58 percent of total new construction. During the rest of the 1970s only 6997 publicly assisted units were constructed, 14 percent of the period's total new construction. Meanwhile, housing abandonment continued unabated. More than 39,000 housing units were demolished, condemned, boarded up, or otherwise removed from the housing stock each year between 1970 and 1978 (Stegman 1985: 225).

If the bulldozer symbolized New York City's large-scale redevelopment during the 1950s and 1960s, its equivalent for the 1970s and 1980s was the dumpster. With the virtual halt of new housing construction, private residential rehabilitation became the city's most important real estate activity. Rental apartment buildings and single-room-occupancy hotels were rehabilitated and converted into cooperatives and condominiums at an unprecedented pace, and industrial and warehouse space was changed into residential and commercial lofts. Neighborhoods such as the Upper West Side, Greenwich Village, Soho, and Brooklyn's Park Slope became the scene of gentrification, as middle- and upper-income households purchased newly or yet-to-be rehabilitated apartments, displacing previous low- and moderate-income renters. By converting rental units into co-ops or condominiums, landlords could escape the strictures of rent control and sell residential units at market prices. Of course not all conversions involved residential displacement: in Soho, for example, manufacturers, not households, yielded to new occupants (Zukin 1982).

Some of the impetus behind the wave of residential conversions and rehabilitation originated in the J-51 tax abatement program. Enacted in 1955 to facilitate improvements in cold water tenements, the law was revised in 1975 to broaden eligible expenditures and extend benefits to privately financed cooperatives and condominiums, as well as to commercial and industrial space converted into residential units. With indirect government support, banks became much more willing to provide mortgages for conversions. As a result, the number of units underwritten by J-51 doubled between 1974 and 1975. The annual amount of taxes foregone totaled $37.7 million by 1978 and more than $100 million by 1983, with three-quarters of the tax subsidy going to Manhattan, and the benefits largely being enjoyed by upper-income households (Fainstein, N. I. and Fainstein, S. S. 1987).

Global City: 1978—?

The most casual glance around Manhattan today immediately dispels the dire predictions made during the crisis years of the 1970s. The viewer would see towering construction cranes, limousines blocking the streets outside swank restaurants, trendy boutiques and discotheques, prestigous postmodern office towers, and art museums opening entire new wings or establishing separate outposts altogether. Statistics also substantiate the city's swift recovery: total payroll employment increased in every year but one since 1978, and Census estimates indicate population growth as well. Perhaps most telling of all, housing abandonment and tax delinquency rates have been significantly reduced (Stegman 1985).

What accounts for this change in the city's fortunes? There is no single explanation, but much of New York's revival revolves around the city's renewed status as a global city. Wall Street has long been synonymous with financial services and corporate law, Madison Avenue with advertising. As the United States becomes increasingly entwined in the global economy, these advanced services, which have become ever more central to the city's function, provide the financial, legal, and informational connections of the international corporate network. In addition, New York continues to serve as a national center. Indeed, much of the city's spectacular employment growth in financial services—and the new office construction this growth generates—is directly related to the national surge in corporate acquisitions, leveraged buy outs, and other forms of domestic restructuring.

General economic expansion has reinforced New York's traditional leadership in the arts, fashion, communications, and trade. Tourism has also boomed. After a 20 percent decline between 1969 and 1978, total domestic and overseas passenger airline traffic in New York City increased 54 percent from 50.4 million in 1978 to 78.1 million in 1985 (Port Authority of New York 1985: Table II-1). Still more telling, sixteen major hotels were built between 1978 and 1986, providing 10,651 new hotel rooms. The only other comparable burst of new hotel construction since the end of World War II was the 1965–66 period of the New York World's Fair. (Brenner 1987; Winkleman 1980). Despite the increase in the number of rooms, the occupancy rate for first-class hotels increased from about 67 percent in 1975 to 82 percent in 1985 (Real Estate Board 1985b: Table 116). In addition, ancillary service industries posted major employment gains. These businesses, including restaurants, bars, nightclubs, boutiques, cinemas, messenger dispatchers, copy centers, specialty printers, office equipment suppliers, and maid services, serve the dynamic advanced service providers and their relatively affluent professional and technical workers, as well as tourists (Sassen-Koob 1986).

New York can be considered a global city in yet another respect: it has again become a city of immigrants. By 1980 almost one-quarter of New York's population was foreign-born. A similar proportion was composed of Puerto Ricans and an estimated 750,000 undocumented aliens. Not since the great European migrations of the late 19th and early 20th centuries has close to half the city's population been born outside the continental United States (Mollenkopf 1988: 397; Rosenwaike 1972: 141). Unlike the previous wave of immigration, the new immigrants are primarily non-white, and most have arrived from the Caribbean, Latin America, and Asia.

Continuing Social and Geographic Inequality

Not all of New York's population, businesses, and neighborhoods prospered from the city's position at the pinnacle of the global financial and corporate system. Goods-producing and goods-handling industries continued to suffer employment declines. Hispanic and non-white residents have found employment opportunities limited in the expanding advanced service industries, particularly as professional and technical workers. Census data indicate that between 1970 and 1980, city residents have continued to hold about 80 percent of all New York City jobs, but transit and other surveys indicate that commuters account for an increasing proportion of the city's better-paid, professional and managerial workforce (Tobier and Stafford 1985; Sassen-Koob 1986).

Little of the city's economic dynamism has spread to the outer boroughs. Manhattan accounted for about three-quarters (74 percent) of the city's total private employment growth from 1978 to 1985, and essentially all of its new office construction (Real Estate Board 1985b). While the outer boroughs also possess service-based economies, their service industries are quite different from Manhattan's. Whereas the leading service-related employers in Manhattan are business and financial services, in the rest of the city they consist of health and social services (NYCCEE 1985). Residential patterns also reflect Manhattan's dominance. Between 1950 and 1980 the proportion of employed Manhattan residents in professional, technical, and managerial occupations nearly doubled, from 24 to 44 percent; in the rest of the city it rose by 2 percentage points, from 21 to 23 percent (See Figure 2.4).

The Built Environment

New York's economic recovery sparked a burst of private and public investment in the city's built environment. The impact of the revived economy was evident in the changing aggregate assessed valuation of the city's taxable real estate. After remaining more or less unchanged from 1971 to 1977, total assessed valuation in current dollars increased 46 percent between fiscal 1978 and 1986, from $37.9 to $55.3 billion. More than eight-tenths of the increase occurred in Manhattan, where total assessed valuation rose by 78 percent. In inflation-adjusted 1983 dollars, the value of Manhattan taxable real estate increased by $925.5 million from 1978 to 1986; in the rest of the city it declined by more than $10 billion. No less revealing of the growing disparity between the fortunes of Manhattan and the outer boroughs, Manhattan's share of the city's total assessed valuation increased from

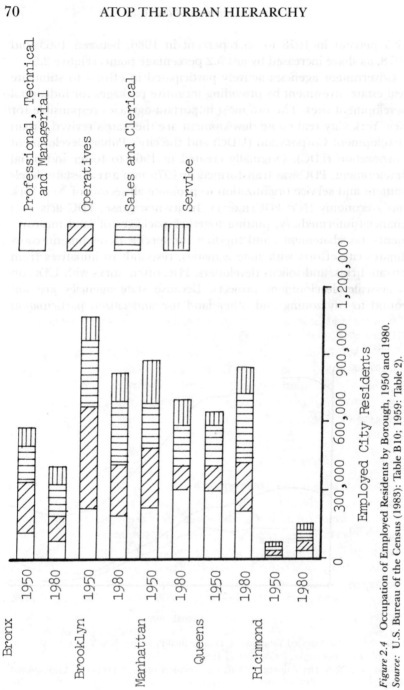

Figure 2.4 Occupation of Employed Residents by Borough, 1950 and 1980.
Source: U.S. Bureau of the Census (1983): Table B10; 1959: Table 2).

47.5 percent in 1978 to 58.1 percent in 1986; between 1963 and 1978, its share increased by just 5.2 percentage points (Figure 2.5).

Government agencies actively participated in efforts to stimulate real estate investment by providing incentive packages for individual development sites. The two most important agencies responsible for New York City real estate development are the state's revived Urban Development Corporation (UDC) and the city's Public Development Corporation (PDC). Originally created in 1966 to foster industrial development, PDC was transformed in 1979 into a real estate development and service organization to promote all sectors of New York City's economy (NYCPDC n.d.:1). In its new guise, PDC acts as a financial intermediary, putting together packages of land improvements, tax abatements, and funding for specific development, coordinates city efforts with state activities, responds to initiatives from private firms, and solicits developers. PDC often works with UDC on large-scale development projects. Because state agencies are not bound to city zoning and other land use and citizen participation

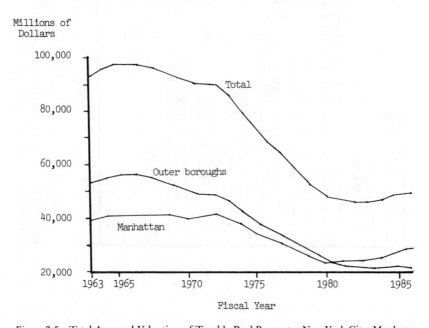

Figure 2.5   Total Assessed Valuation of Taxable Real Property: New York City, Manhattan and Outer Boroughs, 1963–1986 ($ 1983).
Source: New York Department of Finance, Division of Real Property. Unpublished data.

requirements, UDC involvement can greatly expedite the development process.

Among major development projects completed in New York City since 1978, PDC took primary responsibility for a gargantuan Marriott Hotel in midtown and for the South Street Seaport. The Marriott Hotel designed by John Portman and built on the Times Square site of three Broadway theaters over the vehement protests of the theater community, was partially subsidized with federal Urban Development Action Grant (UDAG) funds and was granted several tax abatements. South Street Seaport, for decades a wholesale fish market in lower Manhattan, was reshaped by the Rouse Corporation into a "festival marketplace" like Boston's Faneuil Hall and Baltimore's Harborplace. It was partly financed with another UDAG grant and additional tax abatements.

UDC to date has been the lead agency for three major development projects: two completed, the other stalled after preliminary approval. It arranged the infrastructure, financing, and logistics for Battery Park City, a multibillion dollar, multitower, mixed use, office-residential complex developed by the giant Canadian firm Olympia and York; and it built the Jacob Javits Convention Center, a long-delayed project located on the far west side of Manhattan, which finally opened in 1986. The UDC is also the primary agency behind the stalled Times Square redevelopment plan. Subsidized by an estimated $650 million worth of tax abatements, this project would totally reshape the appearance and character of one of New York's most distinctive and famous districts' through the construction of 4 million square feet of office space and a 2.5 million-square foot merchandise mart (Fainstein 1985).

With PDC and UDC in charge of the city's development strategy, the City Planning Department increasingly devotes itself to studies of specific zoning changes and development impacts. Its primary concerns have become the use of density bonuses, transfer of development rights, and other types of zoning variances to allow developers to exceed normal standards, in exchange for providing amenities such as plazas, "vest-pocket" parks, and subway station improvements.

Tax Abatements. Numerous private developers have used a variety of tax abatement programs designed to lower New York City construction costs. In 1982, for example, twenty-seven office buildings were erected with the help of more than $42 million worth of Industrial and Commercial Incentive Board (ICIB) tax abatements.[2] Developers of luxury apartment buildings also enjoyed huge tax savings, especially from the 421a tax abatement program. Since its inception in 1971, ostensibly to encourage residential construction on "underutilized" sites, the program has cost more than $550 million in foregone property taxes. More than two-thirds of the 56,000 units constructed under the program are located in Manhattan, where the average initial permitted rent per room exceeds $600 (Hinds 1987a). Among the beneficiaries of the 421a program is the prominent developer Donald Trump, who secured, and successfully defended in court, a $20 million abatement for his Fifth Avenue flagship, Trump Tower. The building, which contains some of Manhattan's most exclusive boutiques and most expensive apartments, was eligible for the subsidy because the previous structure on the site, the elegant Bonwit Teller building, "underutilized" the location's permissible zoning (ibid.). Only in 1985 did the city modify 421a eligibility criteria to disqualify most of Manhattan south of 96th Street.[3]

Infrastructure Rebuilding. New York's capital budget remained minuscule until 1980, when capital commitments were increased almost 150 percent above the previous year's allocation, to $926 million. In 1985, the capital budget totaled $2.3 billion, and more than $40 billion in capital expenditures was planned for the 1984-94 decade (Shefter 1985: 197 Hartman 1985: 142). Major investment priorities for the city's capital improvement plan included the overhaul of the bus and subway system, completion of the long-delayed third water tunnel project, construction of several waste and sewerage disposal facilities, and general street improvements (Hartman 1985: 150).

Housing. Unlike office construction, the pace of new housing construction did not return to pre-fiscal crisis years. Between 1978 and 1986 new construction averaged about 10,000 to 12,000 units per year, an improvement over 1975–77 when housing production nearly halted altogether, but less than half the annual construction totals of the rest of the postwar period. When abandoned, demolished, condemned, and converted units are subtracted from new housing additions, the city's inventory increased by only 11,000 units from 1981 to 1984, despite an estimated population increase of more than 93,000 in these years.[4]

Of the relatively little new residential construction, most was located within Manhattan, and almost all was designed for high-income tenantry. With new one-bedroom apartments renting, on average, for $1400 a month (and co-ops and condominiums commanding an equivalent sum) (McCain 1987), New York City housing became affordable only to professional and managerial workers, along with secretaries and other lower-paid employees willing or forced to double or triple up—precisely the types of workers most closely associated with the ascendant financial, legal, and business services.

Little subsidized low- or moderate-income housing has been built since the fiscal crisis, especially following termination in 1982 of the federal Section 8 new construction program. Of what has been constructed or rehabilitated, much is the result of private initiative. Neighborhood Housing Services (NHS), a national not-for-profit organization, opened six offices in 1982 to provide low-income home-owners with financial and technical assistance and to act as a publicly funded base for low-income housing (Fainstein, N. I. and Fainstein, S. S. 1987: Robbins 1983:12–15). The New York Partnership, a business-based civic organization founded by David Rockefeller developed 2500 low- and moderate-income units and plans to build 7500 more (Hinds 1987b).

Most dramatic of the privately initiated subsidized housing programs is the Nehemiah Plan, a church-sponsored effort to provide low-cost single-family housing in the Brooklyn neighborhood of Brownsville. Originally funded by a multidenominational coalition of Brooklyn churches, the Nehemiah Plan had by 1986 constructed more than 1000 privately owned, unadorned single-family row houses, with thousands of additional units planned for neighborhoods throughout the metropolitan area. Nehemiah housing is mass-produced on large tracts of city-provided vacant land. In addition to land donation, the city government provides financial assistance for purchase price subsidies and construction cost write-downs. New York State assists the program with mortgage guarantees and low-interest loans for individual houses (Zukin and Zwerman 1985:13).

In 1986, the Koch administration announced plans to spend more than $4 billion of capital funds over ten years to subsidize low- and moderate-income housing, the first time since the fiscal crisis that the city chose to use the capital budget for provision of affordable housing. At the time of writing, however, the city has yet to determine the program's substance, and the extent to which the program will sponsor low- as opposed to middle-income housing is still quite uncertain. At present New York's largest low-income housing effort is the Department of Housing Preservation and Development's *in-rem* program for managing and rehabilitating tax-foreclosed properties. As of 1987, the city owned more than 10,000 buildings containing approximately 43,000 occupied units.[5] The program is primarily funded by federal Community Development Block Grant (CDBG) money. Because of the high cost of maintaining thousands of deteriorated and widely dispersed tenement buildings, the *in-rem* program has proven far more costly than the city anticipated when it started the program in 1977. With property values rapidly rising, the city is increasingly eager to auction off its *in-rem* properties to private bidders, although community groups and tenant organizations continue to urge the Koch administration to reserve its *in-rem* holdings for low-income residents.

Contradictions of Economic Restructuring

The benefits of New York's renascence have not extended to all the city's people and neighborhoods. As previously noted, the outer boroughs have seen few effects of the boom, income inequality has increased, and housing production has been inadequate. With extraordinarily low vacancy rates, an unrelenting pace of co-op and condominium conversion, the extremely high rental and purchase costs of new and deregulated apartments, and the failure of public assistance allotments to compensate for rising housing costs, homelessness became a major New York City problem in the 1980s. An estimated 30,000 to 60,000 New Yorkers slept on the streets or in emergency shelters and "welfare hotels" in 1986 (Marcuse 1986; Main 1986; Lambert 1987). Several times as many individuals and families are doubled up with friends and relatives. The homelessness crisis has forced the city to expand the capacity of its emergency shelter system every year since 1982, and to utilize private hotels—especially in the Times Square area—at an average annual cost exceeding $20,000 for a family of four.

The shrinking supply of low- and moderate-income housing may also jeopardize New York's economic viability. With increasing proportions of the city's middle-income workers unable to find affordable housing within the city, and worsening congestion increasing the time and aggravation of commuting, businesses find it more difficult to attract a sufficient workforce at economic wages (McCain 1987; Sternlieb and Listokin 1985:392).

In fact, the prospect of a new wave of corporate flight is increasingly serious. Starting in the spring and summer of 1987, a series of major employers announced plans to relocate all or part of their New York City operations to the suburbs and beyond. These firms include J.C. Penny, Montgomery Ward, the Mobil Corporation, TWA, and KLM Airlines. Most ominous of all, Donaldson, Lufkin, and Jenrette, a brokerage firm, and Deloite, Haskins, and Sells, one of the world's largest accounting firms, have broken ranks within the previously stable advanced services sector. The pressures for office relocation are likely to be further fueled by the expiration of hundreds of long-term, low-rent leases signed during the fiscal crisis years of the mid 1970s (Barron 1987; "Now is the Time" 1987; Lyall 1987; Martin 1987; Narvaez 1987).

New York's future stability may also be threatened by the city's drive to sustain its economic resurgence. The Koch administration's ad hoc approach to planning, particularly its emphasis on site-specific development inducements, involves minimal attention to the externalities produced by the pace and character of the city's development (Fainstein, N. I. and Fainstein, S. S. 1987). The city's infrastructure continues to be overloaded and inadequately maintained, despite the increased congestion resulting from intensive Manhattan development.

Finally, New York City's recovery rests on a narrow economic base. While manufacturing and other goods handling jobs continue to disappear, and clerical and back-office jobs are increasingly dispersed throughout the metropolitan region and beyond, the city's growth derives primarily from financial and other advanced service industries. Financial services are a volatile, highly cyclical industry. Employment in this sector plummeted during the early and mid-1970s; the current expansion may falter as a consequence of the October 1987 stock market plunge and subsequent market instability.

Economic Change and Significant Actors

New York City has always been home for the wealthy and powerful. Although the heads of many of the national corporations headquartered there have taken little interest in development issues, some, particularly those in the financial and real estate sectors, have been active in promoting their concepts of the city's future. Major real estate developers have been especially influential in shaping the city's built environment. They responded quickly to increases in service employment by developing new, ever-larger office structures. Even in the 1950s, while other cities were experiencing little new construction within their CBDs, New York's developers, often part of families that had been doing business in the city throughout the century, continued to build without governmental subsidy.[6]

New York's financial and communications sectors remained essential to the national and world economy. Consequently the city's
core maintained an economic advantage despite very high construction and land acquisition costs, the increased suburbanization of the
workforce, the flight of many corporate headquarters from the city,
and the congestion of the transport system. While the headquarters
of manufacturing firms and the back-office operations of financial
institutions departed, the big brokerage houses, international banks,
law and accounting firms, advertising agencies, and media production
facilities continued to seek the agglomeration economies of Manhattan. The growth of international trade, the increased size of securities
markets, and the space-extensive computerization of offices resulted
in an expanded demand for office space, particularly in new buildings
offering large floor areas, in most of the postwar years.

Builders saw the opportunity for superprofits in the commercial
sector; bankers and insurers were eager to finance new construction.
While government facilitated commercial development, it did so in
the context of identifiable effective demand. A group of architectural
firms, including Skidmore, Owings, and Merrill, which designed
Lever House, the first of the glass-walled high rises, I. M. Pei, and
Emory Roth, set the physical pattern of new development, creating
sheer-walled, free-standing structures, each an individual statement
of its occupant's prestige. In the more recent period of postmodernist
architecture, epitomized by Philip Johnson's American Telephone
and Telegraph building, the tradition of megastructures unintegrated
into their immediate surroundings has continued. With government
as willing partner, developers managed again and again to build
structures far larger than would be permitted under as-of-right
zoning, and until recently they received tax abatements even in the
most desirable and overbuilt sections of midtown. They obtained
many concessions by exploiting the city's incentive zoning, threaten-
ing to withdraw investment, or simply expecting and receiving accom-
modation from grateful city officials.

While economic transformation stimulated quick response, shifting
demographics did not. The changing character of housing need, as
the city's population became increasingly minority and low income,
did not mean that private developers sought to provide housing for a
new clientele or even put much pressure on government for low-
income housing assistance. Blaming rent control, overregulation,
property taxes, and the moral character of the city's new residents,
landlords and developers withdrew from supplying housing to accom-

modate the poorer half of New Yorkers. Only large government subsidies or direct government production had brought new or rehabilitated units onto the market. Once federal and state subsidies ended, big developers focused on luxury condominiums and large-scale conversions. Smaller developers were attracted by the J-51 tax subsidy program, adding to the stock of middle income housing through substantial rehabilitation of tenement buildings and adaptive reuse of loft structures in southern Manhattan and northwest Brooklyn. The consequence was widespread abandonment in northern Manhattan, the South Bronx, and much of central Brooklyn, with gentrification of areas adjacent to the Manhattan core. New York resembled most cities in its failure to construct low-income housing. It differed from them, however, in the intensity of demand at all income levels, which, due to abandonment, displacement, and changing household composition, continued to cause an extremely low vacancy rate throughout the postwar period despite major population losses.

It is extremely difficult to disentangle the extent to which developers responded directly to economic factors and the extent to which their actions were mediated by government (which itself was influenced by the political contributions and lobbying of real estate interests). During the Moses years developers provided the basis of support that permitted him to acquire funding for his infrastructural and housing projects. They participated directly through agreements to construct housing on cleared sites and indirectly through pressures on elected officials. While east-midtown expansion proceeded without governmental intervention, downtown and West Side development, both around Lincoln Center and farther north, resulted from the urban renewal program. The Port Authority built the World Trade Center, the city's largest office complex. More recently the massive development of Battery Park City has depended on public subsidy and management, and the Public Development Corporation has been an intermediary in projects throughout the city. While Staten Island's rapid development has proceeded with seemingly little governmental assistance, its attractiveness to developers resulted directly from government's huge infrastructural investment in the Verrazano Narrows Bridge.

The business elite's international scope made it relatively independent of its immediate environment. New York thus lacked the kind of CBD-oriented effort for redevelopment organized by their business elites that characterized other American cities like Pittsburgh or San

Francisco. David Rockefeller's privately controlled Downtown Lower Manhattan Association instigated a building boom at the southern end of the island. But while Rockefeller influence paralleled that of the Mellons in Pittsburgh, the Rockefellers did not press for a plan for the future development of the entire CBD, as the Mellons had. Nor did they put together a group comparable to the Allegheny Conference in Pittsburgh that has continuously monitored that city's growth. In San Francisco "big" and "little" capital, led by the hotel industry, united behind a common scheme for a drastic restructuring of land use. In New York, however, despite the importance of tourism to the economy, representatives of that industry were surprisingly inactive in encouraging redevelopment. The fiscal crisis, which seriously threatened the stability of key financial institutions, mobilized the business community far more actively and concertedly than had deterioration of the physical environment (Fainstein, N. I. and Fainstein, S. S. 1987).

While a relatively small proportion of New York's business elite directly influenced development policy or participated in construction, a much larger group created the consumption market that has shaped New York's contemporary character. An expanded upper-income consumer class has purchased the high-tech lofts and luxury condominiums with marble bathrooms. This group, augmented by suburbanites and tourists, has patronized the fancy boutiques and decorators, gourmet delicatessens, up-scale restaurants, and trendy department stores. Despite a few beachheads in the boroughs, upper-class consumption has mainly stayed in Manhattan. But the demand for services has indirectly fueled the economies of the boroughs, the home of many of the low-income immigrants and minorities who make the beds, clean the kitchens, and build the customized furniture (Sassen-Koob 1986).

One fraction of the upper class, which can trace its roots to the Progressive Movement of the turn of the century, has significantly affected both planning and social service delivery in the city. Under the auspices of such organizations as the Landmarks Conservancy and Municipal Art Society, it has pressed for historic preservation of outstanding buildings and whole districts. The Regional Plan Association has been an active proponent of transit and land use planning. Parks and environmental protection have been another upper-class interest, and a Rockefeller-founded group, the New York City Partnership, has been the most recent of a string of philanthropic organizations devoted to providing housing for the poor. While the effectiveness of these organizations in influencing public policy has varied, they have nevertheless consistently used public hearings and the courts as vehicles for persuasion. In the instances of preservation and transit, they have contributed to the shift in policy that has substituted rehabilitation for the bulldozer and transit improvements for road-building.

Changing Role of Government

The government of New York City has always actively sought to affect the built environment. Beginning with the 19th century tenement laws and the 1916 Fifth Avenue zoning regulation, New York has pioneered in its efforts to direct development. Well before the federal urban renewal program, Robert Moses headed slum clearance programs using only state and city funds. The city boasts the largest public housing program in the country. But while both city and state government have been active participants in urban redevelopment and housing provision, the character of their roles has changed over the years, with corresponding changes in outcomes.

During the Moses' period, government played a strongly directive role in determining the form of the city through regulation and subsidy to private developers. Once Moses departed, the unifying force that he exerted over public development programs ended. Throughout the 1960s in other cities, such as Boston and San Francisco, the urban renewal agency acted as a powerful, independent, central decisionmaker guiding investment choices. In contrast mayoral control in New York caused governmental activities to become more responsive to community-based interests.

The inauguration of John Lindsay as a Republican mayor in 1966 signaled a political alliance between a portion of the business elite and restive minority groups. Lindsay was one of the group of mayors depicted by Robert Salisbury (1964) as representing a new convergence of power in American cities. This new generation was simultaneously seeking to modernize city government through emulating private-sector management techniques, to attract private development capital and upper middle class residents to the central city, and to increase the share of the urban poor in the proceeds of an affluent society (Stone 1981). Lindsay, more than most, stressed this third aim (Yates 1974). Consequently the city directed its redevelopment funding primarily to low-income areas of the Bronx, Harlem, and Brooklyn. To the extent that major renewal programs continued, under state as well as city sponsorship, they operated on already cleared land and did not provoke the controversies that erupted in other cities.

New York was among the first municipalities to participate in the federal Model Cities Program. The program's basic objective of strongly targeting governmental assistance to a few extremely disadvantaged areas fit well with Lindsay's redevelopment strategy. The 1972 federal moratorium on housing subsidies, however, forced the city to depend on its own resources for low-income housing and to shift almost entirely to rehabilitation rather than new construction. The 1974 election of Abraham Beame, combined with the termination of federal Model Cities funding in the same year, marked the end of the concentrated strategy aimed at improving the most deprived areas.

While Beame did not immediately terminate programs directed at low-income areas, the 1975 fiscal crisis, followed by the election of Edward Koch, produced a new governing coalition and a changed pattern of government activity. Once the Koch administration was in a position to resume major capital spending, it directed its attention mainly to Manhattan. In contrast to urban renewal, under which most large projects predominantly involved housing, the Koch redevelopment program aimed primarily at fostering economic development through stimulating commercial enterprises. Most projects involved private participation in development planning from the outset, and required active brokering on the part of city and state officials in order to put together a plan and financial packaging that would ensure private backing. Each project essentially represented an ad hoc collection of bonding, tax expenditures, city lands, federal dollars, zoning concessions, and private financing, accomplished with no effort toward fitting it into a coordinated development strategy. Negative environmental impacts were ignored, and the overriding of zoning restrictions was justified in terms of the greater good served by developer contributions to public amenities or just economic necessity.

The Koch administration did seek to attract office development to the outer boroughs and did commit capital budget money to housing construction. It has fielded a variety of housing rehabilitation programs and created shelters for the homeless. The relatively small magnitude of these activities and dilatory progress toward achieving results, however, have meant that hypercentralization in Manhattan has intensified and the housing crisis has worsened.

The revivial of capital spending allowed the city once again to invest in infrastructure, especially in the rehabilitation of the subway system. But the cumulative deficit is so great that it will take many years at the present rate of expenditure before the city catches up with the pressures created by the current economic expansion. Unlike the schemes of the Moses' years, except for Battery Park City and a proposed boulevard to replace the West Side Highway, none of the capital projects will have a major impact on the shape of the city. Plans for new subway lines were abandoned and, in response to federal restrictions on automobile-caused air pollution, no plans have been presented to add river crossings into Manhattan.

How much of the city's present building boom can be attributed to governmental stimulus is an unanswerable question. During the transitional period after the fiscal crisis, when real estate interests feared to invest in New York, city officials were extremely active in promoting development. Their role in offering tax abatements and regulatory relief prompted the beginning of what became a self-sustaining boom. But it can also be argued that the principal effect of tax abatements was to raise land prices by lowering the projected carrying cost of structures. The scholarly literature is inconclusive on the impact of tax incentives (Netzer 1986). Certainly New York's government was the beneficiary rather than the cause of the enormous growth of the financial industry that was centered in New York. Whether, without government intervention, this industry might have departed cannot be ascertained.

Labor and Community Actors

New York has a long tradition of both neighborhood activism and labor involvement in housing regulation and provision. During most of the Moses' years, communities, despite serious effort, failed to block displacement by highway construction and urban renewal. The traditional political leadership of parties and interest groups had lost its neighborhood roots during the period and had little strength or inclination to oppose lucrative development. But community organizations, in conjunction with organized labor did manage to preserve rent regulation, despite heavy opposition from real estate interests (Lawson 1986). Also during this time, labor unions, acting both through their own organizations and as participants in the United Housing Foundation, built thousands of units of low- and moderate-income housing.

The early 1960s involved very high levels of community mobilization. Agitation to block highways and urban renewal, rent strikes, and demonstrations against school segregation all preceded the passage of the 1965 federal poverty legislation. As a consequence, the urban renewal program exhibited a new responsiveness to community input by 1962, as Robert Wagner, in his last term of office, made a number of concessions to minority demands. Once Lindsay was elected, New York's politics were transformed by the incorporation of minority interests into the governing regime. The governmental reorganization following the fiscal crisis, however, once again excluded these interests; thus, while other large cities were electing black mayors, New York produced an administration oriented toward the white middle class.

New York's economic revival coincides with the administration of Mayor Edward I. Koch. Originally elected in 1977 as a reform candidate, Koch quickly cultivated a political base comprised of middle- and working-class Jewish and white Catholic residents. Conspicuously absent from the Koch coalition were blacks and Hispanics. Few minority candidates have been elected to high-ranking positions, and in 1987 only two non-white elected officials (one black and one Hispanic) sat on the powerful Board of Estimate. Two main factors underlie the political ineffectiveness of the non-white and Hispanic population. First, it is fragmented by multiple social divisions and political rivalries, some quite longstanding (Shefter 1985; Mollenkopf 1988). Second, it has had extraordinarily low electoral participation rates—the lowest of all major cities (Shefter 1985: xv–xvi).

Nevertheless, neighborhood groups and citywide civic organizations have continued to wield some influence over policy. Community opposition to major projects has been largely ineffectual, except in its defeat of Westway, the proposed replacement for the West Side Highway. Many smaller projects, however, were shaped in anticipation of community objections. Community housing development corporations used public funds and private sector loans to build or substantially rehabilitate housing of moderate income homeowners (see Olstein 1982). Tenant organizations, formed to combat landlord failure to provide adequate services, were able to collect rent moneys withheld from landlords and to use them on needed services and repairs (Lawson 1983). The community boards offered a voice for neighborhood interests, although their effectiveness varied considerably, depending on their composition and their relationships with political officials. Since their function was primarily reactive, they could do little to promote a positive vision of their neighborhoods; because they had only advisory powers, they were usually unable to affect projects with strong mayoral backing. Many projects, nonetheless, were susceptible to their input, and developers on the whole preferred to have them on their side (Wiseman 1981).

Economy, Geography, and Politics

A simple model of cumulative causation would argue that New York's already dominant position within expanding sectors of the national economy determined its continuing economic ascendancy. Given the engine of economic investment and a developed built environment conveniently emptying out as a consequence of industrial decline, the current dynamic might seem inevitable. Indeed, the geography and physical form of New York's earlier industrial development did prove surprisingly conducive to the accelerated growth of an economy based on advanced services. At the peak of the dual-based economy, hundreds of thousands of manufacturing jobs were located in Manhattan, primarily in loft buildings adjacent to both midtown and the financial district. The central location and compact vertical form of these structures differentiated them from the sprawling, abandoned factory sites of the Midwest. As deindustrialization proceeded, these buildings were converted relatively easily to office and residential use. Combined with new, denser construction in existing office and upper-class residential districts and on underutilized sites, conversions allowed quick response to new demand.

Such a theory, however, would never explain failures, shifts, and new developments. New York's future at various points, but particularly in the mid-1970s, hung in the balance (see Vogel 1986). While the continuation of a strategy directed toward the needy could no longer be sustained in the context of financial crisis and political backlash, the outcome of its termination did not have to be economic growth. Continued capital flight and population decline appeared just as likely.

Instead, a complex set of volitional factors pushed New York in the direction of a restructured economy and geography. A history of community resistance to demolition-based renewal preserved viable neighborhoods and environmental amenities, which then proved attractive to upper-income workers. Where obtacles to business expansion existed, either because of physical boundaries like the water's edge in lower Manhattan or inappropriate uses, government intervened to produce development opportunities. Direct business intervention in the affairs of city government saved it from insolvency.

The mandate provided by economic decline and fiscal crisis restrained New York's characteristically contentious public unions and suppressed the redistributive demands of low income groups, resulting in public policy strongly oriented toward the needs of capital. With governmental activity directly benefiting developers and large corporations, employment increased, but within a two-tiered wage structure with a shrinking middle (Sassen-Koob 1986). The poverty population grew, and the poor and working class could find nowhere to live. New York's present path of development therefore reflected the wishes of large financial and real estate corporations, but mediated by geography and politics. The extent to which the surplus thus created will ultimately trickle down into housing and services for the mass of New Yorkers remains in doubt and rests in part on changes in the governing coalition.

Notes

1. For accounts of the fiscal crisis's origins and denouncement, see Alcaly and Mermelstein 1977; Morris 1980; Shefter 1985; and Tabb 1982.

2. In 1983 the ICIB program was modified to provide automatic tax abatements for new development located only within outer borough business districts.

3. The city's J-51 program providing tax abatements for residential conversions, as described above, was similarly amended in 1983.

4. Although arson, housing abandonment and condemnation continued to reduce the net number of housing units added to the city's inventory, their incidence was far less during the post-1978 period than it was during the early and mid-70s. From 1970 to 1978, an average of 3274 units were lost each month to the city's housing stock. From 1978 to 1981, the average rate of loss was 2250 units per month, and from 1982 to 1984, it was 1917 units per month (Stegman 1985).

5. Interview with Ron Suser, Director of Fiscal and Policy Analysis, New York City Department of Housing Preservation and Development.

6. Prominent among them are the Rose, Durst, and Zeckendorf families.

CHAPTER 3

Urban Restructuring: An Analysis of Social and Spatial Change in Los Angeles

Edward Soja, Rebecca Morales, and Goetz Wolff

> I should be very much pleased if you could find me something good (meaty) on economic conditions in *California* . . . California is very important for me because nowhere else has the upheaval most shamelessly caused by capitalist centralization taken place with such speed.
>
> Letter from Karl Marx to
> Fredrich Sorge, 1880

The area circumscribed by a 60-mile radius from downtown Los Angeles, which encompasses the built-up area of five counties (Los Angeles, Orange, San Bernadino, Riverside, and Ventura), is one of the largest industrial metropolises in the world. Moreover, since the late 1960s, it has experienced a concentration of industrial production, employment growth, and international corporate finance that may be unparalleled in any advanced industrial country. Between 1970 and 1980, when the entire United States had a net addition of less than a million manufacturing jobs, the Los Angeles region added 225,800 (while New York lost 329,800). In the same decade, total population grew by 1.3 million, the number of nonagricultural wage and salary workers increased by 1.315 million, and an extraordinary office building boom marked the emergence of Los Angeles as a

---

This chapter has been reprinted from *Economic Geography* (Vol. 59, No. 2, April 1983, pp. 195–230) with the permission of the authors and the editor. It has been revised from the original version.

global city of corporate headquarters, financial management, and international trade (Security Pacific National Bank 1981a).

Sustaining this rapid centralization of industrial activity, financial control, and corporate wealth has been a series of structural changes that have significantly modified the social and economic geography of the region. A comprehensive process of urban restructuring has been taking place since the late 1960s, affecting the organization of the labor process and the composition of the workforce, the location of industry and the sectoral distribution of employment, the organization of the working class, and the patterns of class conflict. These changes have instigated substantial aggregate economic growth and expanding concentrations of affluence, as well as extensive job layoffs and plant closures, deepening poverty and unemployment, the reemergence of industrial sweatshops reminiscent of the 19th century, the intensification of ethnic and racial segregation, and increasing rates of urban violence and homelessness.[1]

In many ways, the Los Angeles region appears, paradoxically, to combine the contrasting dynamics of both Sunbelt and Snowbelt cities, adding to this mix many of the features of intensified industrialization characteristic of Third World export-processing zones. This has created a peculiar composite that resembles an articulated assemblage of many different patterns of change affecting major cities in the United States and elsewhere—a Houston, a Detroit, a lower Manhattan, and a Singapore amalgamated in one urban region.

To make sense, both theoretically and politically, of this distinctive combination of expansionary growth and urban social and spatial restructuring requires an interpretive perspective that can set the particular local experience into a broader context. The restructuring of the Los Angeles region is not *sui generis;* it is part of a worldwide process of structural change in the organization of capital and labor that arose from the series of economic and political crises marking the end of the postwar boom. Accordingly, we begin our interpretation of urban restructuring in Los Angeles with a brief survey of the contemporary restructuring process as it is being manifested within the capitalist world economy in general, and specifically within the United States. What initially may appear as paradoxical or unique within the Los Angeles region can be more appropriately understood as a particular concentration of several different patterns of social and spatial restructuring, identifiable within the larger economic system. To demonstrate this relationship, we engage in a detailed empirical examination of the effects of urban restructuring in Los Angeles since the late 1960s.

The Urban Restructuring Process

Urban restructuring is an integral part of the crisis-induced reorganization of capital and labor. Since the late 1960s, significant and widespread changes have been taking place in the social and spatial structure of capitalist urbanization, introducing major modifications in the urban patterns that prevailed in the post-World War II period. In general terms, these changes indicate an emerging transformation of the state-managed capitalist metropolis, in conjunction with the increasing role of global capital to shape urban social and spatial relations. More specifically, the urban restructuring process in the United States and other advanced capitalist countries can be linked to a series of manifest tendencies reflecting contemporary attempts at intensification and extensification in the organization of capital and labor relations. Among the most important of these tendencies are the following:[2]

• The increasing centralization and concentration of capital, most typically in the form of large conglomerates combining diversified industrial production, finance, real estate, information processing, and other service activities;

• A more pronounced internationalization and global involvement of productive and finance capital, sustained by new arrangements for credit and liquidity and by heightened capital mobility (associated with a decreasing role of purely domestic capital in the national economy);

• A growing loss of local control and regulation of increasingly footloose capital, combined with increasing expenditures of public funds to attract or maintain capital investments (resulting in intensified territorial competition among government units);

• An accelerating rationalization of manufacturing sectors, especially those that led the postwar boom (automobiles, steel, construction, civilian aircraft, consumer durables), expressed in a varying mix of deindustrialization and plant closures, the introduction of new labor-saving technology, increased internationalization, and more direct forms of labor discipline (such as deunionization, labor givebacks);

• A selective reindustrialization based primarily on high-technology and less-unionized sectors that are best able to compete within an international market or achieve some protection against international competition through the local or nation state;

• Rapid growth in those employment sectors (including old as well as new industries; office, retail and business services; banking and international finance and trade) that can most easily avail themselves of cheap, weakly organized, manipulable labor pools, especially immigrants and women;

• An overall decrease in the relative proportion of manufacturing employment (led by older heavy industries), accompanied by an even more rapid increase in tertiary employment, contributing to significantly reduced (if not negative) rates of growth in wage levels and real income for workers and in aggregate statistical indices of productivity in the national economy;

• Deeper segmentation of the labor market, marked by a more pronounced polarization of occupations between high-pay high-skill and low-pay low-skill workers and reflected in a greater segmentation-segregation of residential space based on occupation, race, ethnicity, immigrant status, income, and other employment-related variables;

• Major locational shifts of industry and employment concentrations associated with the decline of older, established manufacturing areas and the accelerated growth of new centers of industrial production, reproducing at many different scales what is commonly described as the Sunbelt-Snowbelt shift in the United States.

• Increasing fiscal crisis associated with reductions in certain social services, pressures to abandon the welfare function of public planning and to weaken public employee unions, and more generally to transform the role of the state established during the postwar boom.

All of these tendencies will not be evident in every metropolitan region, nor will the overall direction and pace of change necessarily be the same. As we must emphasize, the restructuring process involves active struggle and conflict under conditions of crisis, with no predetermined outcome. The struggle and competition are not only between capital and labor, but are occurring between different fractions of capital, different segments of the working class, and in association with often incompatible functions of the state. Moreover, unique locationally specific conditions will filter the effects of these tendencies in particular urban regions, contributing to their uneven development over time and space. Recognizing these complicating factors, we turn next to an interpretation of the urban restructuring process in Los Angeles.

Restructuring in The Los Angeles Urban Region

Los Angeles never experienced the intensive geographical centralization of production that characterized the 19th-century industrial capitalist city and shaped the early expansion of most large American cities east of the Rockies. Although founded in 1781, the city of Los Angeles remained a small peripheral outpost until a century later, when the urbanization process had become more decentralized, extensive residential suburbanization had begun, and clusters of separately incorporated municipalities started to rim the central metropolitan city. The rapid population growth between 1880 and 1920, when Los Angeles County expanded from 35,000 to nearly a million inhabitants, was thus primarily shaped by the social and spatial relations of the monopoly capitalist city.

Governmental, financial, and commercial activities were concentrated in the downtown core, and a sizable industrial zone developed just to the south, toward the port of San Pedro (annexed in 1909) and adjacent Long Beach (to this day the second-largest city in the multicounty region). The prevailing pattern of residential and industrial location, however, was already polynucleated and decentralized, with relatively low overall densities. Even with the aggressive annexation policies that increased the size of the city of Los Angeles from 85 to 362 square miles in the decade 1910–1920, the incorporated areas of the county grew more rapidly in population than the city itself. From 1920 to the present, the city of Los Angeles was never again to experience an intercensus population growth rate greater than that in the suburban areas of the county (Hoch 1981).

From 1920 to 1940, Los Angeles County added nearly 2 million inhabitants, roughly divided evenly between city and suburbs. Petroleum refining and the aircraft industry were solidly established, and during the depression four major auto manufacturers opened assembly plants, which attracted rubber, tire, and other auto-related industries to the area. Los Angeles remained, however, an economic center of relatively small firms, engaged in food-processing, garment manufacturing, furniture production, tourism, and movie-making. Despite a history of vigorous workers' struggles, Los Angeles also remained a preeminent center of effective labor control, an area where the open shop was virtually a law in the fifty years following the 1890s depression.[3]

The impact of the Great Depression, although somewhat cushioned and delayed in Los Angeles, given its particular employment mix, was accentuated by the influx of large numbers of the homeless and unemployed seeking jobs and housing. This accumulating and manipulable labor pool, sustained through the depression by New Deal programs and California State welfare policies, smoothed the way for massive war-based expansion of the economy. Manufacturing boomed from the beginning of World War II, moving far ahead of the previously larger service and trade sectors in employment by the early 1960s. During the Korean War period, 1950–1953, total employment increased by 415,000 jobs, 95,000 in the aircraft industry (by then reoriented from an emphasis on aircraft frames to a more diversified aerospace-electronics-guided missile manufacturing). By the early 1960s, the city of Los Angeles contained 2.5 million people, matching almost exactly the total population of the surrounding incorporated areas. Los Angeles County's population exceeded 6 million, more than double its 1940 size.

The Los Angeles region was the exemplary American "growth pole" of state-managed capitalism, with its economy keyed directly to defense expenditures, governmental housing assistance and mortgage programs, and the propulsive industrial growth sectors of the national economy. A low density sprawl of residences and workplaces was meshed with a network of freeways, and another round of decentralization brought new industrial and residential expansion to Orange and other surrounding counties. One of the largest urban industrial zones in the world stretched more than twenty miles from downtown to the port, cutting through rigidly segregated areas of black and poor white workers, tens of thousands of whom had migrated there during the war. The downtown core, never as dense or as developed as in major eastern cities, was reduced further as a regional focus with the accelerated growth of peripheral shopping centers and massive suburban expansion. Flexing their muscles again, powerful corporate interests crushed what had promised to be one of the largest public housing programs in the country under the banner of "fighting socialism" (Parson 1982), shifting the focus of public expenditure toward major renewal programs aimed at reviving the central city business district and upgrading the extensive areas of deteriorated housing surrounding it.

As the quintessential center of state-managed capitalist urbanization, Los Angeles also epitomized the crises borne by it from the mid-1960s to the global recession of 1973–1975. The Watts riots in 1965 and the less widely known Chicano demonstrations challenged the foundations and ideological legitimacy of the post-World War II economic order and marked a period of widespread urban rebellion in the United States and western Europe.[4] Recession in 1969 and 1970 ended a decade in which many different trends were either reversed or rapidly accelerated. The proportion of the Los Angeles County workforce employed in manufacturing peaked at 32 percent, and then began to decline precipitously with the concurrent surge of employment in services, wholesale and retail trade, finance, and government. The aerospace sector intensified its shift away from airframe construction to electronics and ordinance, contributing to a dramatic increase in industrialization in Orange County. The relative economic stagnation in Los Angeles County was reflected in enormous increases in welfare expenditures. Total welfare payments more than doubled between 1964 and 1969, while Aid to Families with Dependent Children nearly trebled.[5] After the end of the 1973–1975 global recession, there was a brief period of recovery and rapid economic expansion in Los Angeles and elsewhere, but only after a significant social and spatial restructuring had begun.

Since 1979, another round of deepening crisis has accelerated the restructuring process. Recognizing three subphases (roughly from the 1960s to the early 1970s, 1972 to 1979, and from 1979 to the present), it is possible to identify a series of empirical trends in the restructuring of the Los Angeles region, trends that can be linked back to the historical and theoretical arguments introduced earlier.

The Changing Sectoral Structure of Production and Employment

Postwar employment growth in the Los Angeles five-county region has been rapid and relatively steady. Around 0.5 million new jobs were added in the 1950s, more than 0.8 million in the 1960s, and more than 1.3 million between 1970 and 1980, pushing the regional total to more than 5 million today. Other large urban areas—Atlanta, Miami, Dallas, and Houston—grew at a somewhat faster rate from 1970 to 1980, but even Houston's net addition of 685,900 nonagricultural wage and salary workers was barely half the L.A. total (Security Pacific National Bank 1981b).

Accompanying this aggregate job growth has been a significant change in the sectoral and spatial distributions of employment manifested clearly in the late 1960s and continuing to the present, a restructuring of employment patterns that is largely masked by persistent expansion in job numbers. Some of the changes, such as the declining share of manufacturing in total employment and the concurrent expansion of the service and trade, and finance, insurance, and real estate sectors, reflect broad national trends. So too does the relative decline in governmental employment (especially federal), in dramatic contrast to the preceding decades. Other changes, although not unique, are more specific to the L.A. region, at least in their particular combination.

To describe the broad patterns of sectoral growth and change, considering both national trends and localized divergences, a series of shift-share analyses were conducted for the L.A. region on employment changes across all sectors and within manufacturing for three time periods, 1962–1967, 1967–1972, 1972–1977, based on available Census of Manufacturing data (Morales et al. 1982). Particular attention is given here to estimated regional share indices, which represent the residual number of jobs "gained" or "lost" after considering aggregate national growth rates and national sectoral growth patterns.[6] Regional share values are presented in Figure 3.1 for seven sectors (excluding government) in the region as a whole, and for Los Angeles, Orange, and San Bernardino-Riverside counties.[7] Also shown are sectoral growth patterns (including government) for the 1960s and 1970s.

Major changes between the two decades include the increasing percentage growth of manufacturing and construction and the decelerating growth of most other sectors, with the decline most pronounced for government. The accompanying regional share values for the whole period 1962–1977 bring out the relative growth of regional manufacturing even more prominently, with most of the +92033 value accounted for by a +75865 for the period 1972–1977. Also evident is the marked contrast between Los Angeles County sectoral growth patterns and those in surrounding counties, especially Orange, which show positive increases in virtually every category, topped by manufacturing and trade. What these regional share values show is an internally differentiated and increasingly decentralized urban area, which is growing much faster than the rest of the country in trade, finance, insurance, and real estate, and especially manufacturing, and slower in services and construction.

Although its margin has been decreasing considerably, manufacturing remains the leading employment sector in the region. More-

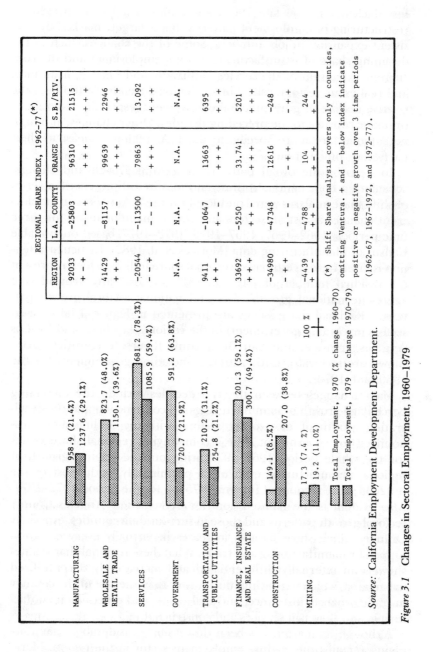

Source: California Employment Development Department.

Figure 3.1 Changes in Sectoral Employment, 1960–1979

over, relative to the rest of the United States, manufacturing has been expanding significantly, reinforcing Los Angeles' postwar position as a leading industrial growth pole in a slowly and selectively deindustrializing advanced capitalist world. According to Bureau of Labor Statistics estimates, of the less than a million net increase in manufacturing jobs for the entire country from 1970 to 1980, the Los Angeles region accounted for 225,000 more than the next two leading urban areas (San Francisco and Houston) combined (Security Pacific National Bank 1981b). In contrast, New York, Chicago, Philadelphia, and Detroit together lost a total of 651,000 jobs. Within manufacturing, this job growth has been concentrated primarily in durable goods production (68 percent), led by the machinery, electrical machinery, primary and fabricated metals, and transportation equipment subsectors (SIC codes 33–37 accounted for 45 percent of total manufacturing employment growth). By far the leading subsector in nondurable goods manufacturing was apparel, which grew nearly 60 percent between 1970–1980, representing 12 percent of manufacturing employment growth and the net addition of more than 32,000 jobs.

Probing more deeply into these changing employment patterns, especially with regard to manufacturing and to the geographical distribution of changes across the five counties, brings out the strikingly composite character of the region and its structural reorganization. Since the 1960s, Los Angeles has shifted from being a highly specialized industrial center focused on aircraft production to a more diversified and decentralized industrial-financial metropolis. This shift has been the product of a combination and complex linking together of several different patterns of restructuring, which exist individually in other major regions but appear as an integrated ensemble in Los Angeles to a degree that is perhaps unmatched anywhere else in the country. On the one hand, the region has been experiencing a characteristic Sunbelt expansion of high technology industry and associated services, centered around electronics and aerospace, at a rate that compares with developments in Houston or northern California's Silicon Valley. At the same time, however, there has been an almost Detroit-like decline of traditional, highly unionized heavy industry, a deindustrialization centered in the huge industrial zone stretching from the downtown south to the twin ports of San Pedro and Long Beach. This combination of stereotypically Sunbelt and Snowbelt dynamics has produced many of the features of a recycled labor force successfully disciplined to sustain a new round of industrial expansion based upon more manipulable pools of highly skilled and unskilled workers. In this sense, a better comparison might be made to the current industrial "revival" of the Boston region (Harrison 1981).

Added to this combination (and very much an integral part of it) has been the growth of "peripheralized" manufacturing and service sectors that resemble the superexploitative industrialization of a Hong Kong or Singapore, based on a tightly controllable supply of cheap, typically immigrant and/or female labor. Many of the same conditions that characterize the numerous export processing zones that have multiplied throughout the Third World have developed within the L.A. region, well before the idea of "enterprise zones" was suggested by the Reagan administration.

Finally, Los Angeles has also emerged as a control and managerial center for international capital, the New York of the Pacific Rim, a global capitalist city of major proportions. This has brought about a dramatic transformation of downtown Los Angeles and the corridor, running along Wilshire Boulevard twenty miles to the Pacific, into a major focus for transnational capital headquarters, financial, accounting, and insurance firms, and a full range of supportive business, entertainment, hotel, and restaurant services. Once true to its popular description as "a hundred suburbs in search of a city," Los Angeles now has a downtown whose size is becoming commensurate with its global economic influence.

Through this combination of changes, Los Angeles has concentrated many different aspects of the contemporary restructuring process in one region. As the following examination of each of these aspects will show, the result of this distinctive mix has been the emergence of a particularly successful example of the social and spatial reorganization of capital and labor in response to economic crisis and social unrest.

The Expansion of "High-Tech" Industry and Services

Table 3.1 presents employment growth statistics between 1972 and 1979 in the aerospace/electronics (A/E) cluster of seven industrial sectors, which is the core manufacturing segment of the L.A. region and the largest such employment concentration in the United States, perhaps in the world. During this period, the A/E cluster grew by 50 percent, adding more than 110,000 jobs and raising its percentage of total manufacturing employment from 23 percent to 26 percent. Leading this growth were the electronics sectors, especially electronic

Table 3.1 Employment Change in the Aerospace/Electronics Industries

SIC Code	Sector		Total Employment: 1972	Total Employment: 1979	% U.S. Employment in sector 1972	1979
372	Aircraft and parts	*Region*	108,501	100,956	21.8	19.2
		LA Cty	103,076 (95.0)	90,153 (89.3)		
		Orange	3,581 (3.3)	7,369 (7.3)		
		SB/R/V[a]	1,844 (1.7)	3,434 (3.4)		
376	Guided missiles and space vehicles	*Region*	not a separate SIC category	56,805	—	44.4
		LA Cty		47,297 (83.3)		
		Orange		7,500 (13.2)		
		SB/R/V		2,008 (3.5)		
357	Office and computing machines	*Region*	20,146	30,967	9.2	9.1
		LA Cty	15,815 (78.5)	14,431 (46.6)		
		Orange	3,969 (19.7)	15,886 (51.3)		
		SB/R/V	362 (1.8)	650 (3.5)		
365	Radio and TV equipment	*Region*	8,016	8,695	6.6	9.3
		LA Cty	8,016 (100)	7,514 (86.4)		
		Orange	—	1,181 (13.6)		
		SB/R/V	—	—		

366	Communications equipment	Region	50,179	64,158	11.7 12.1
		LA Cty	27,699 (55.2)	36,698 (57.2)	
		Orange	22,480 (44.8)	25,984 (40.5)	
		SB/R/V	—	1,476 (2.3)	
367	Electronic components and accessories	Region	28,043	53,384	8.6 11.4
		LA Cty	19,715 (70.3)	29,308 (54.9)	
		Orange	4,879 (17.4)	17,510 (32.8)	
		SB/R/V	3,449 (12.3)	6,566 (12.3)	
382	Measuring and controlling devices	Region	7,224	17,485	7.9 8.1
		LA Cty	7,224 (100)	12,807 (73.2)	
		Orange	—	4,266 (24.4)	
		SB/R/V	—	412 (2.4)	
	TOTAL	Region	222,109	332,450	
		LA Cty	181,545 (81.7)	238,208 (71.6)	
		Orange	34,909 (15.7)	79,696 (24.0)	
		SB/R/V	5,655 (2.6)	14,546 (4.4)	
	Total as % of regional manufacturing employment		23	26	

[a]SB/R/V refers to the counties of San Bernardino, Riverside, and Ventura.
Source: Department of Commerce, *County Business Patterns*, 1972 and 1979.

components and accessories (SIC 367), while aircraft and parts (SIC 372), still the largest single manufacturing sector at the three-digit SIC level, declined slightly.

This cluster covers not only aerospace and electronics but also combines civilian and military-related production, all of which have become increasingly difficult to separate. Indeed, what ties the seven industries together most directly is a shared dependence upon technology arising out of Department of Defense and NASA research and development activities and a heavy reliance on military and defense contracts. The L.A. region has been a leading recipient of prime defense contracts ever since the war, averaging around 10 percent of the total in recent years. Employment directly attributable to military spending in the A/E sector in 1978 was at least 70,000, probably even higher, and there is no doubt that the recent increases in defense spending are further swelling these figures substantially, albeit somewhat more slowly than expected ("L.A. Leads Area" 1982).

The rapid expansion of this cluster of high tech industries represents an augmentation of employment equivalent to the addition of a Silicon Valley to the L.A. regional economy,[8] and is greater than the entire increase of manufacturing employment in Houston over the same 1970 to 1980 period. Moreover, it has been closely associated with significant changes in the geographical distribution of industry and in the organization of the labor process, changes that relate closely to the rise of Neo-Fordism.

Geographically, what might be called the "new Houston" of the L.A. region is centered in Orange County and in the area around Los Angeles International Airport (LAX), with a smaller subcenter emerging in the west San Fernando Valley (see Figure 3.2).[9] Employment growth in these areas has been part of the development of what some have called "outer cities," a contemporary manifestation of the urban decentralization begun in the 19th century.[10] Rather than being satellites of heavy industry and blue-collar workers or of suburbanized office and retail nodes, these new outer cities are large conglomerations of technologically advanced industry and services, huge new shopping and leisure-oriented complexes, and high-income and expensively housed technicians, managers, and professionals, sprawling science-based New Towns described by one developer as having a "work oriented, highly scientific, no-nonsense atmosphere" (*Los Angeles Times*, August 23, 1982).

The atmosphere so described referred specifically to the LAX region, which contains a resident population of about 550,000, but

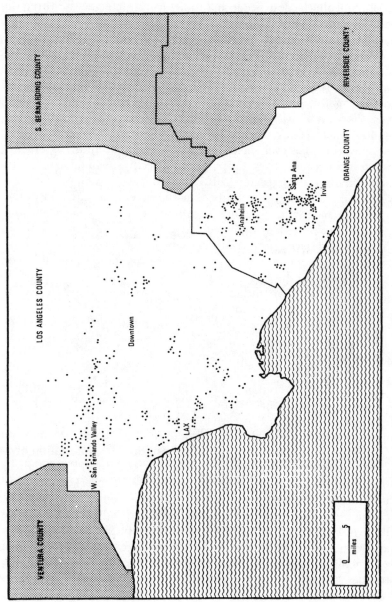

Figure 3.2 Location of Electronics Component Plants, 1981

an estimated daytime population of more than 750,000 and more adjacent hotel and office space than any other urban airport, a product primarily of the past fifteen years. Also clustered around the airport focus are such aerospace and electronics corporations as Hughes Aircraft (the largest military electronics producer in the country, which in its several locations employs more people throughout the region than any other single manufacturing employer), Hughes Helicopter Division and offices of the parent Summa Corporation, Northrop Aviation, North American Rockwell, TRW (specializing in guided missiles and space vehicles), Xerox, the Aerospace Corporation, and Control Data, as well as major banks, insurance companies, and business service organizations. Such communities as Marina Del Rey, Redondo Beach, and El Segundo have received thousands of new residents since 1970, primarily those employed in the occupations that have experienced the largest percentage increases in the country: computer systems analysts, designers and other professional and technical workers, managers and administrators, computer equipment operators, bank tellers, and so on (Leon 1982). The LAX region also contains some of the largest areas of undeveloped urban land in the country, currently being proposed as the sites for massive new housing and office projects, the most ambitious under the aegis of the Summa Corporation.

Of even greater magnitude has been the growth of Orange County, especially in the sprawling development masterplanned by the Irvine Company around Irvine New Town, Tustin, and Newport Beach. While aircraft production has remained highly concentrated in Los Angeles County, the electronics industry has become more decentralized. About 33,500 new electronics jobs were added to Orange County during the 1970s, mainly around the booming Irvine complex, the densest cluster of the more than 500 electronics firms currently operating. Total manufacturing employment in the county is now estimated to be 255,000 (Houston had 251,000 in 1980), of which nearly 60 percent are in various high tech sectors (California Business Magazine 1982). Further indication of this wave of expansion in the 1970s can be seen by comparing the employment growth rates of Los Angeles to Orange County in certain key service activities: business services (69.2 percent and 232.5 percent); banking, credit, and securities (26.3 and 161.4); insurance (10.2 and 124.3); real estate (39.2 and 133.0); health (48.4 and 123.9); legal (80.0 and 186.3). From all available evidence, this trend has continued, if not accelerated, since 1979, with 30,000 jobs added in Orange during the recession year April 1981 to April 1982.

The decentralized expansion of the high tech industries into these science-based outer cities has had important repercussions on the labor process. It has contributed to increasing labor control by further dispersing and segregating certain segments of the workforce and by polarizing workers into a balance of very high-skilled, capital-intensive operations (such as engineering and circuit design) and low-skilled, labor intensive processes (such as the cutting of wafers and packing of circuits).[11] The latter process can take maximum advantage of cheap, unskilled, non-unionized labor supplies (or be exported overseas, an always effective bargaining threat). Workers in the middle are thereby reduced in numbers and influence (draftsmen are bypassed by engineers, machine operators and traditional office workers are mechanized or computerized out of jobs), while knowledge of the whole production process by the individual worker is further fragmented.

Associated with these changes has been a marked reduction in unionization and the attendant improvement in what is called the business climate. Following national trends, the percentage of California workers in unions declined from 30.9 percent in 1971 to 23.5 percent in 1979, figures close to those for L.A. County. The change in Orange County was even more pronounced, dropping nearly ten percentage points over the same period, to 13.8 percent. Orange County manufacturing saw an almost total collapse of the unionized workforce, moving from 26.4 percent to 10.5 percent, representing an absolute decline of more than one-quarter of the 1971 union membership.[12]

Selective Deindustrialization:
Plant Closures, Lay-offs, and Capital Mobility.

Closely associated with the rise of high-tech industries has been an accelerated decline in older, established manufacturing activities, especially over the past four years. During this period, Los Angeles automobile production, once second only to Detroit, virtually disappeared, as did the entire rubber tire industry (Goodrich in 1975, followed more recently by Firestone, Goodyear, and Uniroyal) and a major portion of the auto-related glass, steel, and steel products sector. Counting a few major "indefinite" layoffs, more than 70,000 workers have lost their jobs due to plant closures since 1978, almost

75 percent of the jobs in the auto, tire, steel, and civilian aircraft sectors.[13] Most (about 75 percent) of this job loss was concentrated in the old manufacturing belt running from downtown Los Angeles to the ports of San Pedro and Long Beach, and second in a band stretching east of downtown into San Bernardino County (to the industrial area called the "Inland Empire"). Even Orange County has not been totally immune, although the firms closed there have been relatively small ones (Figure 3.3).

Industry has been decentralizing from its traditional core in L.A. County for decades, and some plant closures and business failures are to be expected in any urban economy. The quickening pace, however, and the particular sectoral and locational focus of recent closings indicates a more conjunctural interpretation. It is no coincidence that actual and threatened plant closures have been concentrated in areas and industries that are the most highly unionized, that pay relatively high blue-collar wages, and that have employed large numbers of minorities. The corporations involved also represent the core of U.S. domestic capital—General Motors, Ford, Firestone, Goodyear, Lockheed, McDonnell Douglas, General Electric, Kaiser, U.S. Steel, and Bethlehem Steel—all major leaders and beneficiaries of the postwar boom. The boom and successful working class initiatives fostered a national decentralization and rapidly rising real wages and benefits in these core, primary sector industries. Crisis and recession, however, have subsequently engendered major changes in the postwar order.

An interpretation of plant closings in Los Angeles, therefore, brings us back to the broader processes affecting the contemporary restructuring of capital and labor. Faced with excess capacity, heavy foreign competition, and falling profits, domestic capital in the United States has moved in many different directions over the past fifteen years in its effort to rationalize older heavy industries. Some large corporations (Lockheed and Chrysler are the obvious examples) have survived primarily through massive state subsidies, often reinforced by labor givebacks (essentially another form of subsidy). Others have moved out of their traditional industrial specialization to conglomerate more diverse activities, at times "milking" their older and often still profitable plants to capitalize other segments of the conglomerate network (Bluestone and Harrison 1982). U.S. Steel is one of many examples of this diversification. Another related strategy has been a pronounced internationalization—of investments, production, and profits—representing a partial abandonment of domestic labor.

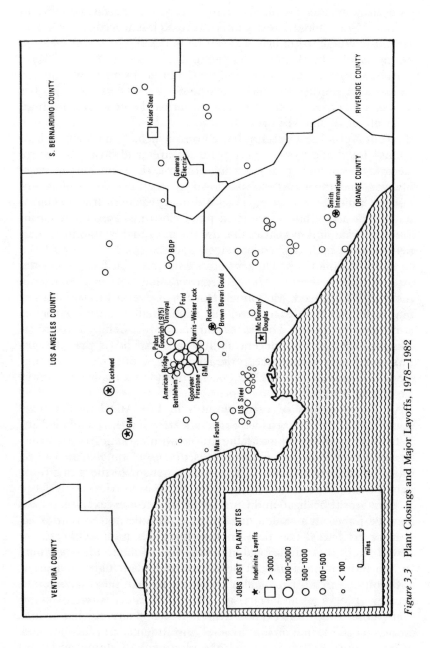

Figure 3.3 Plant Closings and Major Layoffs, 1978–1982

There is also some recent evidence of a corporate strategy of reconsolidation into older areas of production, particularly in the auto industry, to take advantage of advanced forms of mechanization (such as the use of robots) (Anderson 1982).

All these strategies have several key features in common. They are aimed at a restoration of increasing profits under conditions of crisis and general economic decline. They also have involved an accelerated pace of capital mobility and locational change, extending not only throughout the United States but abroad as well. And they have been accompanied by vigorous attempts to discipline and restructure the labor force, especially the most unionized sectors. This whole process of corporate restructuring and labor discipline has been facilitated by state policies, ranging from a tariff system that encourages internationalization, through direct government bailouts, anti-union legislation, and tax policies that indirectly encourage relocation to "greenfield" sites rather than modernization of older plants.

This attempted restructuring of both capital and labor has made certain areas in the Los Angeles region resemble parts of Detroit or the South Bronx, at least in terms of selective deindustrialization, population decline, extraordinarily high unemployment rates, increasing crime, and general urban decay.[14] A more appropriate comparison, however, may be with Boston and other parts of New England, where a deep and prolonged process of labor disciplining, plant closures, and capital flight has created the basis for a renewed expansion based on high-tech industries and services and a polarized labor force increasingly segmented with respect to the technical division of labor in the electronics industry.[15] This has allowed the Boston region to be added to the list of booming national electronics centers (along with Silicon Valley, Houston, and Orange County) and to have maintained relatively low levels of unemployment due to an expansion of low-paid jobs.

The deindustrialization and recycling of labor in Los Angeles has been described as a "K-Marting" of the population. When the president of the United Electrical Workers Local was asked what jobs her 1000 members—the majority of whom were skilled women earning $10 to $12 an hour—would be able to find after General Electric closed its flatiron plant in Ontario (San Bernardino County), she replied: "Clerks at the local K-Mart store." In recent years, however, even retail trade has felt the impact of deepening recession, with increasing store closures and bankruptcies.[16] Concurrently, the "public face" of plant closings must also be recognized. Although state and local governments accounted for more than 10 percent of regional job growth in the period 1972 to 1978, a fiscal crisis, exacerbated by the Proposition 13 "tax revolt" in 1978, led to a severe contraction in the expansion of government employment. Indeed, state and local government employment declined by 3 percent between 1978 and 1981 and was accompanied by a concomitant reduction in public services.[17]

Whereas the public sector had previously absorbed large portions of the growing labor force, that buffer against expanding unemployment is now gone. The leading areas of job growth in L.A. County today, according to California Employment Development Department projections, are very revealing. The following figures present estimated average annual job opportunities and 1982 average wages: secretaries-typists (17,637, $4.70–$8.20), bookkeepers (4,820 $9.40), assemblers (3,928, $5.50), cooks (3,630, $5.70–$7.10), cashiers (3,539, $5.50), sewers-stitchers (3,493, $4.50), janitors (3,469, $5.00–$6.80), registered nurses (3,440, $10.10–$11.60), waiters-waitresses (3,394, $3.35 +), and real estate agents (3,254, N.A.). Except for janitors and real estate agents, all are occupations primarily held by women. Given current conditions, however, male competition is likely to increase significantly over the coming years.

"Peripheralization" and the Role of Undocumented Labor

Tied directly into the restructuring process has been an enormous influx of immigrants into Los Angeles, primarily from countries along the Pacific Rim. The magnitude and diversity of the immigration since the 1960s can be compared only with the wave of European immigrants to New York City in the late 19th and early 20th centuries. If one includes the increasing black population (now approaching one million), the county of Los Angeles has become a Third World metropolis. Thirty years ago, Los Angeles County was more than 85 percent Anglo. Today, Hispanics (or Latinos), blacks, and Asians together compose more than 50 percent of the population, with the Latino segment expected to surpass Anglos (non-Hispanic Whites) as the largest single group some time in the present decade. Although proportionately smaller, the Asian population, especially Filippinos, Chinese, Thai, Vietnamese, and Koreans, has also expanded at a very high rate in recent years. Koreans, for example, grew from fewer than 9000 in 1970 to perhaps as many as 180,000 in 1982.

Greatly underestimated in the ethnic map of Los Angeles (Figure

3.4) derivable from the 1980 Census (Western Economic Research Company 1982a) is the large undocumented or illegal immigrant population, numbering somewhere between 0.4 million and 1.1 million.[18] Mexicans are by far the largest portion of this group, but almost every country in the world is represented. Together with the majority of the new legal immigrants over the past decade, the undocumented population has provided the Los Angeles economy with perhaps the largest pool of cheap, manipulable, and easily dischargeable labor of any advanced capitalist city. While transforming the cultural geography of Los Angeles, it has also radically altered the local labor market by introducing a peripheral workforce and working conditions that approximate those existing in the huge export processing zones of East Asia or in the Mexican *maquiladoras*.[19]

Accompanying this peripheralization and mass immigration has been a process of intensified segregation based on ethnicity and income (Kushner 1981). Using a simple Index of Dissimilarity, a recent study showed a marked increase in what was called ghettoization for the Latino population, with percentages of Hispanics exceeding 95 percent in some parts of the *barrio* of East Los Angeles (*Los Angeles Times,* June 4, 1981). Black ghettoization declined slightly, but the black population of L.A. County was by 1970 one of the most geographically segregated in the country. Comparisons with New York City (Manhattan), Chicago, Birmingham, and other large cities marked Los Angeles to be, across all groups combined, the most highly ghettoized. An examination of census tract income data also shows an increasing concentration in the lowest income tracts since the 1960s, particularly in the ring of communities surrounding downtown, south-central, east Los Angeles, and the Pacoima–San Fernando area in the San Fernando Valley—precisely those areas which stand out in Figure 3.4 as more than 50 percent Hispanic or black.

Closely tied to the peripheralization process and the resulting pool of cheap manipulable labor has been the rapid expansion of the garment and apparel industry, noted earlier as being one of the leading manufacturing growth sectors in the regional economy. Almost 20 percent of the net increase of manufacturing jobs in Los Angeles County between 1970 and 1979 was in SIC 23, apparel. Most of this was concentrated in women's, misses', and juniors' outerwear which, because of its need to be flexibly adaptive to rapidly changing fashions, has tended to be more labor-intensive, less technically innovative, and more organized in small shops than the more standardized men's garment sector (still heavily concentrated in New York City).

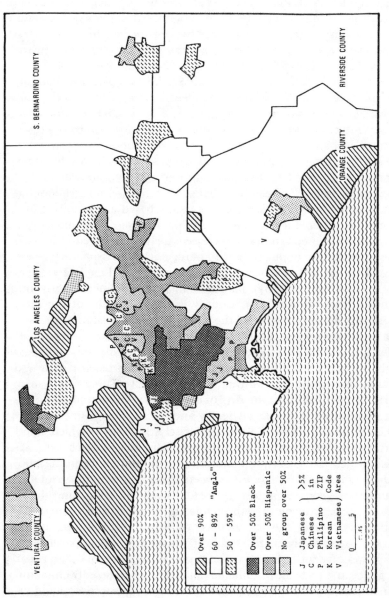

Figure 3.4 Distribution of Major Ethnic Groups, 1980

The apparel industry in Los Angeles, for this and other reasons, is very volatile, with many openings and closings each year. Although California Employment Development Department figures show a decrease in employment for the apparel sector in 1980 in L.A. County, the County Health Department noted that 2746 garment factories were founded and licensed in the same year.

Estimates of current employment in the garment industry range up to 125,000, with perhaps 80 percent consisting of undocumented workers and more than 80 percent being women. Only 20 percent of the industry is unionized, and in a recent investigation by the County Health Department, nearly 80 percent of the shops surveyed fell below legal health and safety standards (Wolin 1981). Similarly, labor standards enforcement officials found in 1979 that more than 80 per cent of L.A. County garment firms were in violation of minimum wage and/or overtime provisions. Garment factories, which bring to mind the unsanitary working environments, long working hours, meager wages, and other exploitative labor practices of the sweatshops of the 19th century, have multiplied rapidly throughout the Los Angeles region. They exemplify vividly the localized effects of the recomposition of the regional labor market due to massive immigration.

It must be recognized, however, that immigrant labor forms a key part of the entire rationalization and restructuring process in Los Angeles, affecting virtually all sectors of the regional economy. In the last decade, undocumented workers have become particularly important in three employment areas (Morales 1983). The first consists of small, highly competitive firms that depend on low-skilled, often transient labor that can be paid extremely low wages. This would include not only the garment industry but also other light manufacturing activities: hotel, office, and restaurant services, and even many firms in electronics. In Los Angeles, many companies too small or, for other reasons, unable to go abroad have expanded locally due to the advantageous approximation of Third World labor market conditions. They are the primary violators of labor standards, health, and safety laws, the revivers of sweatshop conditions, and the subcontractors most likely to turn to home work (the taking of assembly work home by workers to do on a piece rate basis, be it sewing articles of clothing or cleaning circuit boards for electronic components). Much of the expansion in office space, restaurants, and hotels has been facilitated by the specialized labor market conditions provided by undocumented workers.

A second group of employers, overlapping somewhat with the first, pay at least the minimum wage and are able to operate within the legal boundaries of what constitutes adequate employment. Given that the minimum wage produces an annual salary for a family of four (with only one worker) that is below the federally determined poverty level, many U.S. residents cannot afford to take these jobs. The immigrant workers who do accept employment in these firms— which include food processing, glass, plastics, and metal fabricating— are almost forced to be transient, for they too cannot support their families on such low wages. The outcome of Project Jobs, the factory sweep by the Immigration and Naturalization Service and Border Patrol during the last week of April 1982, in nine U.S. cities, including Los Angeles, sustains this interpretation. A follow-up study in Los Angeles showed that 80 percent of the undocumented workers were back on the allegedly good-paying jobs, expected to be eagerly taken up by the native unemployed, within three months (*Los Angeles Times* August 12, 1982).

The third major group of employers of undocumented workers in Los Angeles are firms in those core, primary sector industries that are undergoing major structural changes. One study of auto-industry firms that employ undocumented workers found that the companies usually pay well and may even be unionized, but the employers seemed to value having easily controllable workers who could be released when necessary (Morales 1983). For these firms, the employment of undocumented workers represented a temporary strategy, maintaining production until a longer-term market solution could be established, such as moving to Mexico or elsewhere overseas, changing the product line, or automating. Most of these firms were subcontractors or subsidiary branches forced to bear the market uncertainties passed on to them by the main assemblies or headquarters.

To this pattern must be added the expansion of the Los Angeles economy across the Mexican border. Not only has the periphery been brought into Los Angeles, but many Los Angeles-based firms have reached into the most proximate periphery to construct plants in the nearby U.S.–Mexican borderlands. Of the more than 200 U.S. firms listed in a recent congressional hearing as having factories in the Mexican border towns of Tijuana, Tecate, and Ensenada, approximately half were headquartered in Los Angeles (U.S. Congress, House Committee on Ways and Means 1976). They include not only such giant corporations as Hughes Aircraft, Northrop, and Rockwell but dozens of small firms involved in apparel, food processing, furniture, auto parts, and electronics. The boundaries of the L.A. regional labor market thus need to be stretched to include this special outlier, which occupies an important postion in the urban restructuring process.

Internationalization and the Concentration of Industrial and Financial Control

Over the past fifteen years, Los Angeles has drawn ahead of San Francisco and consolidated its position as the financial hub of the western United States and the primary gateway to the Pacific Basin. Moreover, it has emerged to rival New York City as a management and control center for global capital, a development that is tightly intertwined with the combination of trends previously discussed. The internationalization of the labor force has been accompanied by both an expanding global reach of firms and institutions based in Los Angeles and a large-scale penetration of the regional economy by foreign capital. The result of this two-way movement has been a growing concentration of finance, banking, corporate management, control, and decision making functions that has significantly transformed the urban landscape (Figure 3.5).

By 1980, the Los Angeles region was second only to the twenty-one-county Greater New York area in total deposits and savings in financial institutions. The gap remained large ($294 billion to $104 billion) but had narrowed in the 1970s, while Los Angeles leads by a substantial margin in the holdings of savings and loan associations and credit unions (Security Pacific National Bank 1981b). The largest California banks are still almost evenly divided between Los Angeles and San Francisco, but eleven of the twelve largest U.S. banks headquartered outside California have their sole California office in Los Angeles (*Bartlett's Guide to Commercial Banking* 1979). The L.A. region has been increasing its share of Fortune 500 headquarters and contains more than 60 percent of California's largest industrial firms.[20]

Complementing this domestic concentration is the increasingly international character of banking and finance in Los Angeles. Crocker and Union Banks are owned by British firms, the Bank of California is owned by the Bank of Tokyo, and the former Manufacturers Bank is now Mitsui Manufacturers. Recent newspaper headlines are indicative of this trend: "Singapore Group to Buy American City Bank," "Danish Bank Signs Preliminary Pact to Buy Long Beach Bank," "First L.A. Bank Okays Takeover by Italian Firm." Of the 78

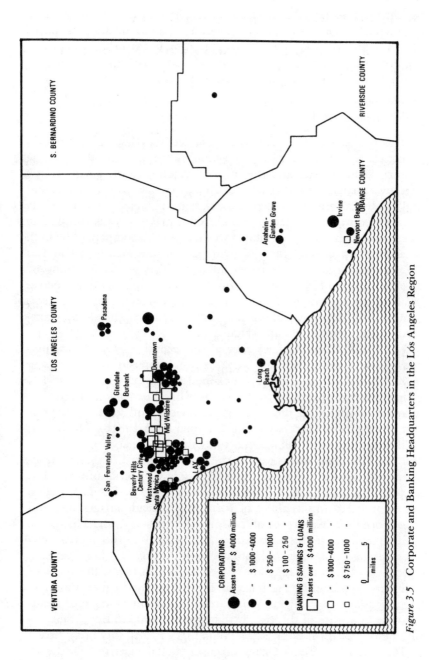

Figure 3.5 Corporate and Banking Headquarters in the Lós Angeles Region

foreign agents of international banks in California, 57 are based in Los Angeles, the largest number being Asian, especially Japanese (ibid.). Four of the "Big 8" international accounting firms are located in downtown Los Angeles, occupying nearly 400,000 square feet of office space, and a fifth is in the Mid-Wilshire area. All are British owned.[21]

Accompanying this expansion has been a major office building boom. The low-density sprawl of the Los Angeles region and the unusually low level of development of the downtown area resulted in many prime locations being undervalued, compared to the office markets of other major world cities. This latent potential for expansion has only recently begun to be fully realized primarily in conjunction with a major influx of foreign capital, the expansion of military and defense based industries,[22] and the availability of cheap labor to service high-rise office buildings and related food provision and hotel activities, all important features of the contemporary restructuring process. More than 30 million square feet of high-rise office space was added between 1972 and 1982, representing more than a 50 percent increase. Although accurate figures for smaller scale office buildings are not available, all evidence points to an equivalent boom. New buildings recently completed or under construction (with 45,000 square feet or more) as of October 1982 contain another 20 million square feet in Los Angeles County (*Los Angeles Times* October 3, 1982), while similar estimates for Orange County run well over an additional 6 million square feet.

Nowhere has the internationalization, financial expansion, and office boom in Los Angeles been more visible and pronounced than in the downtown area. Today, downtown Los Angeles contains more than a third of the high-rise office space in the region, thirteen major corporate headquarters (including Atlantic Richfield, Union Oil, First Interstate Bank, Security Pacific Bank, Crocker Bank, and Coldwell Banker, the nation's largest real estate broker),[23] and the southern half to the Pacific Stock Exchange (including its computer headquarters). An unusually high turnover of landownership (a third of all land parcels recently surveyed by the *Los Angeles Times* had changed hands at least once since 1976) and continuing land bargains (although rental rates are among the highest in the country, the price of land remains well below comparable sites in Chicago, Manhattan, San Francisco, or Denver) have drawn in large domestic and foreign capital at a rapid pace. It is currently estimated that at least twenty-one of the seventy-five most valuable properties on the downtown's western edge are owned by foreign companies or by partnerships with foreign-based companies (*Los Angeles Times* April 25, 1982). Japanese capital (in the Crocker Bank Plaza, the Bonaventure Hotel, the New Otani Hotel) and Canadian firms have been the most active, Canadian capital built the new Manufacturer's Life Insurance building (more than 400,000 square feet of office space) and is to build the proposed new California Plaza development (to include 3.2 million square feet of office space, 220,000 square feet of retail space, 750 residential units, a 100,000 square foot museum, and a five-acre urban park). British, Chinese, German, Dutch, Swiss, and Iranian interests have also invested heavily in the downtown. The remaining high-value properties are owned by bank subsidiaries (about a fifth of the total), insurance companies, oil companies, the Times-Mirror Corporation, and other industries and local businesses.

Downtown Los Angeles is the anchor of a control-headquarters complex that stretches westward to the Pacific in Santa Monica and contains such major nodes as Beverly Hills, Century City, and Westwood. In this almost unbroken ribbon of office development are another forty-nine major corporate headquarters and an additional one-third of the region's 100 million square feet of high-rise offices (Western Economic Research Company 1982b). The rapidly growing western half of this ribbon has specialized in professionals and service-oriented tenants, with 25 percent of recent office leases made to attorneys alone, and much of the remainder to business service firms, engineers, architects, and accountants (Coldwell Banker 1981). Recent completions and current construction are expected to add 5.5 million square feet of new office space to the whole Wilshire Corridor, matching the equivalent new additions to the downtown area.

Branching off from this corridor is the LAX region, a center for aerospace and related high-tech industry, services, and military activities. This booming outer city contains 7.5 million square feet of high-rise office space (an increase of 150 percent in the past decade) and many additional major projects under construction, which were expected to add another 5.4 million square feet of high- and low-rise office space between 1982 and 1984. This new space, added to the growth of the Wilshire Corridor and downtown, comes to a total of nearly 17 million square feet currently being brought on the market.

The Orange County outer city matches the LAX area in high-rise office space and high-tech orientation, but it has become an even larger concentration of medium-sized research, development, and management firms and middle-market banking (to the point of claiming the title of Wall Street West). The primary office clusters are in Santa Ana-Orange and along the MacArthur Boulevard Corridor, stretching from just south of the Latino *barrio* of Santa Ana to the luxury resorts of Newport Beach. Thousands of small and many large firms are located in these areas, which also contain or connect with the University of California-Irvine, John Wayne International Airport, several of the largest regional shopping complexes in California, and major branches of the financial and banking firms headquartered in the city of Los Angeles. The total inventory of office space in Orange County reached almost 25 million square feet in mid-1982, up from 17.6 in December 1980 ("California Business Magazine" 1982).

Smaller nuclei of corporate headquarters and office buildings are found in the San Fernando Valley (which between 1977 and 1980 absorbed more new office space than any other area in L.A. County and is currently adding 2.4 million square feet in new construction), the San Gabriel Valley (Burbank, Glendale, and Pasadena), the port-industrial complex of San Pedro-Long Beach (the third-busiest in the United States after New York and New Orleans), and in such locations as the City of Industry and the City of Commerce. The latter sites are peculiar cities, with very small residential populations. They were incorporated primarily as industrial parks during the postwar boom and remain relatively free from the tax burdens associated with providing local social services (Hoch 1981). Both Industry and Commerce have moved over the past ten years from heavy manufacturing to warehousing and distribution, and now to research and development activities and corporate management.[24]

It is not surprising that the office boom and internationalization process have spawned a major increase in highly specialized industries that service the growing concentration of control and management functions. Employment in the finance, insurance, and real estate sector grew by 47 percent between 1972 and 1979 (vs. 32 percent nationally), and even higher rates of growth were experienced in various business services (SIC 73), especially in management consulting and public relations. Particularly revealing is the new service category temporary help, for which the L.A. region has one of the highest concentrations in the country.

All these developments have contributed to making the Los Angeles region an epicenter for global capital, an internationally defined growth pole that combines substantial industrial production, rapidly expanding financial management and control functions, and a social and spatial environment unusually conducive to international invest-ment.[25] Under these conditions, overseas capital has continued to flow into Los Angeles even during the current deep recessionary period, not only into real estate, office development, banking, and industrial production but also into a wide range of supportive services: hotels and restaurants, luxury shops and boutiques, country clubs and recreational facilities, entertainment, and the media. Twenty years ago, this international presence was virtually nonexistent.

Conclusion

The pace and scope of urban restructuring in the Los Angeles region since the 1960s has been truly extraordinary. More than any other major urban area, Los Angeles has combined and linked together many different structural shifts and readjustments arising in response to the still deepening crisis of contemporary capitalism. Out of this amalgamation of trends has emerged a restructured social and spatial environment organized for more effective labor control and for the restoration of rising profits, at least for certain key fractions of capital. Selective deindustrialization and reindustrializa-tion have been occurring simultaneously, polarizing the labor force and resegmenting the labor and housing markets. A growing cluster of technologically skilled and specialized occupations, claimed to contain the largest concentration of scientists, mathematicians, and engineers in the world, has been complemented by the even more rapid expansion of a massive reservoir of low-skill, poorly organized, low-wage workers, fed from above by a recycling of labor out of declining heavy industry and pressured from below by a growing pool of Third World immigrants and part-time workers. Home work and sweatshop conditions, labor code violations and job accident rates, the complete abandonment of job search, and the amassing of an expanded "underclass" have all increased concurrently.

Sprawling, low-density Los Angeles has always been a centrifugal, fragmented metropolis with a pervasively privatized urban environ-ment, with a reputation for more unlisted phone numbers, more fenced or walled-in residences, and more conspicuously consump-tion-oriented households than any other American city. Its rapid population growth before 1960 was built most heavily upon a stream of migrants from small-town America, who were eager to fulfill personal dreams and to escape the constriction of small-town social life. An accommodative urban spatiality absorbed the newcomers into a compartmentalized mosaic of municipalities and household clusters, connected by the automobile into spread-out networks rather than propinquitous communities. In much of Los Angeles the casual pedestrian was an oddity—or a walking threat to the civic order.

In so many ways, Los Angeles epitomized the state capitalist metropolis as we have described it. It was also directly and immediately affected by the crises that emerged in state-managed capitalism at the peak of its postwar economic expansion. The already socially fragmented and geographically segregated labor force combined with a still tractable land market filled with speculative bargains (not the least of which was the underdeveloped downtown) to provide a particularly attractive and manipulative context for the transformation of the quintessential state capitalist city into an internationalized focus for global capital, an emerging global capitalist city. A heavy stream of foreign investment, along with a concentration of banking, finance, and corporate management (itself increasingly involved in global economic ventures) fueled an office-building boom and reshaped the urban landscape, while selective deindustrialization and massive immigration peripheralized and disciplined the labor force and segmented it even more finely than before. Long dominated by real estate and development interests and with no strong tradition of local community solidarity, the congeries of local governments tended to be willing and encouraging partners in this expansion, even when fiscal stress resulted.

The growth of global capital is keyed to local control over labor and the accentuation of capital mobility, enabling investment to move anywhere higher profits can be assured. The "settling" of global capital in the Los Angeles region (however temporary it may be) is an implicit recognition of its accommodative ecology. It is not surprising, then, that there has been relatively little direct reaction and mass resistance to urban restructuring. The struggles that did develop have tended, for the most part, to be relatively weak and disconnected. Indeed, the ineffectiveness of collective struggles against deindustrialization and plant closures, union breaking, heightened capital mobility and economic dislocation, increasing unemployment, declining real wages, increasing ethnic segregation, fiscally decimated local communities, reduced public services, and unresponsive local governments has been an integral component of the urban restructuring process.

Will the urban region that has combined the many facets of

contemporary restructuring most completely become the locus for a particularly pronounced political response to continuing crisis and further restructuring efforts? Or will Los Angeles continue in the vanguard of a reconstituted capitalism, successfully able to recover from the current crisis and, with the assistance of new exogenous "shocks" to the global economy, to establish the basis for renewed economic expansion? These are not academic but political questions.

Acknowledgments

Valuable research assistance for this paper was provided by Marco Cenzatti and Suha Ulgen. We also wish to thank Martin Wachs, Eugene Grigsby, Trevor Campbell, Ned Levine, Richard Peet and, especially, Richard Walker for their useful comments and suggestions on an earlier draft.

Notes

1. A recent article in the *Los Angeles Times* (December 26, 1982) on the "new homeless" in the United States estimated the number of homeless in Los Angeles County to be 30,000, 40 percent of whom are considered mentally ill. Homelessness in Los Angeles and throughout the United States is thought to be greater today than in any other time since the Great Depression.

2. For an in-depth analysis of these tendencies see pages 196–205 of the original version of this essay.

3. Perry and Perry (1963: xii) claim that "With the possible exception of San Francisco in the 1920s, it is doubtful if the labor movement has ever faced anti-union employer groups so powerful and well organized as those in Los Angeles."

4. The Chicano demonstrations ranged from high school boycotts in 1966 to the Chicano Moratorium antiwar demonstration in August 1970. The latter involved 30,000 people and was thought to have been the largest Hispanic political demonstration in recent U.S. history.

5. *Fact Sheets*, published by the Los Angeles County Department of Public School Services in 1979, noted a 1964–1969 rise of total welfare payments from $20.3 to $43.7 million and of AFDC payments from $7.4 to $22.2 million. Although not as severe as in New York City, urban fiscal problems and related austerity programs (including financial bailouts, cuts in public

services, and reductions in public employment) have characterized the city and county of Los Angeles since the early 1970s.

6. Shift-share analysis breaks down the actual employment change in a sector into three components: national growth (the number of jobs that would have been added assuming the sector grew at the aggregate national growth rate across all sectors); industrial mix (the number of jobs that would have been added or lost assuming that the sector changed at the same rate it did at the national level); and regional share (the derived change in employment after national trends are accounted for). For example, the actual increase of 219,288 in regional manufacturing employment 1962 to 1977 is apportioned into +393,853 (reflecting a national growth rate of 48% for all sectors together), −265,598 (showing the negative growth of manufacturing nationally), and +92,033 (an indication of the degree to which the region departed from national norms).

7. Ventura County was excluded due to problems of suppressed data in the Census of Manufacturing. It is included, however, in all other regional statistics.

8. Total employment for the same seven sectors in Santa Clara County, California (which contains Silicon Valley) was 146,658 in 1979. Its employment is ahead of the L.A. region only in office and computing machines, is slightly less for electronic components, and much less in the other sectors.

9. The data for Figure 3.2 were collected by David Angel (Department of Geography, UCLA). All maps were drawn by Marco Cenzatti.

10. Other examples of these outer cities include Silicon Valley in Santa Clara County, the Texas "Metroplex" between Dallas and Fort Worth, Nassau and Suffolk Counties on Long Island, Florida's "Gold Coast" between Fort Lauderdale and Palm Beach, and the string of communities along Routes 128 and 495 around Boston.

11. 1980 census data on occupations were not available at the time this essay was written, but existing evidence strongly suggests increasing occupational segregation in the Los Angeles region. See, for example, the series on Orange County in the *Los Angeles Times*, beginning July 4, 1982. For a more general analysis of the residential sorting out of the high-tech labor force in space, see Storper and Walker (1983).

12. Also interesting are figures for average days idle per employee per year (a measure of work stoppages). For 1971–1980, the U.S. average was .44; Los Angeles County scored slightly higher at .48; while Orange County's average was .23, with 1975–1980 figures dropping to an average of .08. Data sources for unionization were calculated from the California Department of Industrial Relations reports on union membership (1974–1980) and Employment Development Department (1982–1983) data. Work stoppage data were calculated by dividing the number of man-days lost in the ten-year period (as reported by the U.S. Bureau of Labor Statistics, 1973–1982) by the size of the workforce (based on annual *Employment and Earnings* (1974, 1977, 1980, 1981)).

13. Measuring plant closings is extremely difficult because of the absence of any centralized reporting agency. Even the Employment Development Department data (California Employment Development Department 1982; "L.A. Leads Area" 1983), the primary source for the estimates used, are considered to be incomplete. Figure 3.3 was based upon firm-specific data collected by the Plant Closure Research Project, a group affiliated with the statewide Coalition Against Plant Shutdowns.

14. Parts of south-central Los Angeles, including Watts, are economically worse off than they were at the time of the Watts riots in 1965. During the 1970s, the area experienced the greatest deterioration of any community in the city of Los Angeles. Population fell by 40,000; the labor force was reduced by 20,000; and by 1977 the unemployment rate hit 11.1 per cent. Median family income in the city areas around Watts fell to $5,887 in 1977, more than $8,000 below the citywide median and $2,500 below the city median for blacks (*Los Angeles Times* April 3, 1980).

15. Harrison (1981) summarizes the findings of the New England Economy Project, a major collection of studies that chart the regional restructuring of New England since World War II.

16. Plant closings have not gone forward without struggle. Leading the effort against economic displacement has been the Los Angeles Coalition Against Plant Shutdowns (LACAPS). As plant closures have confronted various communities, LACAPS has provided organizational and technical assistance (as in the United Electrical Workers fight against the shutdown of the General Electric flat iron plant) and applied pressure on state and local government agencies to help create or increase the level of special services and programs for displaced workers. The coalition was also instrumental in introducing and pushing for state legislation requiring advance notice of plant closings and compensation to displaced workers and affected local communities. It is significant that in 1982 a national campaign that sought to link plant closings, runaway shops, and union busting targeted Litton Industries, the Beverly Hills-based multinational conglomerate, as a leading representative of the corporate assault against the working class. The national campaign resulted in several major demonstrations in Los Angeles, bringing together independent unions, the AFL-CIO, community, and church groups. Reports of these events appeared in the *Wall Street Journal* (December 7, 1982) and *Business Week* (December 27, 1982).

17. Cutbacks in health services, for example, have involved the closing down of health centers, the introduction of new fees for services, direct job lay-offs, and more extensive "contracting out." The latter, affecting other public services as well, reprivatizes public employment and union-organized jobs such as dietary workers, laundry, and client financial services, jobs that are overwhelmingly held by black and brown minorities.

18. For more details on the politically sensitive debates and estimates of the size of the undocumented population in Los Angeles, see Wolinsky (1982) and Cornelius, Chavez, and Castro (1982).

19. *Maquiladoras* are assembly plants in Mexican export processing zones. They have increased rapidly in numbers since the initiation of the Border Industrialization Program in 1965.

20. The number of Fortune 500 firms in Los Angeles increased from 14 to 21 between 1957 and 1982. Information on headquarters of California's largest industrial and financial firms was derived from "California Business Magazine" (1982) and the 1982 *Los Angeles Times* "Roster" of leading California firms (May 18, 1982).

21. The accounting firms are Price Waterhouse; Peat, Marwick, Mitchell; Coopers Lybrand; Deloitte Haskins and Sells; and in the mid-Wilshire area, Touche Ross.

22. It has been estimated that 25 percent to 30 percent of the total new office space in the Los Angeles region is being absorbed by defense related industries (*Los Angeles Times* April 5, 1981).

23. Crocker Bank, now British owned, has a dual headquarters, having added a Los Angeles center to its original headquarters in San Francisco.

24. Los Angeles County (Los Angeles-Long Beach SMSA) has the largest square footage of industrial floor space of any SMSA in the country, estimated by Coldwell Banker (1981) to be 526 million in 1980 (vs. 516 for New York and 512 for Chicago). In Commerce, Industry, and the LAX area, much of this space is currently being recycled into office construction.

25. The formation of world cities is explored in more general terms by Friedmann and Wolff (1982).

CHAPTER 4

Planning for Chicago: The Changing Politics of Metropolitan Growth and Neighborhood Development

Marc A. Weiss and John T. Metzger

Chicago was the premier modern industrial city of the late 19th and early 20th centuries. The city, a tiny hamlet in 1830, grew to a population of 5000 in 1840, 1 million in 1890, 2 million in 1910, and 3 million in 1930. Chicago had 300,000 manufacturing jobs in 1900, and 500,000 by 1920. Its rapid growth in population and employment was based on the tremendous expansion of manufacturing activity and related services. The Chicago area economy has been highly diversified in its manufacturing and has offered a wide range of business and personal services, transportation and communications, and wholesale and retail trade as well. Rebuilding after the Chicago fire of 1871 meant accommodating burgeoning increases in population and employment so that the primary role for urban planning was to shape land-use patterns and coordinate public and private investment in real estate and construction for the massive future growth (Chicago Plan Commission 1942b; Hoyt 1933; Mayer and Wade 1969; Weiss 1987).

By the 1930s, however, the city's relentless expansion hit its first major snag. The long cyclical crisis of the Great Depression revealed a structural decline of the inner zone of neighborhoods immediately adjacent to the central business district. These inner areas constantly had been depleted by the movement of people and jobs to the outskirts of the expanding city limits and to suburban communities, but they had always been replenished by new immigrants and business establishments. For the first time, there was no replenishment—inner

123

zone population and employment opportunities declined, as did real estate values, and physical deterioration increased noticeably. In this context, the role of urban planning became not only the facilitation of overall metropolitan growth by guiding public and private land development but also the promotion of physical reconstruction and redevelopment of the inner areas. Once the Depression ended and World War II began, however, population and employment continued to increase for the next three decades, and the ruling policy assumption of urban planning continued to be that physical development was all that was necessary to accommodate the inevitable growth of the Chicago area economy.

The "inevitable" growth lasted more than a century, but it did not last forever. The city of Chicago lost more than 600,000 people from 1950 to 1980 and, while the suburban population grew rapidly from 1950 to 1970, between 1970 and 1980 the entire metropolitan area essentially stopped growing. Manufacturing jobs in the city of Chicago fell from a 1947 peak of 668,000 to 277,000 in 1982, the lowest number since the 19th century. Suburban manufacturing employment picked up the slack for almost a generation, growing by 315,000 jobs from 1947 to the peak year of 1977. Since then region-wide decline has set in; even the suburbs lost 32,000 manufacturing jobs between 1977 and 1982 (Berry and Cutler 1976; Cutler 1982; McDonald 1984).

This new reality has precipitated a reexamination of the basic assumptions of urban planning. No longer are land-use changes the only strategies and techniques used to accommodate growth. New debates and methods have centered on the issue of stimulating city and metropolitan population and employment growth by promoting business opportunities through financial support, education and training, technical assistance, and other programs. In the new lexicon of "economic development," land planning and development has lost the premier public policy position it occupied for so long in the city of Daniel Burnham. Furthermore, the paramount political position held by the downtown corporate decision makers in the urban planning process is being increasingly challenged by community development organizations, particularly in the inner zone of city neighborhoods. Consequently, new forms of political and economic partnerships are being forged among a wider variety of public and private sector participants than ever before.

Chicago History: Three Periods Of Growth, Planning, and Development

The first major period of modern urban planning in Chicago came with the "City Beautiful" movement, which was spawned by the 1893 World's Columbian Exposition and culminated in the 1909 "Plan of Chicago" written by Daniel Burnham and Edward Bennett and sponsored by the Commercial Club. This period lasted until the early 1930s by which time major portions of the 1909 plan had been completed. The basic thrust of the plan was to establish the modern commercial/corporate downtown area by removing manufacturing, warehousing, rail yards, and other unsightly activities from the central area, and replacing them with parks, boulevards, bridges, and new public and private office buildings. This downtown area was to be linked to expanding middle- and upper-income suburban residential areas by an improved radial system of highways and rail transportation, and suburban housing growth was to be encouraged and protected by a system of regional parks and forest preserves. Finally, Chicago's "front yard," the land along Lake Michigan, was to be reclaimed for recreational use and a long corridor of fashionable residential developments (Burnham and Bennett 1909; Moody 1919).

The business executives who sponsored and lobbied for the 1909 Plan of Chicago were not opposed to the growth of manufacturing in the metropolis. Many of them were executives and directors of large industrial corporations headquartered in Chicago. However, they did not want the dirt, grime, and congestion of the blue-collar world to impinge on their home-to-office white-collar lifestyle. The vision of Daniel Burnham, head of the city's largest architectural firm and well known designer of downtown skyscrapers, and of his fellow members of the Commercial Club was the creation of a "post-industrial" city center. This vision was clearly a part of the 1909 plan and proved to be a remarkably successful concept.

Despite vigorous battles between members of the Commercial Club and central area manufacturers, railroad executives, wholesalers, and other business interests opposed to the Plan, the Commercial Club triumphed. Downtown rail lines were covered over and the air rights were eventually developed for parks, office buildings, and consolidated passenger terminals; the wholesale produce market was relocated to accommodate construction of the bilevel Wacker Drive; the Michigan Avenue Bridge opened up the "Magic Mile" and the "Gold

Coast"; a long and beautiful lakefront park was established; and a vast array of street widening, bridges over the Chicago River, and other improvements were initiated to reconstruct and secure the modern commercial core. Combined with new highways and forest preserves designed to link the downtown to the spreading metropolis, a total of nearly $300 million in public funds was spent in the two decades after 1909 to make the Chicago Plan a reality (Chicago Plan Commission 1933; Mayer and Wade 1969; Walker 1950).

Perhaps the most remarkable aspect of the Commercial Club's plan is that it completely ignored the inner zone of working-class industrial and residential neighborhoods that surrounded the downtown and constituted the great bulk of the city's developed land and its population. The corporate vision of the future took these areas for granted and looked both inward to the central business district and outward to the suburbs as the focus of public investment.

During the second period of modern Chicago planning, from the early 1930s to the early 1970s, this attitude changed. The primary causes for this change were, first, the decentralization of employment and population, particularly during the 1920s, and the failure of new immigrants and businesses to move in and revitalize the now increasingly abandoned "zone of transition" surrounding the central area. The result was declining property values, underutilized facilities, and spreading physical deterioration. The second primary cause was the rapid influx of black people into the inner zone precisely at a time when the demand for their labor was drying up. Chicago's black population jumped from 40,000 in 1910 to 250,000 in 1930 to one-half million in 1950 and one million by 1970. The racial fears and hostility of white Chicagoans generated calls for action to block the spread of the black population into white residential areas and to physically remove blacks from neighborhoods near downtown (Hirsch 1983; Philpott 1978).

The response of the Commercial Club, the newly formed Central Area Committee, and their counterparts among other civic organizations and public officials, was to initiate a new round of planning that produced in 1943 a master plan that focused almost entirely on the vast inner zone that the 1909 plan had avoided. The 1943 plan, written mostly by the famous real estate economist Homer Hoyt, proposed that twenty-two square miles of "blighted" inner city land be completely cleared and then rebuilt with low-density, middle-income housing. The suburbs were to be transplanted to the slums of Halsted Street. Neighborhood conservation techniques were to be applied to many more square miles of inner-zone housing farther from the city's center (Chicago Plan Commission 1941, 1942a; 1942b; 1942c; 1943; Mayer and Wade 1969).

The strategy of urban redevelopment, later embodied in a host of federal programs that included urban renewal, public housing, and the interstate highways, succeeded in saving and expanding Chicago's downtown, rebuilding a few neighborhoods and reviving several others, and further facilitating suburban population and employment growth (Weiss 1981). By the 1970s, Chicago had become the corporate city that the Commercial Club and the Central Area Committee had envisioned, with a great concentration of service and retail jobs in the central area surrounded by pockets of high-income housing, and healthy expansion of housing and jobs on the city's periphery. Despite three decades of rebuilding under the 1943 plan and extensive investment in construction programs by Mayor Richard J. Daley, large portions of the inner zone continued to deteriorate (Berry and Cutler 1976; Berry 1979; Chicago Plan Commission 1958; 1966; Cutler 1982).

The third period of Chicago planning, beginning in 1973 with the Central Area Committee's "Chicago 21 Plan" and widespread neighborhood opposition to the plan's implementation, was characterized by the end of nearly one and one-half centuries of employment growth. By then, even the downtown and the suburbs stopped generating enough new jobs to stem the overall metropolitan stagnation (Chicago Central Area Committee 1973). The loss in manufacturing employment was severe and particularly devastating to the older industrial areas of the city. At the same time, the emergence of neighborhood activism in the political area went far beyond any previous independent efforts to mobilize communities.

The Commercial Club responded to the new economic reality by sponsoring a plan in 1984, "Jobs for Metropolitan Chicago". The significance of plan is that it essentially abandoned the hallowed tradition of Daniel Burnham, Homer Hoyt, and Richard Daley, which stressed physical development and redevelopment to accommodate what was assumed to be continued metropolitan employment and population growth. The 1984 Plan was not a land use plan but an economic development plan that emphasized financial tools, job training, research and education, and other methods to stimulate the growth of private businesses and jobs (Peltz and Weiss 1984). Growth was no longer assumed; it had to be generated. Infrastructure and land planning still had an important role to play, though no longer a preeminent role (Commercial Club of Chicago 1984).

True to tradition, however, the Commercial Club's 1984 plan continued to largely ignore the inner zone. The emergence of a powerful movement of neighborhood-based advocacy and development organizations forced a change in the Commercial Club's position by 1987. Mayor Harold Washington's election in 1983 and reelection in 1987, his control of the Chicago City Council in 1986, and increased dominance in the Cook County Democratic Party after his successful reelection campaign, galvanized a new constituency for "balanced growth," economic development policies designed to promote better jobs and housing for the inner zone (City of Chicago 1984; Mier, Moe, and Sherr 1986). Black and Hispanic groups became increasingly well organized, often joining forces with working-class and middle-class white community organizations to oppose inner city "redlining" by financial institutions; to campaign for neighborhood lending through the Chicago Reinvestment Alliance; to block the prospective money-losing and downtown-oriented World's Fair through the Chicago 1992 Committee; and to support linkage programs and a variety of other strategies to promote housing rehabilitation and industrial and commercial development (McClory 1986; Metzger and Weiss 1988; Squires et al. 1987).

During this period, the problems of the inner zone had extended to many suburban communities, particularly in Cook County, while other parts of the outer ring, most notably DuPage County, the North Shore, and the area near O'Hare International Airport, continued to thrive economically. The suburban periphery was now more divided than ever before between haves and have-nots, along both class and racial lines. Economic development truly became a metropolitan-wide issue, and neighborhood organization and advocacy emerged as a notable feature of regional politics and planning.

The effect of all these initiatives is that both land planning and economic development planning in metropolitan Chicago are slowly changing from the old downtown-suburban partnership to a three-way affair with greater participation by neighborhood organizations from a now greatly expanded inner zone that includes many older suburbs. For the first time, there now exists the genuine possibility that targeted investment programs could actually benefit existing inner zone residents. Such an outcome would contrast sharply with past attempts at private-public rebuilding of these communities through population displacement and racial segregation. Since this third period of Chicago planning is only in the fifteenth year of what should be approximately a 40-year cycle, the full results will not be visible until early in the 21st century.

The Changing Structure of the Chicago Metropolitan Economy

The rapid growth of Chicago during the 19th century was unmatched by that of any other large city in the world up to that time. Chicago's access to the Great Lakes trade through Lake Michigan provided it with a key economic advantage. The development of the Erie and Illinois-Michigan canals, along with lake commerce and railroad construction, facilitated the import of labor and raw materials and the export of finished products. Nearly one-half of the railway mileage in the United States entered Chicago, making the city a major transportation hub and further enhancing its industrial development.

Initially, Chicago developed as a commercial city dependent upon the lakes and railroads, with an economy primarily oriented to serving local needs. After the Civil War, with changes in industrial technology and business organization, Chicago became a national manufacturing center. Several industries emerged during this period and remained prominent through the early 20th century: meat packing, agricultural machinery, men's clothing, and furniture manufacture. Through the import of iron ore and coal, the Chicago region also became a leading center for the iron and steel industry. By the turn of the century, the number of people employed in Chicago's manufacturing industries had reached nearly 300,000 (Chicago Plan Commission 1942b; Hoyt 1933; Mayer and Wade 1969).

The growth of manufacturing in Chicago continued through World War I, as factories spread west and along the branches of the Chicago River, and as a large iron and steel complex developed on the city's south side in the Lake Calumet region (see Figure 4.1). After 1919, manufacturing firms began to locate farther from the central city. The process of decentralization continued to the beginning of World War II and resulted in the creation of industrial districts on the city's outskirts and in suburbs like Cicero (ibid.; Buder 1967; Monchow 1939). Iron and steel and printing and publishing became the dominant industries, while electrical equipment, chemicals, and allied products advanced as important production sectors. During this period of industrial development, the work force of earlier Irish and

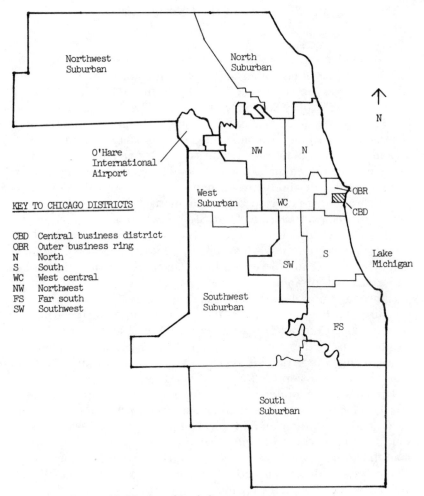

Figure 4.1   Geographic Districts of Cook County.

German immigrants was supplanted by new immigrants from southern and eastern Europe and, after World War I, by blacks from the South and immigrants from Mexico (Abbott 1936; Holli and Jones 1984; Philpott 1978; Spear 1967). By 1940, the city's population exceeded 3 million, and another million persons resided in the region's suburbs.

The impetus of wartime production rejuvenated Chicago's manufacturing base in the years during and shortly after World War II. In the following three decades, the decentralization of population and manufacturing that had begun prior to the war took off. A regional system of expressways, radiating northwest, west, southwest, and south from Chicago's central area, was completed by 1964 and opened up new areas for residential, commercial, and industrial development. The city of Chicago annexed land on its outer northwest limits and opened O'Hare International Airport in 1955. The airport replaced Midway Airport on the city's southwest side, in an already developed area that could not be used to meet the growing commercial air traffic. By 1974, O'Hare had become the world's busiest airport and an important transportation and communications hub for the regional economy (Berry and Cutler 1976; Cutler 1982; Getis 1985; Mayer and Wade 1969; McDonald 1984).

Table 4.1 shows the historic patterns of population and manufacturing employment. With the 1970 census, the suburban share of the metropolitan population was, for the first time, greater than the central-city share. The region's population grew slightly to 7 million persons by 1980, with 4 million located in the suburbs. The central-city population fell by more than 600,000 between 1950 and 1980, a loss of 17 percent. In the same span, postwar migration nearly tripled the city's black population to 1.2 million, which accounted for 40 percent of the shrinking city-wide total by 1980. The rate of black population growth has slowed somewhat since 1970, but Chicago's Hispanic population has doubled to more than 400,000 in the last decade, amounting to 14 percent of the city's total. Chicago's Hispanic community is roughly 43 percent Mexican, 32 percent Puerto Rican, and 7 percent Cuban, with the remainder coming from other Latin American countries. The Hispanic population is projected to reach 600,000 by 1990, which would be 20 percent of Chicago's total.

With these demographic changes has come a drastic change in the central-city economy. Manufacturing employment within the city limits in 1982 was at a lower level than at any other point in the 20th century. By 1972, a majority of manufacturing jobs were concentrated in the suburbs. Growth in financial and service employment has

Table 4.1   Population and Manufacturing Employment in the
Chicago SMSA, 1940–1982

	Total	Chicago City	Balance of SMSA
Population			
1940	4,569,643	3,396,808	1,172,835
1950	5,177,868	3,620,962	1,556,906
1960	6,220,913	3,550,404	2,670,509
1970	6,978,947	3,366,957	3,611,990
1980	7,103,624	3,005,072	4,098,552
Manufacturing Employment			
1947	825,840	668,056	184,784
1954	842,641	614,847	227,794
1958	846,943	569,356	277,587
1963	848,097	508,797	339,300
1967	966,500	546,500	420,000
1972	892,100	430,100	462,000
1977	865,900	366,000	499,900
1982	744,600	277,000	467,600

Source: U.S. Department of Commerce, Bureau of the Census, *Census of Population,*
1940–1980; *Census of Manufactures,* 1947–1982.

Note: The Chicago SMSA contains Cook, DuPage, Kane, Lake, McHenry and Will
counties.

picked up some of the slack, but these jobs have been concentrated
either in the central business district or in outlying suburban growth
nodes, and are often inaccessible to inner-city and minority residents.

Table 4.2 illustrates the changing sectoral distribution of employment in the Chicago metropolitan area since 1950. Manufacturing, as
measured by employment shares, fell from 38 percent to 26 percent
of the economic base between 1950 and 1980 and is no longer the
largest sector. The service sector has become the largest, growing
from 17 percent to 27 percent of the local economy during the 30-
year span.

This economic transformation has changed the nature and quality
of employment for inner-zone residents and has produced new patterns of development in the downtown core and suburban ring. In
the following sections of this chapter, we will explore the political
conflicts and planning responses that have occurred within the different areas of the Chicago region by examining the roles and activities

Table 4.2   Employment Shares by Industry in the Chicago SMSA, 1950–1980

	1950	1960	1970	1980
Agriculture	0.9	0.7	0.6	0.6
Mining	0.1	0.1	0.1	0.1
Construction	4.6	4.7	4.8	4.2
Manufacturing	37.5	34.2	31.7	26.5
Transportation, communication and public utilities	10.2	8.5	8.1	8.5
Wholesale trade	4.1	3.9	4.8	5.1
Retail trade	16.0	14.1	16.0	15.9
Finance, insurance and real estate	4.6	5.1	6.0	7.7
Services	16.9	18.2	23.5	27.3
Government	3.9	4.0	4.4	4.1
Industry not reported	1.2	6.5	—	—
Total percent	100.0	100.0	100.0	100.0
Total employment (in thousands)	2,361.8	2,511.6	2,852.0	3,238.9

Source: U.S. Department of Commerce, Bureau of the Census, *Census of Population,* 1950–1980

of various public and private actors in stimulating physical and economic growth and in shaping the built environment.

The Central Business District

The "Loop," Chicago's central business district (CBD), is the economic anchor for the entire metropolitan area and is as well the functional center for government, business, commerce, culture, and entertainment. Downtown Chicago is also a prime site for corporate service activities, solidifying the city's position as a node for national and international business. Throughout the century, public and private planning for this central area has been preoccupied with two goals: expanding downtown growth and development and then preserving it from the encroachment of impoverished inner-city neighborhoods.

The establishment and preservation of the CBD can be traced to two historical periods of planning in Chicago. The first was shaped by Daniel Burnham's 1909 plan for the Commercial Club of Chicago. The Burnham plan facilitated the exit of manufacturing from the urban core by transforming the downtown area into a regional base for financial and professional services. The second era was influenced by the Chicago Plan Commission's comprehensive efforts of the 1940s. The CBD spawned by the Burnham Plan was redeveloped, and surrounding slum neighborhoods were acquired and cleared for urban renewal during the 1950s and 1960s. This redevelopment strategy pushed the physical boundaries of the Loop outward and produced a land-use barrier to the "blighted" inner residential zone situated between the "new" downtown and the decentralized manufacturing district.

By the end of the 1950s, the Chicago Central Area Committee, a key private downtown planning organization, had joined Mayor Richard Daley to form a "pro-growth" coalition of real estate developers, trade unions, and Loop property interests that mobilized the necessary public support and private investment to further transform and reconstruct the CBD. The Chicago Plan Commission's 1958 "Development Plan for the Central Area of Chicago" outlined the agenda for the next two decades. By the 1980s, its objectives had essentially been accomplished: the expansion of regional and administrative functions; the development of new government buildings (the Daley and Dirksen buildings), a university campus (the University of Illinois-Chicago Circle), an exposition center (McCormick Place), and residential neighborhoods (the South, West, and North Loop) in the CBD; the elimination of blight; the selective reconstruction of Loop retail areas (the State Street Mall); and transportation development through added mass transit, parking, and rail lines (Chicago Plan Commission 1958).

The "Chicago 21 Plan" of 1973, the last of the 16 area plans from the city's 1966 Comprehensive Plan, focused on middle- and upper-income residential development to preserve the economic viability of downtown and enhance the local property tax base. The goal of the Central Area Committee was to avoid the complete surrounding of the Loop by low- and moderate-income residential areas by constructing new housing in the South Loop and gentrifying the neighborhoods of Pilsen, Chinatown, Humboldt Park, and Cabrini-Green adjacent to the CBD (Chicago Central Area Committee 1973; Chicago Plan Commission 1966).

The plan did result in the construction of self-enclosed, self-sustaining middle-class housing projects in the CBD. The 939-unit Dearborn Park complex was the first "new town-in-town" arising from the Chicago 21 Plan, and was soon followed in the South Loop by the

River City development (South Side Planning Board 1983). The gentrification strategy was blocked by neighborhood opposition, but residential re-use of light industrial districts in the CBD has occurred in the Printer's Row and River North areas of the Loop.

The redevelopment of the West Loop is anchored by the new $200 million Presidential Towers residential complex, which sits on land cleared by the city's Madison Street Urban Renewal Plan of 1959 (Chicago Plan Commission 1951). Presidential Towers consists of 2,346 rental apartments in four, 49-story towers, with 100,000 square feet of commercial space, a parking garage, and indoor athletic facilities. Overall, the annual production of downtown rental housing has grown sharply, from 499 units in 1979 to 1,388 in 1984. In addition, 2,742 condominium units were added to the downtown housing stock between 1979 and 1984, of which 1,944 were new units and 798 were part of re-use or renovation projects (Ludgin and Masotti 1985).

On the face of it, public-private planning has been successful in preserving the continued growth of the CBD. Chicago's Loop has emerged as one of the "hottest" real estate development locations in the nation. Between 1962 and 1977, 32 million square feet of office space was added to the CBD, bringing the total amount of downtown office space at that time to 80 million square feet. Most of this new space was for corporate headquarters and offices and professional service firms. More recently, commercial and residential real estate development has expanded outward, spreading south to Roosevelt Road, west to Halsted Street, and north to North Avenue. A study by Northwestern University's Center for Urban Affairs and Policy Research found that from 1979 to 1984, this enlarged downtown zone gained 36.4 million square feet of new or upgraded office space, 14,670 residential units, 2.5 million square feet of retail space, and 6600 hotel rooms (Ludgin and Masotti 1985). Table 4.3 shows the annual growth in total projects and investment during this period.

The redevelopment of Chicago's CBD in the three decades following World War II was accomplished by an injection of private investment supported and guided by public sector actions in the form of writing-down the costs of acquiring and clearing land, providing construction and development subsidies and capital improvements, and implementing the necessary land-use controls. Public plans represented the coalescing of interests, goals and strategies among private groups like the Central Area Committee and the various constituencies in Mayor Richard Daley's coalition. Since the announcement

Table 4.3   Completed Commercial and Residential Development
Projects and Annual Investment in Downtown Chicago,
1979–1984

	Projects	Investment (in millions)
1979	11	$ 99.6
1980	17	336.3
1981	26	466.5
1982	34	552.8
1983	47	1,019.9
1984	32	857.9

Source: Mary K. Ludgin and Louis H. Masotti, *Downtown Development: Chicago 1987–1984* (Evanston: Northwestern Press, 1985), pp. 39, 42.

of the "Chicago 21 Plan" in 1973, however, the full implementation of a central-area strategy has been slowed by political conflict over downtown land use and development. The Daley coalition of machine Democrats, trade unions, real estate developers, and downtown businessmen was unified by a common political and economic platform of downtown redevelopment (Banfield 1961; Hirsch 1983; Holli and Green 1984; Rakove 1975; Royko 1971). This coalition began to dissolve amidst the neighborhood displacement and racial transition that accompanied postwar urban renewal, thereby weakening the machine's control over municipal government.

Low-income and working class blacks and whites in the inner-zone neighborhoods of the city formed the political base of the Chicago Democratic machine during the 1950s, the beginning of the Daley era (Allswang 1986). These constituencies were "demobilized" and dissipated by the urban renewal programs of the 1960s. Many of the ethnic whites in the central area, with rising personal incomes and mobilized by fears of neighborhood racial transition, moved to the city's periphery and became the new electoral base of the Democratic political machine. Daley's vote among middle-class whites between 1955 and his last election in 1975 grew from 38 percent to 74 percent. At the same time, the overall voter turnout in four uncontested Democratic mayoral primaries between 1959 and 1971 fell from 471, 674 to 375,219 (Allswang 1986).

The blacks, lower-income ethnic whites, and the new groups of Hispanics that were left in the central neighborhoods and adjacent areas became the target of community organizing and neighborhood development efforts during the 1960s and 1970s. Voter turnout doubled in 1975 when Daley faced three primary opponents—a black, a white liberal, and an ethnic conservative.

In 1979, black mobilization was key to the defeat of Daley's incumbent successor, Michael Bilandic, and the election of Jane Byrne. Mayor Byrne aligned herself with machine factions of the Democratic Party after her election, however, and alienated blacks with her stances on issues relating to the city schools, the police, and public housing. A massive voter registration drive between 1979 and 1983, which added 150,000 new and mostly black voters to the rolls, propelled Congressman Harold Washington to victory over Jane Byrne and another machine candidate, Cook County State's Attorney Richard Daley, the son of the former mayor, in the 1983 Democratic mayoral primary. A record black turnout pushed Washington to his narrow general election victory over Republican Bernard Epton, whose campaign was buttressed by defecting white Democrats. Washington's status as the leading black independent politician in the city, along with the links he forged with Hispanics and with white liberals in neighborhoods such as Hyde Park near the University of Chicago, was critical to his success (Holli and Green 1984; Joravsky and Camacho 1987; Kleppner 1985; Travis 1987).

Washington's election, along with the victory of several of his supporters to the city council on a platform of neighborhood development and racial equity, signified the decline of the old downtown planning consensus in Chicago. Neighborhood groups from communities adjacent to the CBD opposed downtown planning on two fronts: fear of gentrification and displacement, and lack of access to the private planning process. These interests had accumulated power since the "Chicago 21 Plan" was introduced, and became the base of Harold Washington's electoral coalition (Squires, et al. 1987).

The changing structure of power in Chicago was highlighted further by the demise of the proposed 1992 World's Fair. Chicago's corporate elite designed the plan for the fair as a tool to expand the boundaries of the CBD southward. The physical and transportation improvements proposed in the plan attempted to build upon the recommendations of the "Chicago 21 Plan", by providing public infrastructure for the development of a new "city within the city" on the near south lakefront (Little 1985). The Chicago 1992 Committee, a community-based research and advocacy group, was formed by neighborhood activists to raise opposition to the "top-down" planning process for the Fair and prevent displacement of low-income residents. The efforts of the committee were key as public fears grew over the large, tax-supported subsidies being targeted to a shaky World's Fair that was projecting a budget deficit without showing clear civic benefits. Political support for the fair dwindled, and it died in 1985 (McClory 1986).

In response to this growing constituency of neighborhood interests, Mayor Washington initiated the Linked Development Task Force, which issued a report exploring ways to link neighborhood-based development with burgeoning downtown growth through exaction fees on new office construction in the Loop (Bennett 1986; City of Chicago 1985). In 1987, the city negotiated its first linked development agreement with the developers of the luxury high-rise Presidential Towers on the near West Side. The Byrne administration had earlier provided over $100 million in public subsidies of land and financing costs for the project. In the linkage agreement, the Washington administration refinanced the original bond sale for the project and issued an additional $55 million of debt for the final phase. In return, the private developers agreed to establish a $17 million Low Income Housing Trust Fund, and to develop 120 units of senior and handicapped housing.

These initiatives caused strains in Washington's relations with downtown-oriented business constituencies who, for the first time, did not have an aggressive "partner" and advocate for their interests in City Hall. Washington sought alliances with business in his battles over political reform issues with the City Council, which until 1986 was controlled by a majority bloc of machine aldermen. During his first term, Washington courted business support for reforming the local distribution of federal Community Development Block Grant funds, speeding up the planned renovation and expansion of O'Hare International Airport, and passing a municipal bond issue to fund neighborhood infrastructure improvements. A coalition of interests around city-wide planning and development, however, has not yet emerged between the business community and Chicago's minority and neighborhood constituencies. Mayor Washington's 1987 re-election, following endorsements by Chicago's two major daily newspapers and by the business press, suggested that he had developed a working relationship with downtown business elites equal to that of black mayoral administrations in Detroit and Atlanta without alienating his electoral base. After Harold Washington's sudden death in late 1987, black Adlerman Eugene Sawyer was elected Major by a City Council coalition of white and black machine politicians. Mayor Sawyer's ascension will probably not weaken the downtown support cultivated by Washington, but it has divided and confused neighborhood constituencies, which remain highly mobilized.

A proposal for a new $170 million football stadium and health complex on the near west side adjacent to the CBD will be one test of City Hall bridge-building between downtown and neighborhood constituencies. The plan is spearheaded by the Illinois Medical Center Commission, the urban renewal arm of a multi-hospital complex located on the near west side. The plan includes a new stadium for the Chicago Bears and an adjoining sports medical facility sponsored by the Medical Center. Housing values are expected to increase in middle-income residential neighborhoods near the University of Illinois campus, but these development projects will also displace up to 1500 mostly low-income black residents.

Harold Washington endorsed the proposal, as did the Midwest Community Council (MCC), a long-standing neighborhood-based organization on the west side. MCC is sponsoring a ten block low- and moderate-income housing and commercial redevelopment in the community and has won the support of the Medical Center for the project. Other community organizations, particularly the Interfaith Organizing Project (IOP), have opposed the stadium plan. The IOP, a coalition of twelve west-side churches, blocked the Illinois Legislature from expanding and reconfiguring the Medical Center Commission into a "West Side Development Commission" during 1986, and has protested the lack of community participation in developing the stadium proposal.

In addition to the political question, the economic prospects for continued residential development in and near Chicago's CBD are somewhat unclear. The market may not exist for all the new housing being developed downtown, particularly if young, white-collar professionals begin to move out of the city after forming families. This decision will probably be influenced by the quality of city services and the public schools, and housing costs in the CBD. Mayor Washington, School Board President George Munoz, and corporate leaders had worked to forge a business-school "compact" for educational reform. Efforts in this direction, however, have been stalled by labor disputes, fiscal crises, and conflicting proposals for school decentralization.

Strategies to improve city services and stabilize the finances and curriculum of the public schools may become more prominent in future plans and development for the CBD. The allocation of educational resources as part of a narrow, downtown-oriented strategy, however, will only intensify patterns of uneven development in the city. This was illustrated in 1984 when the School Board purchased five townhouses in Dearborn Park to operate as a school for 30 to 55 students who lived in the Loop middle-class residential project. Twelve blocks to the south, 139 students from the low-income Hilliard Homes public housing project attended school in eight dilapidated trailers. The high level of neighborhood mobilization in Chicago during the 1980s has altered the public-private downtown coalition to such an extent that any public spending targeted to the central business district must be packaged as a "partnership" that includes the city's low- and moderate-income residents.

The Inner Zone

Since the industrial decentalization of the early 20th century, the inner zone of land that surrounds Chicago's central business district and spreads out to the older suburbs on the city's border has been developed as the location for both manufacturing firms and working-class neighborhoods. Plant closings and the drop in manufacturing employment over the last few decades have devastated many of these areas, particularly the west and southeast sides of the city. In the wake of this job loss, older neighborhoods like Lawndale and South Chicago have deteriorated, and historic patterns of racial discrimination and disinvestment in businesses and housing have continued. The ability of local government to deal with these problems has diminished in the last twenty years due to fiscal crises brought on by a declining tax base and federal spending cutbacks in urban housing and economic development programs.

The impact of this upheaval in the inner industrial and working-class zone has been harsh. Between 1972 and 1983, nearly 200,000 manufacturing jobs left the city, a decline of 41 percent. Table 4.4 indicates that this drop was heaviest in the southern and western sectors of the city. In the same period, suburban Cook County lost over 50,000 manufacturing jobs. Again, Table 4.4 shows that the suburban loss was most extreme in the county's southern and western sectors because of the presence of older industrial suburbs such as Cicero, Harvey, and Chicago Heights.

The decline of the steel industry, at one time an integral part of the region's economic base, has been dramatic. Between 1972 and 1983, Cook County lost nearly 27,000 jobs in primary metal indus-

Table 4.4 Location of Manufacturing Employment in Cook County, 1972–1983

	1972	1983	Percent Change 1972–1983
Chicago, total	435,425	258,012	−40.7
Central business district	14,421	9,727	−32.5
Outer business ring	81,910	53,703	−34.4
North	68,348	41,819	−38.8
South	57,608	30,937	−46.3
West Central	58,980	30,954	−47.5
Northwest	60,733	39,776	−34.5
Far south	48,347	25,261	−47.8
Southwest	44,787	25,628	−42.8
Unclassified	291	206	−29.2
Suburban Cook, total	293,779	241,063	−17.9
Northwest	64,017	76,888	+20.1
Southwest	84,039	50,622	−39.8
West	63,365	48,771	−23.0
North	45,585	40,394	−11.4
South	34,057	22,547	−32.2
Unclassified	2,716	1,841	−32.2
Total	729,204	499,075	−31.6

Source: Illinois Department of Employment Security, *Where Workers Work in the Chicago SMSA,* 1983 edition, Table 8, pp. 33–34, Table 2, pp. 9–10; 1972 edition, Table 8, pp. 30–31, Table 2, p. 8.

tries, a drop of more than 50 percent. Empty steel mills on Chicago's south side highlight these changes. The southeast side was formerly the home of three large integrated mills—Republic Steel, International Harvester's Wisconsin Steel, and U.S. Steel's South Works. In 1980, Wisconsin Steel was abruptly shut down, leaving 3500 steelworkers jobless. South Works, which had a post-World War II employment peak of 15,000, has been gradually phased out, while layoffs have also reduced the workforce at the Republic Steel plant. A 1982 survey found 22,450 persons unemployed on Chicago's southeast side and a massive unemployment rate of 35 percent (City of Chicago 1986; Markusen 1985b).

Other industries in the inner zone have also been hurt by changes in the local and national economy. In 1984 Hasbro Industries purchased the Milton Bradley Company. Milton Bradley was the owner of a Playskool Toys plant that had been a fixture on Chicago's west side for fifty years. Two weeks after its purchase of Bradley, Hasbro announced that it would close the Playskool plant, leaving 700 workers—two-thirds of whom were black or Hispanic and many of whom were women—unemployed. In 1980, the city of Chicago had sponsored a $1 million Industrial Revenue Bond (IRB) to finance the plant's expansion. The closing of the plant prompted the city to file a lawsuit against Hasbro/Bradley for breaching the IRB agreement. The lawsuit was dropped in early 1985 when Hasbro agreed to keep the plant running temporarily and assist the laid-off workers with job placement. However, few of the Playskool workers were able to find comparable employment. The case of the Playskool shutdown illustrates the inability of local employment sectors to absorb effectively manufacturing job loss and the disproportionate impacts of unemployment on women and minorities.

The residential neighborhoods within the inner zone have been hard hit by industrial decline. Chicago lost 5 percent of its rental housing stock, or 40,145 units, between 1970 and 1980, and many other aging units not demolished or abandoned have fallen into decay and disrepair. In addition, an analysis of 1982 mortgage lending data by the National Training and Information Center revealed that the city of Chicago received only 23 percent of all conventional home mortgages in the metropolitan area. the total dollar amount of housing lending activity in the city fell by 73 percent between 1980 and 1982. This lower amount was concentrated in areas adjacent to the CBD at the expense of white working-class and minority neighborhoods (National Training and Information Center 1983).

Changes in the inner zone have had profound implications for blacks. The residential neighborhoods that surrounded declining industrial districts became areas of rapid racial transition (Berry and Cutler 1976; Berry 1979). Declining neighborhoods inherited by blacks have promised little in the way of employment opportunities (Greenberg 1981). An example of economic decline on Chicago's west side is the empty International Harvester factory. Sitting on a huge 53-acre site, it once employed 14,000 workers before closing in the late 1960s.

As a result of these economic changes, areas of the city's south and west sides have become wastelands of abandoned factories, burned-out housing, and rampant criminal violence (Brune and Camacho 1983). These neighborhoods have the most extreme concentrations of poverty in Chicago. In the Oakland community on the south side, three-fifths of the residents were living below the poverty line in 1980; the unemployment rate was 30 percent; one-fifth of the residents lived in overcrowded housing; and the median family income of $6000 was the lowest of any community in the city. In East Garfield Park on the west side, an area devastated by riots following the assassination of Rev. Martin Luther King, Jr. in 1968, the population declined by 53 percent between 1960 and 1980; 43 percent of the residents lived below the poverty line in 1980; and 55 percent of the rental housing stock was abandoned between 1950 and 1980. In addition, black working-class neighborhoods have suffered from disinvestment in small businesses and housing. In 1982, census tracts with a minority population of 40 percent or more received only 8 percent of the total housing lending in the Chicago SMSA, despite accounting for nearly 40 percent of the SMSA's census tracts.

Conflicts over land-use within the inner zone can be traced to the political conflict described earlier over urban renewal in the CBD. The displacement of low-income minorities from the central area by postwar redevelopment plans intensified the competition for residential land in the inner zone. Due to the existing patterns of racial segregation, land-use conflict emerged between a growing black population that was dispersed by urban renewal but constrained by residential racism, and working-class whites unable to escape the cental city for the suburbs (Berry 1979). The construction of high-rise public housing ghettos, such as the Robert Taylor Homes that stretched for miles on the south side, was the local political machine's strategy to resolve the racial land-use conflict (Hirsch 1983; Meyerson and Banfield 1955).

Community-based advocacy organizations proliferated in the inner zone during the 1960s and 1970s with the support of the Industrial Areas Foundation, created by Chicago organizing theorist Saul Alinsky, and the grassroots-oriented programs of the federal government's "War on Poverty" effort. These neighborhood organizations emerged as the most significant opposition and alternative to the Daley machine when it controlled and dominated local elections in the 1960s and early 1970s. Richard Daley was suspicious and distrustful of the "neighborhood movement," thinking it was unnecessary and subversive. This hostility from the entrenched machine forced community organizations into local electoral politics. Mayor Daley's percentage of the black vote between the 1955 and 1975 Democratic mayoral primaries fell from 80 perent to 48 percent. The election of independent Democrat Harold Washington as mayor in 1983 on a neighborhood and reform platform signalled the growing mobilization of the inner zone. Mayor Washington consolidated this new political base in the 1986 special Aldermanic elections, when four of his allies won in remapped black and Hispanic wards, giving him control of the City Council. By 1988, independent Hispanic politicians had wrested control of the city's four Hispanic-majority wards from the Democratic Party machine, completing another aspect of the political transformation of Chicago's inner zone.

In addition to their accomplishments in altering the city's political climate, community-based organizations (CBOs) play a vital role by organizing residents, providing services, and undertaking development projects. These groups have grown in sophistication and capacity, serving as a base for community action and development that often proves to be more accountable and flexible in meeting local needs than government and business efforts. Across the country, state and local governments are designing a greater number of programs that include and build upon the existing capacity of CBOs. Banks, corporations, and foundations are targeting inner-city CBOs for grants, technical assistance, and loans (Weiss and Metzger 1987, 1988).

The recognition of CBOs by the Washington administration is illustrated in the city of Chicago's 1984 Development Plan, "Chicago Works Together." The plan cited increased job opportunities, balanced growth, and neighborhood-based planning and development as its primary goals. Under Mayor Washington's leadership, the city stepped up its efforts in neighborhood business revitalization and housing rehabilitation, often using CBOs as vehicles for public policy implementation (City of Chicago 1984; Mier, Moe, and Sherr 1986). The Kenwood-Oakland Community Organization estimates that the Washington administration funnelled $10 million in job training and housing funds into the south side neighborhood in four-and-a-half years. The city's "delegate agency" program allocated $2.7 million to 108 community groups for economic development activities during 1988.

CBOs have also been able to successfully negotiate and implement urban development programs for the inner zone in conjunction with private corporations and financial institutions, aided by certain government regulatory and funding support. Between 1984 and 1986, the Chicago Reinvestment Alliance, a city-wide neighborhood development coalition, utilized the provisions of the federal Community

Reinvestment Act to leverage neighborhood lending agreements to-talling nearly $200 million from Chicago's four largest banks. First National, Harris, and Northern Trust Banks agreed to create a five-year lending pool for housing, commercial, and industrial develop-ment in inner-zone neighborhoods. Continental Illinois Bank agreed to create a home improvement loan partnership with funding sup-port from the city and state governments. The Continental program is being administered by a consortium of CBOs in conjunction with the Chicago Energy Savers Fund, a $15 million energy conservation loan program financed by the city and Peoples Gas, a major local utility company. The Community Reinvestment Act and its compan-ion legislation, the Home Mortgage Disclosure Act, enable citizens groups to document lending patterns in their communities and to challenge merger and branching applications of banks and savings institutions for failing to meet community credit needs. These agree-ments are perhaps the most successful use of federal community reinvestment regulations to date, due to the size and scope of the programs—which include increased grant commitments from each bank foundation for community development—as well as the role played by CBOs in loan packaging and program review (Metzger and Weiss 1988).

The city of Chicago has targeted its community development fund-ing to support these neighborhood lending programs, and local corporations have organized the Chicago Equity Fund to raise syndi-cation proceeds for corporate equity injections into low-income mul-tifamily housing projects financed under the programs. CBOs have expanded their activities and added staff and resources in utilizing the loan programs to implement redevelopment projects in the inner zone. For example, the City-Wide Development Corporation of the Chicago Association of Neighborhood Development Organizations packaged 43 real estate and small business development projects totalling $13.9 million between 1984 and 1986. The Chicago Rehab Network and Neighborhood Housing Services, two non-profit hous-ing developers operating in neighborhoods across the city, have been instrumental in implementing single- and multi-family housing pro-jects through the bank programs. All this activity has generated additional resources for CBOs in Chicago. In 1988, the Local Initia-tives Support Corporation and the MacArthur Foundation established an $11.3 million Fund for Community Development to support the operations of 30 neighborhood organizations over the next eight years, with the goal of leveraging $150 million in new private investment for the development of $85 million in housing projects.

In addition to the strategy of recognizing and strengthening CBOs as vehicles for inner-zone revitalization, a variety of public-private initiatives have emerged since the 1970s under the heading of "economic development" to rebuild declining industrial districts and create jobs for inner-zone residents. Under Daley's administration, inner-zone economic development was not a major policy. The 1966 Comprehensive Plan called for the creation of urban industrial parks, along with transportation development, to spur economic growth on the far south (Dan Ryan Expressway), southwest (Crosstown Expressway), and northwest (O'Hare public transit line) sides of the city (Chicago Plan Commission 1966). Chicago's first economic development agency, the Mayor's Council of Manpower and Economic Advisors, was created in 1972 and later became known as the Economic Development Commission, a private blue-ribbon panel tied to the Central Area Committee that prepared overall economic development plans for the city government through funding from the federal Economic Development Administration. The Chicago Department of Economic Development was created in 1980 and initiated business development and assistance programs and task forces for industrial revitalization.

The Economic Development Commission was reorganized by the Washington administration to take a more aggressive role in land assembly and financing for industrial development. The Commission has embarked on a strategy of building new industrial parks in the inner zone that, through energy efficiency, landscaping improvements and effective marketing, can compete with comparable suburban facilities. One of these parks is slated for the site of the closed Wisconsin Steel mill. The city has worked with local development corporations on these and other projects, such as the re-use of the closed Playskool Toys site, to redevelop vacant manufacturing plants for new industrial and commercial uses. The city is also creating "protected manufacturing districts" in industrial areas of the inner zone that are competing for land and space with residential and commercial development that is spreading outward from the expanding CBD. Perhaps the most significant economic development accomplishment of the Washington administration was the stimulation of minority business growth through city contracting policies. Between 1985 and 1987, the city government awarded $74 million in city contracts to minority-owned firms, most of which were either located in the inner zone or owned and operated by inner-zone residents.

The combined efforts of CBOs, economic development agencies, banks, corporations, and small businesses in forging partnerships to rebuild Chicago's inner industrial zone have been unable to match the rapid economic expansion and growth generated by private investment in the CBD and in the "boom" corridors of the suburban ring. In some areas, inner-zone redevelopment has, at best, only arrested the decline triggered by forces of national and international economic restructuring beyond the control of local public-private planning (Bluestone and Harrison 1982; Checkoway and Patton 1985; Fainstein et al. 1983; Markusen 1985a; Noyelle and Stanback 1984). The key change has been in the growing political mobilization of inner-zone residents and the creation of new development entities that can now broker with public and private sector actors to target resources toward disinvested areas and monitor the outcomes so that some of the benefits actually accrue to inner-zone residents. Harold Washington cultivated this theme as the core element of his electoral strategy and attempted to redirect city government to support it. On issues such as linked development, neighborhood reinvestment, and plant closings, coalitions were established between blacks, Hispanics, and working-class whites in the inner zone (Bennett 1986; Squires et al. 1987; Metzger and Weiss 1988).

These constituencies became divided in the immediate aftermath of Mayor Washington's death in late 1987. His slim Council majority was splintered when six of the city's 18 black aldermen joined with the 23 members of the white ethnic opposition bloc to elect Eugene Sawyer as mayor. He was elected over Alderman Timothy Evans, a close ally of Mayor Washington who was supported for mayor by 12 black, four Hispanic, and three liberal white aldermen. Mayor Sawyer's election split the black community. In the first city elections following his victory, four of the six black aldermen who supported him were defeated in Cook County Democratic ward committeeman races. The new mayor faces the challenge of reuniting minority and neighborhood groups. A divided black vote would hamper his relection prospects and could lead to the election of a white, and possibly Republican, mayor for Chicago.

The Suburban Ring

The suburban ring of the Chicago region encompasses suburban Cook County, along with all of DuPage, Kane, Lake, McHenry, and

Will counties. The area west of the inner zone has experienced rapid growth in population and employment over the last two decades, benefiting from the location of new industries, corporate headquarters, and office-financial-service-hotel complexes. The development of the suburban ring from farm hinterlands to a new regional zone of economic development has been catalyzed by a sprawling network of highways and the presence of O'Hare International Airport (see Figure 4.2).

Growth has been concentrated into three areas: the suburbs of north and northwest Cook County near O'Hare Airport, the suburbs in the northwest "corridor" formed by the Tri-State and Northwest Tollways, and the western suburbs of DuPage County adjacent to the East-West Tollway. The north and northwestern suburban communities of Schaumberg, Des Plaines, Elk Grove Village, and Northbrook experienced large increases in population and private sector employment during the 1970s, which more than doubled in some areas. Woodfield Mall in Schaumburg is the retail base for the area and is Chicago's largest regional shopping center in both sales and size (Cutler 1982).

In DuPage County, where private sector employment grew by 83 percent between 1972 and 1983, the East-West Tollway "corridor" of growth is anchored on the east by Oak Brook and on the west by Naperville. Oak Brook is the site of many corporate headquarters, including McDonald's Corp. and Waste Management Inc., and the Oak Brook Mall, the region's second-largest shopping center. Argonne National Laboratory and Fermi Lab have stimulated high-technology development in the county. Naperville is one of the fastest-growing municipalities in the nation with private research parks, laboratories, and office buildings locating in its vicinity. Naperville's population is projected to rise from 1984's 56,000 to 100,000 by the end of the century. Between 1980 and 2005, DuPage County's population is projected to grow from 658,858 to 930,000, and its employment is predicted to rise from 274,600 to 444,000.

State and local governments have responded to this explosion of growth by improving infrastructure and transportation in order to rationalize existing development and sustain continued expansion. The construction of the DuPage County Tollway will link the East-West Tollway office corridor between Naperville and Oak Brook to O'Hare Airport and the commercial, office, and light industrial development adjacent to the airport in northwest Cook County. This project, along with the completion of the Thorndale Avenue highway

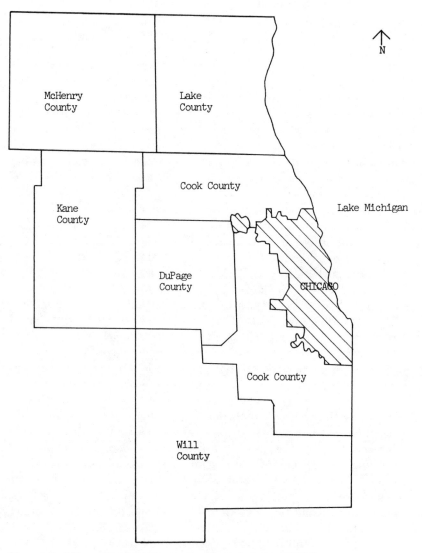

Figure 4.2 Chicago Standard Metropolitan Statistical Area (SMSA).

extension in DuPage County, is being financed primarily by the state of Illinois. The suburban, white-collar constituencies of northwest Cook and DuPage counties form an important part of Governor James Thompson's statewide electoral base.

The Illinois Department of Commerce and Community Affairs (DCCA) is the key economic development agency for Governor Thompson, who has been in office since 1976. DCCA, along with Governor Thompson's "Build Illinois" initiative announced in 1985, have been critical of the development of Chicago's suburban ring. Between 1981 and 1988, DCCA's appropriations in the state budget grew by 462 percent, far outpacing the state's General Revenue Fund, which grew by only 33 percent. During 1987, McHenry County was the largest per capita recipient of DCCA project spending, with a per capita amount over four times larger than of Chicago and Cook County combined.

The western and southern sectors of Cook County have not shared in the growth experienced by the other outlying areas of the suburban ring. Communities such as Cicero, Berwyn, Blue Island, and Maywood experienced declines in population and manufacturing employment during the 1970s similar to those of the inner-zone neighborhoods of Chicago. In addition, some of these communities have growing proportions of minority and low-income residents, establishing yet another link to the inner zone. Before his death, Harold Washington's growing involvement in Cook County Democratic Party politics was an attempt to build bridges to these constituencies and develop a broader coalition and agenda for inner-zone redevelopment. Washington became involved in supporting candidates for county-wide races, particularly for the Cook County Board of Commissioners, the governmental coordinating body of the county's suburbs. The growing suburbs of northwest Cook County attempting to align with the other expanding outlying areas, view their interests as diverging from those of the declining districts of suburban Cook County. This northern tier of Cook County townships successfully lobbied the Thompson administration to create a separate service district and Private Industry Council to administer the Job Training Partnership Act program in their area.

In addition to the political conflicts over economic development in suburban Cook County, land-use conflicts within the suburban ring have arisen over the environmental disruption caused by the rapid pace of development. The initial plans for the DuPage County Tollway called for the demolition of the Morton Arboretum, but the efforts of suburban environmentalists have preserved the site. Residential growth in Naperville has placed stress on that city's provision of water and sewers, as well as on transportation and other services, prompting local planners to consider a moratorium on new building permits. Overlapping political jurisdictions have slowed the resolution of these and other conflicts over development in the suburban ring. Private investment has continued to generate commercial, industrial, and office expansion in the outlying growth corridors. While office development in the suburban ring is nowhere near the level of that in the CBD, overall growth in this outer zone should sustain itself into the near future, existing side-by-side with the decline in the inner zone and the "inner zone" suburbs, and the continued development in Chicago's central area.

Conclusion

For more than a century, Chicago was a city of destiny. Growth was its watchword, and massive public and private works were undertaken to facilitate and accommodate relentless physical expansion. This was the essence of urban planning.

In the 1980s, planning has come to mean not just growth, but balanced growth; not just expansion, but revitalization. The policy implications of this meaning are currently being debated by many competing factions. Powerful constituencies for downtown and suburban development are facing new participants at the negotiating table—representatives from low- and moderate-income inner zone neighborhoods. Community organizations are battling for a larger share of regional economic benefits and new methods of allocating resources. Electing Harold Washington as Chicago's mayor was their greatest triumph, and now they are fighting to maintain hard-won political gains in the wake of his death. For the Commercial Club, the Central Area Committee, and suburban promoters, finding ways of including these newly-mobilized community groups and addressing their problems may be essential to the future success of planning for metropolitan Chicago.

CHAPTER 5

Houston: Hyperdevelopment in the Sunbelt

Joe R. Feagin and Robert A. Beauregard

Houston is best known for its spectacular 20th-century growth. It is not famous as a city of historic, civic events (as is Boston), a city of momentous social movements (as labor historians might say of Chicago), or a city of unique neighborhoods (such as New Orleans with its French Quarter). When one thinks of Houston, it is of shipping, oil refining and petrochemicals, and real estate investment. Houston's distinctive economic identity and postwar spatial development dominate its national image. It is a contemporary city, a city apparently without history. The present is what matters in Houston, and the ability to expand space and accumulate capital.

Time and space in postwar Houston are not regulated by the pace of traditional factory production, the intrigues of ethnic and union politics, nor the strictures of governmental planning, but by the rapid accumulation and circulation of capital, massive population growth fueled by in-migration and speculative property development. From the 1900s to the mid-1980s, the chronological net of capitalism and its spatial manifestations were different in Houston than in the older industrial cities facing stagnation or decline. In 1983, with its economy in shambles, time and space in Houston took an unfamiliar turn.

In the boom period, capital was more abundant, circulation faster. Time was literally speeded up. Profitable opportunities arose suddenly and disappeared just as rapidly. Investors were prepared to move on as new developments restructured the landscape of accumulation. Migrants hoped to get rich quick in a city where anyone could become an entrepreneur. The turnover time of fixed capital was shortened by the availability of capital and rapid shifting of

153

investment potentials. The bounty of much flat, unimproved land and the physical form of the city enabled capital to devalue and value space easily as it moved outward from the city's center. With money one could overcome distance, flee social problems, and ignore the negative externalities of development. Space was boundless, and people were unconstrained by proximity to deal with public problems.[1] The bust of the mid-1980s changed all that, making painfully clear that the profusion and rapid movement of capital "radically transforms and fixes the meanings of space and time in social life and defines limits and imposes necessities upon the shape and form of [Houston's] urbanization" (Harvey 1985:1).

The intersection of capital, space, and time in Houston, however, must be disentangled from the ideology that has been an integral part of the city's history. The material relations of its urbanization have always been clothed with a hyperbolic boosterism touting laissez-faire capitalism, unfettered growth, and individual opportunity. In Houston the heavy hand of government is non-existent, and obstacles to capital accumulation scarcely exist. This is the private city (Warner 1968) taken to an extreme, a city whose business elites have always involved themselves deeply in regional, national, and global economic competition.

While one must recognize the heavy ideological core of Houston's development, one must nonetheless resist its seductive appeal. Capital investment and accumulation hinge partly on a sense of the future, a positive outlook that lures other investors, garners State support, and entices consumers. That temporal dimension is especially pronounced in property development. Optimism about a bright future can blind us to the real ways in which capital is being invested, labor controlled and the city built. It can set in motion binges of speculation that generate boom-and-bust cycles in the economy. It can lead to property development whose benefits fall wholly in the pockets of capitalists, leaving labor no less susceptible to the caprices of capitalism.

In exploring the postwar spatial transformations of Houston, we must give this capitalist ideology its due, but not let it deflect attention from how capital has actually operated. Laissez-faire ideology, in this case, is far from reality. The purpose of this chapter is to interweave the material and the ideological as they have joined to create the city of Houston and to structure its postwar growth. Four themes will dominate: (a) the pro-business ideology of community leaders and the related, weak, physical and regulatory barriers to development leading to unrestrained, haphazard growth characterized by decentralized and deconcentrated commercial and residential development; (b) the importance of local government absence in structuring the ideological environment for development, and federal and state governmental presence in creating infrastructure; (c) the existence of large property development companies with national and international connections, able to undertake large-scale planned developments; and (d) the economy's specialization in a small number of economic activities which makes Houston susceptible to boom-and-bust cycles. After establishing the roots for these forces in the early history of Houston, we will look more closely at the nature of its spatial development and the unique political economy that conferred it.

Historical Background

In 1836 two northern entrepreneurs, Augustus and John Allen, set out on a real estate venture at the headwaters of navigation of the Buffalo Bayou, approximately 45 miles inland from the Gulf of Mexico and 25 miles from Galveston Bay.[2] For $5,000 they purchased land that they hoped would become "a great interior commercial emporium of Texas" (Writer's Program 1942:xi). They also managed to have the nascent city designated (albeit briefly) the capitol of the Republic of Texas; by 1837, 1200 people inhabited the site. Its location close to the bay, and its proximity to rich soil for farming cotton, sugar, and grain and to ample forests for lumber, granted Houston a natural advantage as a transshipment point. Throughout the 19th century, however, Houston had to compete with Galveston, a city on a low-lying island between the bay and the Gulf of Mexico (see Figure 5.1) Houston did not fare well; since its waterways could not handle deep-draft ocean-going vessels, Galveston became the main port of the region. In the 1840s, the Texas Congress authorized the city government to build and maintain wharves for its bayou could still receive shallow-draft steamboats and sloops. A port was thus established, which in 1845 handled more than 11,000 bales of cotton.

Throughout the last third of the 19th century, Houston's port operations were secondary to its function as a railroad hub. Beginning in the 1850s and rapidly expanding in the 1870s, numerous regional rail lines converged on the city. By 1880, nine railways had been built. The tenor of Houston's economic development was set, an economy

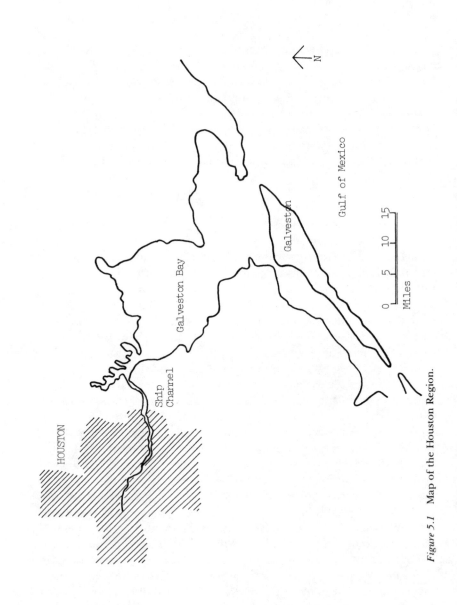

Figure 5.1 Map of the Houston Region.

based almost exclusively on commerce. Even though a textile factory opened in 1869 and 64 manufacturing establishments were evident in Harris County in 1870, the major activity was commercial. During the Civil War the city served as a military supply depot, and throughout these early decades the city building process—the construction of streets, drains and sewers, and market houses, and the awarding of franchises for municipal services from street railways to gas lighting—focused on commerce (Platt 1983:29). Transportation to and within the city was the key to the movement of goods from one mode of transit to another. Warehouses, banks, and cotton-brokerage companies facilitated trade. Not until the 1870s and 1880s did an industrial component emerge, and that consisted mainly of shops engaged in the construction and repair of railroad equipment. The pace of economic activity was regulated by harvests, brokerage house transactions, and the schedules of the railroads.

During the 1890s Houston began to decentralize. Once a compact city structured around the rail lines and the port, it extended one and one-half miles beyond the city center and into suburban areas serviced by the electric street railway (ibid.:134). Franchise rivalries pushed the boundaries ever outward. The population went from 27,557 to 44,683 over the decade, and by 1900 more than 210 manufacturing establishments were producing wearing apparel, iron and metal products, heavy machinery, foods, and printing material. City building became a political struggle as technical problems were solved, and two opposing groups fought over the future of Houston. The "regulars" supported growth, public service franchises, and limited government; the "dissidents" favored municipal ownership and an improved quality of life for residents. Franchises were granted by the regulars, municipal services were extended, city finances were rationalized, and electoral processes were rearranged, all under the banner of good, businesslike government. For two brief periods, the union-backed dissidents tried unsuccessfully to reverse the consolidation of business control. By 1910, the stage of commercial capitalism was overlaid in palimpsest fashion with a stage of industrial capitalism (Feagin 1984a, 1985a). Houston was becoming more than a regional marketing center dealing mainly in cotton, lumber, and grain, and was developing into an oil-centered economy.

Two events made the early 20th century a turning point in Houston's history: a major hurricane and tidal wave in 1900 that devastated Galveston, leaving 6000 dead and thousand homeless, and the discovery of oil in 1901 at Spindletop near Beaumont, 90 miles to the northeast. The destruction of Galveston demonstrated the vulnerability of that city to natural disasters and enabled Houston to vanquish, finally, its regional rival. The establishment of the Spindletop oil field created a new market not just for shipping and trading but also for production (such as oil refineries, drilling equipment) and circulation (for instance the financing of oil exploration). Both events caused local business elites to renew their efforts to resolve Houston's waterfront deficiencies.

Since the 1870s, numerous improvements had been made to the channel of the Buffalo Bayou. Dredging and widening were constants, and in 1908 the Turning Basin was completed, but Houston needed a deep-water channel if it were truly to gain regional dominance over Galveston. With federal assistance, a ship channel was constructed in the channel of the Buffalo Bayou. Opened in 1914, it enabled the city to exploit the oil and gas pipelines that had extended to the city since 1905; facilitated the development of oil and gas refineries, oil tool and well equipment firms, and other service companies; and set in motion an industrial ensemble focused on natural resources. Major oil companies established themselves in the area; the Texas Company (Texaco) in 1908, the Gulf Company in 1916, and Standard Oil in 1918. By the 1910s, Houston had become a center of oil-related production, a major port, and one of the world's major extractive economies. In addition to oil, lumber and minerals (such as sulfur, salt, and lime) were also accessible. Robert Wood, a top executive at Sears, Roebuck, noted around this time that "within a 200-mile radius of Houston more wealth is taken from the soil than from any equivalent area on earth" (cited in Feagin 1988: Chapter 3).

In the late 1910s and 1920s, Houston entered a stage of oligopoly-industrial capitalism, with large firms increasingly directing the oil industry and port development, and later petrochemicals. Trade had fallen off during World War I, but after the armistice, trade and commerce expanded. During the 1920s, Houston experienced a major construction boom. Industrial development clustered along the ship channel. New residential developments were built, one of the most noteworthy being the exclusive River Oaks area for the city's elite, just west of the downtown. Annexations in 1925 added 25 square miles to the city's land area. Skyscrapers became more abundant and created a new skyline. Yet throughout this binge of investment, Houston remained a commercial-distribution center: in 1929 its ratio of wholesale-retail employment to manufacturing employment was 1.0 to 0.7, whereas that for the nation was 1.0 to 1.3 (Buchanan 1975:

36). By 1930, Houston had become the largest city in Texas (292,352 people) and the third-largest port in the United States, surpassing New Orleans.

A big boon for Houston's development was the opening of a vast new market for oil products: automobiles and trucks. This link between Houston and Detroit greatly expanded demand and spurred exploration. The huge East Texas oil field was developed in the 1930s, and by 1939 it had 26,000 wells. The structure of the oil industry in Texas changed from one composed of small firms to one of two dozen giants. Oil accounted for more than one-half the jobs in more than 1200 oil companies and supply houses in the Houston area. Still, Houston was not able to avoid the depression totally. Private construction diminished, and unemployment rose. Strikes were common, and 25,680 families lived in substandard housing. In a modest way, the federal government stepped in to assist with new housing, and a few subsidized projects were constructed. The first, Houston Gardens, opened in 1935 just north of the central business district and brought about one of Houston's earliest futile calls for land-use zoning (Babcock 1982). New Deal programs helped to alleviate the pains of unemployment and contributed to the enhancement of the city's infrastructure, including additional work on the ship channel and frequent attempts at flood control. Still, Houston's population grew by 32 percent during the 1930s, and *Fortune* magazine, in December 1939, labeled Houston "the city the Depression missed," a fate attributable in part to the rising demand for oil.

By the 1940s the economy had begun its upturn. Building construction increased in intensity as war mobilization expanded. Houston did well during World War II. War materiel production and shipbuilding were robust, and a major steel plant was built to support these activities. Federal funds flowed into the high-tech petrochemical industry to help meet the demand for aviation fuel and synthetic rubber. After the war the Houston metropolitan economy continued its expansion without stuttering, as happened in many other cities. Investment for wartime activities had established an infrastructure and plant capacity that could be exploited for peacetime markets. The chemical and oil industries were strong, and the port, now second in the nation in foreign commerce, continued to do well. The population had increased over the decade of the 1940s by more than 55 percent to 596,163, and automobile registrations had increased by almost 90 percent to 322,000, phenomena that were central to Houston's spatial development.

Houston thus entered the postwar period with a population of more than a half million inhabitants within a city of approximately forty square miles. Economically it was dependent on agricultural marketing, shipping, oil refining, and related activities. Major manufacturing firms shared these orientations, being comprised mostly of food, chemicals, petroleum, iron and metal goods, and heavy machinery. Heavy industry was arranged to the east and southeast of the downtown area along the ship channel and Galveston Bay. The more expensive, white residential developments had been built to the west and north, with some institutional development (such as Rice University, hospitals, and some hotels) located to the south of downtown. The city's low-income, racially segregated neighborhoods were mostly clustered along the east side of the downtown area, with some neighborhoods near industrial districts. (The exception is the black Fourth Ward to the west near River Oaks.) Railroads crisscrossed the city. In the 1940s and 1950s, the central business district was typical of modern American downtowns. Houston, although it sprawled for miles, could still be termed a city with a single center.

As the city boomed through the 1960s and 1970s, the spatial pattern of development took a different path. The city's rapid growth, large size, major infusions of capital, and unregulated and unrestrained environment for development created a multinucleated city of residential and commercial enclaves, a city unlike the industrial cities of the North. In 1942 Houston was described in this way: "Skirted by rich Texas prairies, tremendously productive of oil wells, cotton, lumber, and cattle, the city combines major industrial developments that are like the East, the culture and lush verdure of the South, and the enterprise of the West, plus a medley of pine trees, smokestacks, huge moss-hung oaks and arriving and departing ships that is entirely its own" (Writers' Program 1942:2). Except for the shrinkage of the prairies, many of these same descriptions were still accurate in the 1980s, but within a profoundly different spatial structure.

Patterns of Development

Houston's postwar development has been characterized by rapid growth virtually unrestrained by physical and governmental barriers to investment. The result has been the creation of the prototypical sprawl city. The built environment, nonetheless, varies dramatically in density. Huge transportation networks, particularly the more than 240 miles of freeways, and the emergence of large-scale development companies—some specializing in planned, multiuse, often high-density developments—contributed to a multinucleated pattern of development. Houston went from a downtown-centered metropolitan pattern just after World War II, to eighteen "centers" spread across wide expanses of flat, undifferentiated landscape, with various land uses juxtaposed in complex mixtures by economic and political forces.[3]

Rapid Growth

If any one trait of Houston comes readily to mind when one considers its postwar history, it is the city's rapid growth. In 1940 Houston was the 21st-largest city in the country with a population of less than 400,000 (see Table 5.1). By 1980 the population was close to 1.6 million, and Houston had become the fourth-largest city. Throughout this period, the city experienced a more than threefold expansion and has grown faster than almost any other large American city, with its most dramatic population growth occurring between the 1950s and the early 1980s. Moreover, it has able to avoid the fate of older cities outside the South and West which, even when enmeshed in growth, lost position, both relatively and absolutely, to the surrounding suburban ring. This was not the case in Houston. While the city's share of the metropolitan population has fallen since 1960, the decline has not been precipitous. The reason is annexation.

"Extra-territorial jurisdiction" is a provision of the Texas Annexation Act of 1963 that prevents communities within five miles of a major city from incorporating without permission, and requires developers of subdivisions to submit their plans to the city of Houston planners in order to maintain conformance with utility requirements and specifications. Incorporation would negate the possibility of annexation, while subdivision review supposedly protects the city from a costly annexation. Annexation in Texas, moreover, can proceed without a popular referendum. As a result, the city of Houston has been able to expand its boundaries to absorb new growth on the fringe, thereby protecting itself from the decentralization of capital and people. Incorporation of adjacent communities, in fact, began as early as 1891 and has been a frequent occurrence since then (Buchanan 1975). In 1940, the city was 25 square miles in land area; by 1980 it had expanded to 565 square miles. The importance of annexation is captured by the fact that within its boundaries of 1940,

Table 5.1 Selected Characteristics: City and Metropolitan Area, 1940–1980

	1980	1970	1960	1950	1940
City population	1,594,086	1,233,505	938,219	596,163	384,514
Decade growth rate[a]	(29.2)	(31.5)	(57.4)	(55.0)	
SMSA population	2,905,350	1,999,316	1,430,394	947,500	646,869
Decade growth rate[a]	(45.3)	(39.8)	(51.0)	(46.5)	
City/SMSA population ratio	0.55	0.62	0.66	0.63	0.59
City percent non-whtie	27.6	26.6	23.2	21.1	22.4
City/SMSA non-white ratio	0.83	0.82	0.87	0.71	0.83[a]
Occupied dwelling units:					
City	602,719	427,880	282,626	158,470	107,530
SMSA[b]	1,027,069	668,454	353,320	232,265	141,345
City/SMSA ratio	0.59	0.64	0.80	0.68	0.76

[a] Numbers in parentheses indicate percentages.
[b] In 1940 the metropolitan area had yet to be delineated though Harris County was considered Houston's metropolitan district.

Sources: Data were taken from Bureau of the Census decennial reports: Detailed Population Characteristics, Social and Economic Characteristics and Census of Housing, selected years.

the central-city core, Houston actually lost population between 1940 and 1980 (Jackson 1985:155). Without its annexation power, the city would have fallen into the category of "declining central cities." Instead, it remained prosperous until the oil price crash of the mid-1980s.

Such giant steps in population size do not come simply from natural increase. In 1980, approximately one-quarter of the metropolitan area's residents who were five years or older had lived outside that area in 1975. Out-of-state migrants, moreover, were not mainly individuals fleeing the declining Rustbelt, as the "regional shift" media perspective of the late 1970s implied. Rather, less than one-half of these interstate migrants came from the northeast and north central regions. The proportion of migrants from the South and West has been declining since 1940, but Houston's metropolitan population growth has been fueled as much by intraregional migrants—the South has consistently dominated as a locus of origin—as it has by interregional ones. Moreover, migrants from Texas always exceeded out-of-state migrants during the postwar period. Thus, while surbubanization has been foreshortened by annexation, extrametropolitan spatial shifts in population have been mainly intraregional and intrastate.[4]

Local Economy

The large migration can be explained, in part, by Houston's relatively low unemployment rates, in comparison to the nation and other large cities, between 1945 and 1983. Resident city employment has increased almost threefold since 1950, while resident employment within the metropolitan area has had a twofold increase, the similarity clearly attributable to the absorption of new development within the city's boundaries via annexation.[5] Both the metropolitan area and the city have thus experienced major additions to the economic base. Metropolitan, new capital expenditures for manufacturing increased fourfold between 1958 and 1982 in constant dollars, and the amount of value-added tripled. Within the city, the manufacturing growth rates from 1954 to 1982 were more than 600 percent for new capital expenditures, and more than 500 percent for value-added.[6]

Over the postwar period, Houston's economy and the resultant economic growth were centered on a small number of industries. Since 1947, three industries have dominated value-added in manufacturing within the metropolitan area: petroleum products, petrochemicals and allied products, and nonelectrical machinery which includes oil field machinery and tools (see Table 5.2). While the petroleum products industry has been dominant in value-added and is central to the energy-based image of the Houston economy, its growth from 1967 to 1982 was anemic relative to the previous time period and to other major industries in the region. Because of its relatively capital-intensive nature, the petroleum products industry's contribution to manufacturing employment is less significant than other industries. That is most apparent when one looks at the major manufacturing industries within the city. There, while petroleum products was a major contributor to value-added in manufacturing in 1982, it contributed relatively few jobs to the local labor market. Moreover, more of this industry is located outside the central city, but within the metropolitan area, than within it: approximately 75 percent of the metropolitan jobs in petroleum products and 60 percent of the metropolitan value-added.

Also intriguing are the similarities between the major industries within the city and those outside it. This situation contrasts with metropolitan areas in the Northeast and Midwest, where sharp divergences can be found between central-city manufacturing and suburban manufacturing (Black 1980). Printing and publishing, along with food and kindred products, have become slightly more important in the city than in the metropolitan area as a whole, and stone, clay, and glass production seems concentrated within the city, but otherwise the major industries are the same. The spatial disparity of industry between the central city and the surrounding area is not readily apparent, because it is not very great. For Houston one begins to question the use of such terms as "central city" and "suburbs," and not just because of the distribution of industry, a point we will address below.

Of particular importance to the economy since the city's inception has been Houston's shipping and other port activities. In addition to generating a large amount of commercial activity, the port serves as an appropriate location for oil refineries and other similar industries. The focus, however, remains shipping, so much of which has gone though the port that in 1979 it ranked first in terms of foreign trade tonnage and third in total cargo tonnage (Kaplan 1983:197), with foreign trade increasing from $2.4 billion in 1970 to $23.0 billion in 1980. In the early 1980s, Houston's top foreign trading partners were Mexico, Saudi Arabia, and Japan. The number-one export category, valued at $1.7 billion, encompassed construction, mining, and oil field

Table 5.2   Top Manufacturing Industries, 1947, 1967 and 1982

Metropolitan area	Value-added[a] (in millions of 1958 dollars)	Employment
1982 1. Nonelectrical machinery	1,195.0	60,600
2. Chemicals and allied products	1,140.5	31,400
3. Petroleum products	566.7	14,100
4. Fabricated metal products	531.2	37,800
5. Food and kindred products	353.1	12,900
Areawide totals	4,821.5	264,100
1967 1. Chemical and allied products	711.2	17,500
2. Petroleum products	467.1	10,600
3. Nonelectrical machinery	267.9	19,400
4. Fabricated metals	215.9	18,800
5. Primary metals	190.3	13,500
Areawide totals	2,443.0	138,100
1947 1. Petroleum products	120.1	10,955
2. Non-electrical machinery	97.1	11,954
3. Food and kindred products	74.3	7,636
4. Chemical and allied products	65.0	4,500
5. Fabricated metal products	37.0	4,877
Areawide totals	516.8	58,606
City		
1982 1. Nonelectrical machinery	986.2	46,700
2. Fabricated metals	397.2	27,200
3. Food and kindred products	318.4	11,600
4. Petroleum and coal products	230.9	3,500
5. Chemical and allied products	201.7	6,300
Areawide totals	2,908.5	174,600
1967 1. Nonelectrical machinery	252.8	18,200
2. Fabricated metals	194.3	16,300
3. Chemical and allied products	118.2	3,700
4. Printing and publishing	56.1	5,500
5. Stone, clay and glass products	53.1	4,100
Areawide totals	1,318.5	97,900
1947 Areawide totals	344.6	40,563

[a]Sectoral data for the City in 1947 are unavailable.

Source: U.S. Department of Commerce, *Census of Manufactures,* various years

machinery. The second most valuable export category was unmilled wheat and corn, and the third and fourth, organic chemicals and nonelectrical machinery respectively. The major import is crude oil, once a major export, valued in 1981 at $4.5 billion. Steel products, and automobiles, and transportation equipment also constituted major imports for the port.[7]

Government and the Economy

The strength of Houston's industry has other dimensions, not the least of which involve the federal government. Over the long run, one of the most important has been federal involvement in the improvement of the ship channel. Since 1867, the federal government every few years has provided financial subsidies or direct assistance to widen, deepen, and expand the Houston port. The Buffalo Bayou and the San Jacinto River to the east of the city have been made part of the ship channel, extending from the eastern edge of the downtown area to Galveston. Wharves, turning basins, warehouses, ship repair facilities, and a host of shipping-related activities have been constructed. The ship channel has thus become a meandering spine for industrial activity, and for many years directed manufacturing and commerce to the east side of Houston.

In the early 1960s, the National Aeronautics and Space Administration Center came to Houston. It includes laboratories, simulation and training facilities, a mission control center, and office complexes employing more than 10,000 people, mostly administrative, technical, and scientific personnel. Now called the Lyndon B. Johnson Spacecraft Center, it is located to the southeast and three to four miles beyond the city in Clear Lake City. Along with an industrial park developed by Exxon, it helped to spur development in that area and along the I-45 corridor with which it connects with the I-610 Loop Freeway and the downtown. Various phases of the U.S. space program—the attempts to land men on the moon, the space shuttle program, and now the Strategic Defense Initiative—have channeled federal funds into the Houston area, funds that flow from a political rather than economic spigot, thus helping to dampen the area's sensitivity to business cycles.

The reinvigoration of military expenditures in the 1980s and the resulting positive consequences for Houston are reminiscent of earlier war-related assistance to the area's economy (Feagin 1985a). During World War II, the federal government bolstered demand for aviation fuel and synthetic rubber, and subsequent military excursions—the Korean conflict and the war in Vietnam—spurred economic growth in Houston both through the petroleum and chemical industries and through local branches of international construction firms such as Brown and Root, a major contractor for facilities in Vietnam. Wartime demand for ships also helped to expand the Houston Shipbuilding Company which at its peak in the early 1940s employed more than 20,000 workers. During that same time-span, two major oil pipelines were built by the Roosevelt administration, federal funds were used to provide local firms with prime defense contracts, and 250 million federal dollars were spent on defense preparations.

Indirect federal assistance was also forthcoming. Limitations on oil imports, gas pipeline regulations (along with very favorable state regulations), preferential tax treatment for expenses incurred in oil and gas exploration, weak tax penalties for rapidly rising excess profits in oil resulting from the Arab oil embargo in the mid-1970s, and tax policy biased toward new plant and equipment, rather than rehabilitation of old, were some of the many federal laws and regulations of which numerous cities could take advantage, but to which Houston was eminently suited. More recently, Houston has benefited from rising health-care costs and the general expansion, corporatization, and specialization of the health care industry. The Texas Medical Center is one of the largest employers in the area, with more than 26,000 employees, a major teaching hospital with about 8600 students, and a center for cancer treatment, open heart surgery, and biomedical engineering (Kaplan 1983:200). With approximately 29 hospitals and research institutions, it covers 235 acres and has an annual economic impact estimated at $1.5 billion, probably more than for military-space-industrial facilities. The expansion of the Texas Medical Center and the growth of Rice University and the University of Houston, promise a more diversified economy, one that can weather fluctuations in oil prices and dependence on a few major industries. Still, because it emphasizes treatment and not research, the Medical Center has not been prominent in creating spin-offs and only a few med-tech companies exist in Houston (Clark 1984).

Employment

This pattern of economic development has shaped the occupational structure of Houston (see Table 5.3.) In 1980, six out of every ten employed persons were involved in managerial, professional, techni-

Table 5.3   Resident Occupational Distributions, City of Houston, 1940–1980[a]

City Share	1980	1970	1960	1950	1940
Managerial, professional and technical	24.5	·25.3	22.3	21.4	18.7
Sales and administrative support	34.4	29.1	24.6	24.2	23.6
Service, including domestic	11.0	13.6	13.7	14.9	21.3
Farm managers and laborers	0.6	0.2	0.3	0.3	0.2
Precision production	13.7	13.1	12.7	15.1	12.3
Operators and laborers	15.8	18.7	19.4	22.9	22.8
Totals	100.0	100.0	93.0[b]	99.0[c]	98.9[d]
Absolute totals	827,110	515,637	363,636	252,068	161,697
City/SMSA Ratio[e]					
Managerical, professional and technical	0.57	0.65	0.78	0.78	
Sales and administrative support	0.58	0.69	0.80	0.83	
Service, including domestics	0.63	0.70	0.83	0.85	
Farm managers and laborers	0.37	0.21	0.29	0.19	
Precision production	0.50	0.56	0.71	0.71	
Operators and laborers	0.59	0.63	0.74	0.75	
Totals	0.57	0.65	0.77	0.77	

[a]Employed persons 16 years and older for 1960 to 1980, 14 years and older for 1940 and 1950 except those on emergency work in 1940.
[b]Occupation not reported for 25,515 persons, 7 percent of the total employed residents.
[c]Occupation not reported for 1.0 percent of the employed residents.
[d]Occupation not reported for 1.1 percent of the employed residents.
[e]No SMSA existed in 1940.

Sources: U.S. Department of Commerce, Bureau of the Census, *Detailed Population Characteristics* and *Social and Economic Characteristics*, selected years.

cal, sales, and administrative support activities. This distribution reflects the capital-intensity of the petroleum, chemical and shipping industries, the administrative overhead of these firms, and the influence of NASA, the Texas Medical Center, and the universities. Thus while Houston might have the hard-hat image of construction and oil rigs, for several decades the city has been more white collar than blue collar in its employment mix. In 1940, nearly 38 percent of all urban workers were in white-collar occupations. By 1970 the figure was 54 percent, and by 1980, 58 percent. Throughout the postwar period it has exceeded the national average.[8]

This dominance of professional-administrative occupations is further reflected in the temporal pattern of the occupational structure. Only four out of ten persons were engaged in the above-named occupations in 1940. In addition, precision production workers have increased their share of employment, while machine operators and laborers have lost their share, further reinforcing the belief that the production process has become more and more centered on technology and advanced machinery. In fact, many of the white collar workers are employed by oil-petroleum companies. The largest relative drop in occupational share from 1940 to 1980 has been in the category of nonbusiness service workers, including domestics, which declined from employing two out of ten to one out of ten workers over the four decades.

These changes in occupational structure are linked to changes in industrial structure. While the data above on value-added and employment in manufacturing showed relative stability over the postwar years, a breakdown of employment across nonagricultural industries displays a much different picture (see Table 5.4). Rather than stability, what we see is a rendition of the manufacturing-service shift that has characterized the nation since at least 1945. The share of resident employment in the city of Houston has fallen by almost 30 percent since 1940, and that in services has increased by nearly 60 percent. Finance, insurance, and real estate, and wholesale trade have also increased relative to the other sectors. What is so striking about these shifts, however, is that they have taken place within a context of major employment growth, unlike that which has occurred in older industrial cities. Manufacturing employment's share dropped by 30 percent, but its absolute numerical presence expanded by more than 270 percent from 1940 to 1980. Not one of Houston's major industrial sectors lost employment during this boom period.

Across the postwar period, moreover, the occupational structures

Table 5.4   Resident Employment Shares by Nonagricultural Industry
City of Houston, 1940–1980

	1940	1950	1960	1970	1980
Mining	3.3	1.8	2.7	3.1	4.6
Construction	8.2	9.7	7.1	8.1	9.3
Manufacturing	24.0	20.5	19.8	18.5	17.0
Transportation, communications and public utilities	11.3	11.8	9.5	8.2	8.4
Wholesale trade	4.7	5.9	6.5	6.7	6.4
Retail trade	20.4	18.6	13.3	17.2	15.5
Finance, insurance, and real estate	5.5	4.9	5.4	6.3	7.1
Services	18.7	22.8	26.7	28.7	29.1
Government	2.6	2.8	2.9	3.2	2.6
Total	99.9[a]	100.0	100.0	100.0	100.0
Absolute total[b]	155,546	250,415	361,186	512,093	822,040

[a]Discrepency due to rounding.
[b]Data have been adjusted for non-reporting.

Source: U.S. Department of Commerce, Bureau of the Census, *Social and Economic Characteristics,* selected years.

of the city and metropolitan area of Houston have basically paralleled each other. Note that in Table 5.3 the city/SMSA ratios for occupational categories are within a few points of that for the overall ratio. If the occupational distributions were different, the ratios would exhibit much more variation. The exception is farm managers and workers. Houston has always had many fewer such workers, but paradoxically its share has been increasing. Simultaneously, however, the city's ability to retain a healthy share of metropolitan employment has been decreasing. This quantitative shift could likely lead to qualitative variations in city and metropolitan occupational structures, thus making Houston more like cities which have experienced suburbanization without the powers of annexation (Black 1980: Table 4.13; Garn and Ledebur 1980: Table 7.9).

The economic growth that has shaped the occupational distribution has not necessarily brought prosperity to all residents. In 1979, 12.7 percent of the city's population and 10.1 percent of the metropolitan area's were officially poor. The incidence of poverty, moreover, fell unevenly across racial and ethnic categories. While the percent of those falling below the official poverty line in 1980 was 7.2 for white residents of the city, that for the city's blacks was 22.3, and for residents of Spanish origin, 18.0. The corresponding percentages for the metropolitan area were slightly less by one to two percentage points, but in the same general relationship to each other. Of course, this does not speak directly to the influence of sustained economic growth on poverty within the Houston area. Comparing the poverty rates over time for the city, that for all families has gone from 10.7 percent in 1969 to 10.0 percent in 1979: from 25.3 percent to 20.0 percent for black families, and from 15.9 percent to 15.4 percent for families with Spanish surnames or language. To that extent, economic growth has had a slight positive effect upon poverty in the city. The data show a similar pattern of declines for the SMSA. In constant dollars, median family income has increased in the city from $5,713 in 1960 to $8,298 in 1980. The corresponding numbers for the metropolitan area are $5,847 and $9,262. The 45 percent and 58 percent increases, respectively, certainly indicate overall economic growth, if not a strong distributional component. Of course, the bust of 1983–1984 likely had a countervailing impact upon the diminution of poverty and rise in income.

Spatial Disparities

While Houston's economic growth has helped to raise median incomes and the city's ability to annex has enabled it to capture population and employment growth, thus staving off urban decline, disparities between the central city and the surrounding suburban area are still evident, although not nearly as pronounced as might be found in an older industrial city such as Boston or Detroit. The stereotype of Houston is of a city that has absorbed its suburbs; that is, it has captured growth and affluence. Beyond the city's geopolitical boundaries exist new developments ripe for annexation and areas of little value.

As we saw in Table 5.1, the city has been able to maintain a major share of population growth, and as noted in Table 5.3, it has done even better as regards jobs. In terms of the dollar value of economic activity, the city has basically maintained its status quo. In 1958 it had 62.2 percent of the metropolitan area's value-added in manufacturing, while in 1982 its share was 60.3 percent. On the other hand, the city seems to be losing its share of households, down from 77 percent in 1960 to 59 percent in 1980, which indicates a slightly higher household formation rate outside the central city. Average household size since 1950 has been higher without than within the city's boundaries. Moreover, blacks and Hispanics are disproportionately concentrated in the central city. While the city had 55 percent of the metropolitan area's population in 1980, it had 83 percent of blacks and 66 percent of Hispanics. The percentage for blacks was at a postwar high of 87 percent in 1960, up from 71 percent in 1950. Houston has had a significant black population since the 19th century; it was 39 percent in 1880 (Buchanan 1975:37). In 1930 the proportion fell to 22 percent, even though it had increased in absolute terms.

This concentration of minorities in the central city is also reflected in the poverty data. Overall, in 1980 the city had 68.7 percent of all poor persons, 85.9 percent of all poor blacks, and 70.2 percent of all poor Hispanics. Moreover, while median family incomes were roughly similar in the city and the suburbs, the ratio of city to SMSA median family income has been falling, at least since 1960 when they were almost identical. By 1980 the ratio was down 8 percent. In sum, while the city of Houston has been able to maintain its metropolitan position in aggregate terms, the distributional consequences of economic growth have concentrated minorities and poverty within its midst. Intrametropolitan spatial disparities do exist within the Houston SMSA, although certainly not on the scale of that experienced in SMSAs of the Northeast and Midwest. Given its large size and rapid growth, Houston's city-suburban spatial disparities are not immediately obvious.

Spatial Patterns

Sharp spatial differences are ostensibly lost in the unregulated sprawl of the city's urban development. That sprawl is a function of the rapidity of growth, in which soaring demand fueled numerous land development projects, and the lack of barriers to low-density development. The latter is composed of two factors: the paucity of physical barriers to spatial growth, and the absence of land-use planning and coordinated land-use regulations. Houston's flat landscape, uninterrupted except for bayous, presents a different set of geographical constraints than that posed to Boston by shoreline and marshlands; to Portland, Oregon, by its river and hills; or even to Chicago by Lake Michigan on one side. In Houston, the major physical barriers are to the east and take the form of the Buffalo Bayou, the ship channel and, farther away, Lake Houston to the northeast and Galveston Bay to the east and southeast. Galveston Bay and the many small bays between it and the beginning of the channel are nearly twenty miles away and Lake Houston, 15 miles. The most prominent physical barriers are thus far from the center of the city, and the closest barrier, Buffalo Bayou, has been easily managed with bridges and tunnels.

The minimal environmental constraints on the direction of property development are paralleled by a lack of governmental restraints. Many Houstonians pride themselves on being a city without zoning (Babcock 1982). Land-use planning, backed up by legally delineated areas for specific types of development is nonexistent. A city planning department is situated within the local government, but it is not very influential and concerns itself mostly with sewer and water line placement and with documenting the projects of developers (Kaplan 1983:200). Except for the limitations imposed by deed restrictions and by building codes, owners of property can build whatever they wish. Thus fast-food restaurants are found in high priced residential areas, and churches are one parking lot away from multistory office buildings. No planning attempt has been made to group homogenous and compatible land uses into zones, the traditional Euclidean zoning of the land-use planner, or to set up a system of zoning controls to protect property owners from the negative externalities of development. The city government takes a passive role when it comes to regulating growth, preferring to focus its energies on fueling that phenomenon.

Instead, the arrangement of land uses is more a function of land prices and deed restrictions (Fox 1985; Siegan 1972). The latter take effect after the original property has been designated and developed, and require property owners to mobilize in lawsuit or protest to an unwanted land use. Restrictive covenants and civic associations to enforce covenants have been the mechanisms used to protect residential areas since the 1920s. Deed restrictions, as well as private master plans, were generated for the hundreds of shopping centers, garden apartment complexes, industrial parks, and office parks built in the metropolitan area in the postwar period. In 1965 the Texas legislature permitted city governments and local civic associations to enforce private deed restrictions. By the mid-1970s, it was estimated that 10,000 deed instruments covered about two-thirds of the city. One supporter of land-use controls wrote that "Texas is a great place to live, but it is also a place where it's virtually impossible to protect yourself against progress" (Schwartz 1982:24).

The result has been development responding not to natural attributes of the environment nor to a public interest conception of land-use patterns, but to opportunities generated by transportation accessibility and previous investments. Buffalo Bayou and the ship channel clustered commercial, industrial, and even residential development at the headwaters of the bayou and eastward along the water's western edge. To some extent this was a response to land forms, but to a socially created space, not simply a natural one. The coming of the electric street railway enabled growth to spread in other directions. Beginning in the 1920s, highways and the automobile further reinforced this nondirectional deconcentration of land-use activity. In fact, in the postwar period Houston's pattern of development has been closely tied to limited-access interstate highways funded by the federal government and, to a lesser extent, by the state government. Such highway construction began in the mid-1950s and has subsequently spread in all directions.

Houston is well served by interstate highways. Seven spokes meet in a road that rings the CBD, and these spokes are interconnected once again about five miles from the CBD by a circumferential road, I-610. State Highway 6, another eight to ten miles out, provides a second, albeit partial, circumferential. This system of highways—more than 240 miles in length—has created a series of major interchanges almost evenly distributed throughout the Houston region. These interchanges have differentiated the landscape and attracted large-scale commercial and residential developments. Busch Gardens, a major tourist attraction, is at the intersection of I-10 and I-610 to the east, Gulfgate Shopping Center is to the southeast where I-610 meets I-75, and the Astrodome and Astroworld (an amusement park) span I-610 in the southern part of the city. The abundance of limited-access highways has made low-density development possible, and that low-density development has served as a rationale for further highway construction and automobile usage. Such a spatial pattern, when combined with a city government disinterested in public services, has resulted in Houston having one of the most anemic mass-transit systems in the country. The bus system is small and poorly utilized. Only 3 percent of commuters took public transportation to work in 1980, while more than 90 percent traveled in private vehicles.

Despite the lack of directional barriers to development, development is not evenly spread about the center. There is direction and concentration. This can be seen clearly in the spatial pattern of office development. Houston has gone from a city with a clearly recognized center—the downtown—to one with many areas competing with the CBD for prime investment opportunities. The tallest buildings in Houston are located in the CBD, but two of the twelve towers more than 50 stories high are outside the original downtown. The two, next-largest office complexes are the Post Oak area and Greenway Plaza, both sited in the southwest energy corridor. The phenomenal growth of the Houston office market, driven by the rapid increases in oil prices brought on by the Arab oil embargo in 1973–1974, created a fast-paced, speculative market for office buildings. Between 1971 and 1980, 202 office buildings of 50,000 square feet or more were constructed in the metropolitan area (Feagin 1987:175). From then until 1987 another 157 were added. From 1969 to 1986, the amount of office space in Houston increased by almost 800 percent, by 144.9 million square feet. With the severe slump of oil prices in 1982–1983, howver, office construction fell to near zero, and in mid-1987 the office market was still considered overbuilt. Many buildings had high vacancy rates, and owners were willing to grant leasing arrangements containing numerous concessions (Hooper 1986).

Office growth has also not spread evenly throughout the Houston region. Not one, but 18 different office activity centers exist in Houston (see Figure 5.2). In 1986, the downtown contained 25.8 percent of the existing office space, but two other areas—the Galleria-West Loop area at the intersection of I-610 and I-59 and an area farther west beyond I-6—contained 33.9 percent of the existing office space (Coldwell Banker 1986). The fourth-largest office concentration is Greenway/Richmond, just west of the downtown and within the I-610 circumferential.[9] Thus nodes of office development along with a concentration of office space are found to the west and southwest. Office space expansion in the downtown, moreover, has brought about pressure for development in long-existing black wards to the west and northeast, where land is relatively inexpensive and residents are easily displaced (Feagin and Shelton 1985; Hill and Feagin 1987). Certainly this would contradict any possible hint of nondirectional spatial development of the built environment.

Also demonstrating a westward bias is retail development. Excluding the CBD, which had only 2.3 percent of the city's retail sales for 1982 and which had lost 27 percent of its retail establishments since 1972, most of the city's retail space (64 percent) is in the west and there it is clustered in the southwest quadrant defined by I-10 and I-

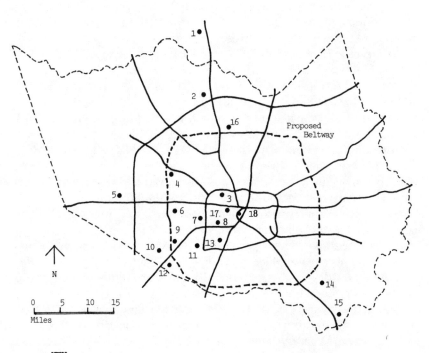

KEY

1. Woodlands
2. FM 1960
3. North Loop/Northwest Freeway
4. Central Northwest
5. West Houston
6. Central West
7. Post Oak/Loop 610
8. Greenway
9. Central Southwest

10. West Belt
11. Bellaire/Loop 610
12. Outer Southwest
13. South Main
14. Gulf Freeway/Pasadena
15. Clear Lake
16. North Belt
17. Allen Parkway/Memorial
18. Downtown

Figure 5.2 Major Existing and Developing Office Activity Centers.
Source: Rice Center, "Questionnaire Results on Office Location Issues in Houston,"
   Research Brief 4 (Houston: Rice Center, 1980), p. 3.

90A (Coldwell Banker 1986).[10] While this is not as sharp a disparity as that for office space, it is more than just a statistical discrepancy. Of the top three major retail concentrations outside the downtown area, two are in this quadrant: Galleria/Post Oak and Memorial City. The largest non-CBD retail concentration is to the northwest nearly 20 miles beyond the downtown, and includes the Woodlands. Significant retail development is also to the east and southeast in the energy corridor.

Further reinforcing the notion that development is nodal in form is the finding that 24.1 percent of all non-CBD retail space is contained in shopping complexes of at least 500,000 square feet of retail space and with at least one national retail department store as an anchor tenant. Another 44.7 percent is in neighborhood or community centers. Of the metropolitan area's 27 major retail centers (MRCs) reported by the *Census of Retail Trade* in 1982, only two are not composed of planned centers. Moreover, Houston has a large number of major retail centers for a city of its population size. Sixteen (or 60 percent) of the major retail centers in the Houston metropolitan area in 1982 were wholly within the city of Houston. The Philadelphia metropolis with 48 retail centers had only two MRCs within its city limits. Such data speak not only to the issues of land area and annexation but also to the relative dominance of the CBDs.

Of the nonresidential components of development, industrial space displays the least-differentiated spatial distribution, even though it still has a slightly westward bias. Only 55 percent of industrial space outside the loop defined by I-610 is to the west (ibid.). Moreover, the northwest quadrant contains the greatest concentration, 41 percent of the total. Still, the largest concentration of the metropolitan total lies within the I-610 circumferential, 84.3 million square feet (40.9 percent). Most of this space is arrayed along the ship channel to the southeast. This area contains 51 percent of all major manufacturing plants with 25 or more employees, as well as three-quarters of the chemical plants, oil refineries, and other oil-related facilities. Steel and other metal operations are also disporportionately located there. The easternmost section, near Galveston Bay, has much of Houston's heavy industry. In the southernmost part are Exxon's huge industrial park (Bayport) and a cluster of newer aerospace and electronics plants near the NASA Spacecraft Center. Manufacturing facilities outside the southeast quadrant are mostly arrayed near major roads and highways, such as I-10 and the Southwest Freeway, and near the Houston International Airport in the far north area of the city.[11]

New residential development repeats the westward pattern. Apartment construction since 1985 has been concentrated in the wedge defined by I-10 and I-90A (ibid.). Within that area, 138,798 new units have been brought on-line, 34 percent of the total. The northwest has added another 23 percent, bringing the total in the west to 55 percent. Trailing far behind is the northeast, with less than 10 percent of the new apartment construction. Houstonians pride themselves on being a city of homeowners, although in 1980 one out of every two city residents was a renter, as compared with one out of every four residents of the metropolitan area outside the central city.[12] The majority of black and Hispanic households, as shown above, are concentrated in the city, are renters, and live disproportionately in segregated neighborhoods, many of which are adjacent to the downtown where there has been significant displacement, due to office development, and signs of gentrification.

With almost 50 percent of the 1980 housing stock having been built after 1960, Houston is a city with numerous planned enclaves of condominiums and detached single-family houses. With the local government playing a minimal role in service provision, many outlying complexes are served by municipal utility districts (MUDs) which utilized tax-exempt bonds to construct infrastructural facilities, with the property owners making annual payments until annexed by the city. If the city cannot provide utility services, the developer can create, with governmental permission, a municipal utility district with the authority to sell bonds for utility construction. By 1986 the metropolitan area had 411 MUDs, about three-quarters of all such districts in the state. Even during the economic downturn in the mid-1980s, developers continued to create new districts in order to raise money for water and sewage infrastructure facilities. The city government is supposed to review the financing proposal and the quality of utility services in terms of future annexation and assumption of operation of the utility systems. As a rule, the city eventually annexes the subdivisions and takes over the utility systems, often incurring substantial debt as a result. While the Houston annexation policy has kept many suburbanites within the official city boundaries, this inclusion has brought with it the problems of inadequately planned utility systems.[13]

Overall, then, data on office, retail, and industrial space and new apartment construction point to a westward bias in Houston's postwar development as well as development around a series of nodes or, in the case of the ship channel and I-10 South, along growth corridors.

Moreover, the original downtown area, while not experiencing absolute decline, maintains its commercial dominance by concentrating the administrative headquarters (or subsidiaries) of leading banks and corporations (such as Texas Commerce Bank, Shell Oil Company), but has lost any residential or retail dominance it might once have had.

The development of nodes of commercial, retail, and residential space has been facilitated by the intersection of rapid growth, abundant capital, and large-scale development and construction firms able to arrange and implement such projects. Postwar residential construction has been dominated by some of the country's largest builders—such as U.S. Home, Gemcraft, General Homes—and commercial development by such large firms as the Gerald D. Hines Interests, a nationally-known commercial developer. Major oil companies created development arms, and investors for national insurance companies and pension funds entered Houston looking for investment opportunities (Feagin 1987:183). Some of them set up property development organizations: Prudential Insurance Company has the PIC Realty Corp., Sears, Roebuck & Co. has the Homart Development Co., and Exxon has the Friendswood Development Company. Capital-rich OPEC countries, the expansion of Japanese investment abroad, and the relative stability and high rates of return of U.S. real estate investments led foreign investors to provide capital for new construction and to purchase existing properties. In 1987, 39 percent of the major office space in the downtown market was owned by international investors (Coldwell Banker 1987).

Rapid growth and major in-migrations required equally rapid and large-scale responses. Only big developers could undertake the vast projects that would respond quickly to demand. While many nooks and crannies were available in the market for small developers, the large developers dominated and created the multinucleated landscape that now characterizes Houston.

One of the major "other downtowns" is Post Oak to the west of the city. Post Oak not only has more first-class shopping space than the CBD, it has more first-class hotels, a 64-story office building, and one of the region's largest shopping malls, the Galleria (Goldberger 1987). This new-style commercial center is situated between River Oaks, the city's most fashionable neighborhood, and the newer development to the west, and itself is adjacent to numerous condominium and residential complexes. River Oaks was one of the first planned communities in Houston in 1923 and opened its shopping center in 1937

(Buchanan 1975; Jackson 1985:259). Then it was a suburb; later it was incorporated into the city. River Oaks has its own privately financed and operated police force, as do other residential enclaves like the Woodlands, twenty miles outside Houston (Louv 1983). Moreover, just southwest of the city a 9300 acre site is being developed with 1500 houses in 34 residential communities, more than a half million square feet of retail space, and 4 million square feet of office and warehouse space to be in place by the mid-1990s (Hooper 1986:220). Also to be included are 300 acres of lakes and a 1.5 million-square-foot shopping center. Shulgen Properties, Inc., is the lead partner in this massive project.

The postwar spatial development of Houston can be described simply as one of multinodal sprawl structured by the ship channel and interstate highways, but having, overall, a westward momentum despite the lack of physical barriers. Within this larger pattern exists a complex juxtaposition of land uses displaying neither the clustered homogeneity that zoning and land-use planning would have imposed nor the anarchy of an unfettered market. Rather, the economics of land with its peak in the CBD, the presence of large-scale developers, and the existence of deed restrictions and vociferous neighborhood groups have served to bring some order to the free-enterprise market. The result has been a clustering of planned, mixed-use developments within a more disparate land-use pattern. Rapid growth, moreover, has made new construction the norm, with hardly any noticeable rehabilitation in progress. Governmentally subsidized urban renewal was rejected. Although a small Model Cities program once existed, it had no significant impact. Gentrification occurs, but is not nearly as extensive as in northern cities. Houston's spatial development thus clearly distinguishes itself from that of Boston, Detroit, Newark, and Cleveland.

Political Economy of Urbanization

Houston's postwar spatial development was structured by a small number of specific relations. The interaction of local business and political elites established the ideological environment for rapid, unregulated growth and minimal public services. The relationship between the local government and the federal government, often mediated by state and local economic elites, enabled the development of essential infrastructure for supporting industrial development, often provided demand for local products, regulated major markets in which Houston-based industries were involved, and facilitated decentralized development. The complex interweaving of oil industry capital, property development firms, and national and international financial entities produced large-scale developers capable of and willing to be engaged in the multiuse planned centers that are the hallmark of Houston's postwar growth. Last, the reliance of the local economy on a few industries created a boom-bust phenomenon that has had important implications for patterns of consumption and reproduction and their spatial consequences.

Local Business, Local Government

Noteworthy throughout Houston's 150 plus years has been a close and mutually supportive relationship between local capital and local government. In fact, it is accurate to state that almost without interruption, local business elites have been the major influence over the structure and functions of local government (see Platt 1983).

Since its first decade, Houston has been ruled by strong business elites which, except for one or two brief episodes in the late 19th century, have been unchallenged in their power and influence. The top politicians of the city, with rare exceptions, have been members of, or heavily dependent on, business elites. The first group to dominate the city was composed of the founding entrepreneurs, the Allen brothers, and a few other merchants. General and cotton merchants were very influential over the next few decades. In the 1880s and 1890s, the merchant aggregation was supplemented with bankers, lawyers, and railroad men. By the late 1920s, oil entrepreneurs had become part of the city's power structure, but they never ruled alone. In the late 1930s the most cohesive clique emerged, the Suite 8F crowd (Murray 1980). It appears to have been the most powerful in the city's history, in large part because of its cohesion and its distinctive personalities, as well as its corporate networks (banking, law, insurance, and oil-gas transmission) and national and international resources.[14] When Suite 8F power waned in the 1970s, a larger and less-cohesive power structure emerged: the Houston Chamber of Commerce moved to the center of business leadership. While this organization is headed by an assortment of corporate executives, its influence in the mid-1980s has been limited by larger contextual factors brought by major disinvestment.

Thus is found in Houston not only a tight relation between government and the economy but also a changing one. Different capitalist fractions have gained political ascendency as the economy has layered banking and railroad service upon agricultural production and marketing, primary commodities upon those sectors, and then added oil, petroleum, and paper processing and manufacturing, to be followed most recently by medical services and space-related activities. In spite of this shifting dominance of economic sectors, the local power structure has been headed by business leaders in every decade since the 1830s. Unions, neighborhood leaders, and black groups have been unable to establish countervailing power. Unions, in fact, have had to struggle against a pro-business and anti-union climate, while benefiting from the boom or being ravaged by the bust, and have, for the most part, confined themselves, as they have throughout the United States, to workplace demands (Mollenkopf 1981). Construction unions are a good example, since they can hardly oppose property development and suffer during downswings. Ethnic, neighborhood-based leaders have been undermined throughout the 20th century by at-large elections and a commission form of government, while blacks have suffered from a southern plantation heritage exacerbated by poverty, discrimination, and police brutality.

Essential to the economy, at least in terms of what government can provide, is an infrastructure supportive of commerce, of movement of goods, and of circulation of capital. To the extent that such infrastructure is unlikely to be provided by capital, the local government has been a key actor in the commercial life and spatial development of the city. The weave of economic elites and political officials is close, and both join forces around the belief that the built environment is meant to serve primarily as the facilitator of capital accumulation.[15] In the postwar period, as mentioned, property interests provided the link between major industries and political intervention, but their involvement was made possible by decades of ideological commitment to the notion that the function of local government is to serve capitalism. Local government has maintained a consistent and strong orientation to growth; growth has meant physical and economic expansion. No attempts have been made to control or limit physical development out of a need to create a more orderly city, reduce the spatial antagonisms among various capitalists, mop up the negative externalities of growth, or provide amenities that might benefit labor and improve the quality of life (Feagin 1985b). For example, Houston ranks far down the list of the country's major cities in land set aside for parks (Babcock 1982:22). Unlike other local governments, that in Houston has minimal interest in protecting capitalism from itself, much less in protecting labor from capital. Accumulation reigns.

Growth is supported, not because it will enhance the tax base and expand the potential for local government to provide community services such as daycare or public amenities such as parks, but because it reinforces an ideological commitment to capitalism and serves the economic elites whose influence is central to local government existence. Houston can maintain low taxes and ignore this aspect of expansion in part because the extraterritorial jurisdictional provision enables it to annex areas of growth. Most important, local government needs capital for very practical reasons.

Throughout the postwar period, the process by which local officials are elected has been one that relies mainly on heavily funded electoral strategies (Murray 1980). All councilmembers, until 1979, were elected at large. Because of the large land area of the city, candidates have been forced to run expensive media campaigns to gain the exposure and name-recognition necessary for election. The funding for such campaigns comes mostly from the business community, thereby linking elected officials and economic elites early in the formers' careers. While the laissez-faire environment might be more influential in gearing local government to business interests, this functional tie (of many) cannot be ignored. The electoral reform in 1979, which changed the structure of city council to five at-large and nine district-based members, has lessened the dependence of some (especially minority) candidates on business community money, but the business community controls more than enough seats to maintain de facto control of the city.

An important consequence of this political economy is Houston's general avoidance of the social costs of growth and the provision of services (such as environmental regulations and police protection) normally expected of local government. Unlike older cities of the Northeast and Midwest, Houston's industrial development was not rampant during an era of Progressive reform, an era in which other cities became deeply involved in housing and building code regulations, water and sewer treatment, social services, and a host of other interventions. Progressive reformers did emerge in Houston, but their concerns were centered on an inefficient, ward-based government whose interests were not always compatible with economic growth. Even Houston's rapid and vast urbanization has failed to generate a more socially interventionist local government. The commitment to maintain a good business climate of low taxes, few regulations, and minimal governmental services (with the exception of projects facilitating local, private investment, such as port facilities, convention center, and industrial parks) has been too powerful to be overridden by social reformers. Social liberals with a conservative business ideology have occasionally taken over the reins of government (Platt 1983), most recently Kathryn Whitmire who was elected mayor in 1981. The police department is generally considered to be undermanned, water and sewage facilities are overloaded, roadways are clogged with traffic, the bus system is inadequate, and social services are miserly at best. In 1977, for example, Houston annexed the Clear Lake City region of approximately 20,000 to 25,000 people but added no police, fire, or street maintenance personnel (Beck and Henkoff 1980). City services were simply stretched thinner across the city, or some areas were further deprived.

The absenteeism of local goverment is particularly pronounced in the area of land-use regulation. Houston prides itself on being the only major city in the country with no land-use zoning; the market determines the location of different land-use activities. Deed restrictions are abundant and have the effect of excluding certain types of uses from areas, but their exclusivity has, in the past, extended to race, and their more common use in more affluent areas leaves the poor no less vulnerable to unwanted land uses. Poor Houstonians rarely resort to political means to protect themselves, while the rich use their political contacts to overcome opposition.

Not only incompatible land uses, as planners term them, stem from the lack of zoning but the absence of any local governmental oversight and regulation of development itself. One consequence is sprawl, mile after mile of low-density development insensitive to problems of transportation and the provision of infrastructure. Developers can continue to accrete projects onto existing development and exploit the low-lying flat land that surrounds the city. The end result has been inadequate water and sewage facilities, onerous traffic congestion (and lengthening commutes), pollution of the bayous, and subsidence as more and more groundwater is pumped out from under Houston. It is ironic that Houston began as a planned town (Reps 1981:29). When the Allen brothers subdivided the land in 1836 they reserved space for schools and churches and provided one full block for a courthouse and another for the capitol of the new Republic of Texas. Since that heyday of planning, Houston's development has followed the dictates of the market, a market regulated by land prices,

large developers, oligopolistic industries, politically influential property interests, and a pro-growth local government. Planning occurs,
but on a subdivision-by-subdivision basis.

Local-Federal Relations

While local government absented itself from regulating growth or
providing public services commensurate with the scale and pace of
urbanization, the federal government's presence enabled Houston to
establish the important infrastructure that supported growth without
destroying the good business climate that the city government sustained. The federal government has provided numerous subsidies
and much assistance to Houston's economy and arguably has been
one of the key agents in the city's growth. At the same time, the city
leaders were deploring big government and its intervention into the
economy, they were aggressively lobbying the state and federal governments for laws, money, and other assistance to enhance the local
economy. The ideology of free enterprise has always been anchored
in a peculiarly capitalist, material base.

Even before the New Deal legitimized federal intervention into local
affairs and shifted its scale, Houston benefited from its intercession.
The Supreme Court's role in clarifying the political economy of public
utilities and municipal bonds enabled Houston and many other cities
in the last decades of the 19th century to continue their pro-growth
orientation. Financially, the federal government has been providing
subsidies to improve the ship channel since before the turn of the
century. New Deal public works programs provided the city with the
basic infrastructure necessary for renewed growth after the depression. During World War II, key industries in Houston were aided not
only by the government's demand for rubber, ships, and fuel but also
by the federal government's investment in defense preparations.

The federal support for interstate highways after the war, along
with the expanded FHA mortgage assistance program, allowed Houston to expand rapidly, while the power of annexation enabled Houston to capture this suburbanization within the city's boundaries. The
subsequent decentralization and deconcentration weakened the city's
core and helped to create the particular urban form that distinguishes
Houston from older industrial cities in the Northeast and Midwest.
More recently, the federal government's locating the NASA complex
in Houston, its contracts with Brown and Root (an international
construction firm), and its tax policies concerning oil exploration,

plant and equipment depreciation allowances, and commercial property development have also facilitated the prosperity the city experienced up to the mid-1980s. More indirectly, the federal government's failure to regulate health costs and to allow the corporatization of health care has definitely been one factor in the growth of one of the city's major employers, the Texas Medical Center.

Since the early 1900s, the federal government has been a major actor in Houston's development. That involvement, in fact, has extended beyond the general support State policies have provided to decentralization. Specific projects deeded to Houston have been instrumental in its pace of expansion; aid to the ship channel, regulation and subsidies for oil and gas exploration, and the Johnson Spacecraft Center are unique to Houston and linked strongly to the ability of city and state elected officials to work with federal officials in directing governmental investment to Houston, a link tied not just to voting power but also to economic power and personal ties. Moreover, federal assistance often has distinct spatial consequences. Decentralization and deconcentration are background themes, but in the foreground are the clusters of property development around the NASA complex, the ship channel, and highway interchanges. Other cities have gained from federal programs and policies, but Houston is particularly blessed.

The Property Development Sector

Translating these opportunities and incentives for capital accumulation into reformulations of the built environment required the presence of a well-developed property development sector of developers, real estate agents, lending institutions, and construction firms. On the other hand, the development of such a sector with its large, nationally active developers led to that growth being shaped into a multinucleated urban form. Planned multiuse centers came to define the landscape, and only large developers had the financial and managerial capacity to acquire the land, develop the projects, and lead it through the implementation process successfully.

As we have seen, many developers were involved with national insurance companies or major oil firms. Others were independent of these intersectoral links but, like Gerald D. Hines, were major actors in real estate around the country. The economy has ebbed and flowed with the price of oil, but it is unlikely that oil capital (that is, the retained earnings of oil and related energy companies) has dominated the financing of property development (Feagin 1987). Rather, two factors seem to be more prominent in generating the demand for development and the capital with which to respond. The first is the ability of finance capital to flow freely throughout the world. For example, finance capital is increasingly controlled within a few large cities like New York, San Francisco, and Los Angeles. Investment officers of insurance companies, large banks and pension funds are immediately aware of each change in Houston's real estate market and its reputation, despite the recent downturn, as a place of profitable investments and thus a destination for national and international capital. Foreign investment thus poured into Houston's office market and multiuse developments in the boom period, and by the early 1970s Houston was a major segment of the world market in real estate. By 1987, 39 percent of Houston's downtown office market was owned by international investors (Coldwell Banker 1987), and numerous development projects have been joint ventures between a Texas company and a foreign investor. Still, while national and international finance capital provided the requisite capital during the boom period, they abandoned the city once the scale of overbuilding became evident and property values fell.

The second factor is the multiplier effect of oil and energy industry growth and decline. The sustained, rapid growth of key Houston industries drew large numbers of migrants into the area, generating massive additions to the labor force, and thus pumped wages and salaries into the economy, as well as being a source for property capital. These new workers required housing, clothes, food, automobiles, appliances and numerous other consumer items, which in turn required apartment complexes, housing developments, retail stores, warehouses, and gasoline stations. The rapidity of economic growth led to a demand-driven property market that needed large developers and substantial outside capital to satisfy the scale of demand. The growth in income enabled numerous households to assume the mortgages and meet the rents asked for new housing, thus completing the financial circuit of residential property development.

Economic Specialization

The concentration of investment and employment in certain industries, despite a multisectoral economy, has always been a major factor in Houston's spectacular growth, but during the mid-1980s it has increasingly been recognized as one of the economy's weaknesses.

Throughout the 20th century, the Houston economy has been favorably positioned in the national and international economy, that is, within expanding sectors. Agricultural marketing and oil and gas exploration and refining have served Houston well. In the last few years, however, specialization in these industries has made it difficult for the city to weather the relatively high U.S. dollar (which diminished exports) and the downturn in oil prices and the glut of oil on the market. The policy prescription is economic diversification.

An example of the response to the relative lack of diversification, which can be exaggerated, is the Houston Economic Development Council (HEDC). In the mid-1980s, the business leadership of the Chamber of Commerce set up the HEDC under the direction of the chair of the board of the Century Development Corporation, one of the largest real estate development firms in North America. The HEDC publicly pinpointed nine categories of business firms as the most important targets for future development: biomedical research and development; research and development laboratories; instruments, particularly medical and computer equipment; communications equipment; chemicals, including plastics and drugs; materials processing research; computers and office machines; engineering and architectural services; and distribution services. The notable omissions were oil, petrochemicals, construction, and most types of manufacturing—Houston's core enterprises. The ostensible reasons were the concern for diversifying the local economy and mitigating the huge losses in employment experienced in these traditional industries during the 1980s recession (Crown 1986).

Whether economic and political elites can reshape the economy to make it immune to cyclical fluctuations and restructurings of capitalism is speculation. More objective is the effect of economic specialization on the uneven temporal and spatial development of the Houston area. The rapid growth of these industries resulted in population growth and a concomitant expansion of the built environment. The pace of that growth had much to do with the deconcentration of the city and the bias for large-scale, multiuse projects developed by big organizations. On the other hand, when the bottom fell out of the oil barrel in 1983–1984, the subsequent economic bust also reverberated spatially. Many oil-based firms went out of business, creating empty commercial and industrial space and not a few foreclosures.[16] Unemployment rose, and households that had purchased housing at boom prices now found themselves with burdensome mortgages and falling property values. To sell was to take a capital loss. Even land prices fell precipitously.[17] Construction virtually came to a halt. The depression in the market for land and property, moreover, was unevenly spread across the city. Some areas, such as the older more-established developments, continued to do well, but newer developments occupied by recent firms and migrants linked to the oil industry did not. Empty office buildings, condominiums, and factories attested to the spatial consequences of economic specialization.[18]

The agents of spatial transformation in Houston thus must include the federal government, large-scale developers, national and international finance capital, local government, migrant households, and the dominant local industries. The complex interaction of these entities, each pursuing his own goals and each responding to a logic of capital accumulation, shaped Houston's built environment in specific ways, ways also influenced by the paucity of physical constraints and an insensitivity to environmental and social costs. Within its ideological discourse, Houston's spatial development has been one of free enterprise unhindered by governmental interference and driven by the market. The reality has been much different; state-assisted oligopoly capitalism is a more accurate description.

Ideology, Time, and Space

The ideology of free enterprise in Houston masks a clear case of state-assisted oligopoly capitalism. One cannot deny that market forces play a role in shaping the built environment, but neither can one avoid recognition of the extent to which the overlapping land, property, capital, and labor markets are constrained by various non-market factors. Deed restrictions and political activism place limits on property development, local and federal government intervention creates an uneven spatial pattern of land and property values, and international political events affecting oil prices and the value of the U.S. dollar along with national conditioning of alternative investment opportunities, make the capital market less than an unfettered forum for exchange. Even the labor market within Houston plays a part in property development. During the boom years, rapid economic growth brought good wages and salaries to the upper third of the income distribution and encouraged residential speculation and excessive property values, all of which collapsed when growth subsided. The inability of the labor market to satisfy all workers, particularly minorities, has left a significant segment of the population poor and forced to occupying low-quality housing near the city's traditional downtown.

This boosterist, entrepreneurial ideology does more than mask the many and important distortions of the free market; it also serves political and cultural purposes. The ideology maintains the legitimacy of a local government that is indifferent to the social needs of all its neighborhoods and citizens, particularly minorities and low-income individuals. The ideology also offers a prescription that combines a sustaining optimism about the future with blatant opportunism: private troubles are eliminated by private actions. Be an entrepreneur, or ride the wave of economic expansion in administrative, sales, technical, and precision production jobs.

The social costs of growth, the exploitation and alienation of workers—phenomena exacerbated by the sensitivity of the economy to sharp shifts—and, most important, the distributional consequences of Houston's prosperity are veiled by an ideology that supports the individual against an elusive and ill-defined monolith. Implicit within Houston's boosterism is not just the straw man of big government, but a statement about social constraints, about the ways in which all societies require conformance to norms, condemn what they define as deviant behavior, and necessitate a consideration of the behaviors and thoughts of others. In Houston, all prosper if everyone takes care of himself. The ideology justifies indifference to and isolation from public troubles. Pollution, traffic congestion, poverty, unemployment, subsidence, and all other problems are simply to be fled. For the local government to collect substantive taxes and undertake the full-fledged programs to solve such intrusions would violate the ideology and make real the monolith of oppression. That certain of these problems are barriers to capital accumulation is recognized; the solution is to turn to the federal government. This is a contradiction, of course, but one easily overlooked since it is merely a highly leveraged, entrepreneurial coup—the city obtains great value with minimal contribution. For many blacks and Hispanics, and for a significant portion of the white population, the material reality of their daily existence makes this ideological gloss on Houston's hyper-development ring painfully hollow.

Time and Space

What might find more consensus among Houstonians is the effect of the pace of capital accumulation upon the rhythm of daily life.

Major infusions of population and capital during the postwar period have expanded the built environment. From 1973 to 1988, with oil prices leaping upward and then downward, Houston first became enmeshed in a frenzy of office construction and employment growth, then in a major recession. In the boom period, capital circulated even more quickly than it had in the past; the time between conception and execution of development projects shortened, properties changed hands as new investors took advantage of speculative values and tax opportunities, and massive amounts of new capital flowed into the Houston area as construction loans and mortgages went into new additions to the built environment. The construction industry was in a frenzy. Middle- and upper-income tenants took advantage of new apartment construction, and homeowners used their paychecks to purchase housing. The mobile population moved about the area to take advantage of housing opportunities. The local government, in turn, was under citizen pressure to respond to property developments and to provide infrastructure to service them, but was limited by low taxes and business opposition.

Life at the workplace and in the home also set a different pace. Throughout the boom period overtime was abundant, and workers probably found it difficult to substitute leisure time for the opportunity to capture some of the prosperity. High employment rates for ordinary workers, however, masked lower wages and benefits than in the Snowbelt. The better-paid workers used their higher income to purchase luxuries. The demands and rewards of the workplace had implications for home life, particularly for those in the bottom half of the income distribution. More household members were working, and for longer hours. Even when they had jobs, wages were low for lower-income families. With the sudden drop in oil prices, high unemployment, and falling incomes, life took another turn. Work-weeks shortened or disappeared, leisure became enforced rather than selected. Many of the unemployed found their daily lives driven by desperation rather than hope. Some became small businesspeople, some took lower-wage jobs, some left town. The press of depression is different from that of growth. Time does not move so quickly for the unemployed, though the first of the month comes around more quickly for those facing mortgage payments and possible foreclosure.

The rapidity of Houston's growth has substituted fortune-telling for history. The past is not important; what will the future bring? Tomorrow's potential financial returns outweigh yesterday's accomplishments. The result is a sense of place without history. While historical landmarks exist throughout the area and people have built up attachments to neighborhoods, there are few monuments and parks, and the symbolism of space in Houston, a symbolism that emerges only out of a rich and revered past, hardly exists. A combination of vast reaches of available land and abundant capital has resulted in numerous large-scale planned developments, rather than in an incremental creation of social space by indigenous and small-scale investors and households.

One consequence has been the scattering of highly concentrated, multiuse developments within a sea of low-density sprawl and a patchwork of open spaces leapfrogged by development. The polar orientation of property development in older, industrial cities is nowhere apparent. The metaphor is more of a grid of nodal investments distorted in its rectilinearity by a web of highways. Yet land prices in the center are not devalued by this pattern of development. Quite the contrary, they remain high—the highest in the metropolitan area and even higher than in a city of comparable size; such as Philadelphia.[19] One would expect equilibrium across nodes, until one realizes that rapid growth engenders speculation, abundant capital distorts values, and investors despite their much-acclaimed risk, tend to be the conservative and the successful, both economically and spatially.

This complex picture also contains a process of devaluation and valuation of space, not in a see-saw pattern whereby earlier spaces are abandoned only to be recaptured by capital, but in a succession of outward movements. Capital continually and haltingly migrates toward the periphery, establishing new nodes or corridors, and then appends to them further developments. Redevelopment is nearly unheard of in Houston. The CBD, because of its importance as an office center, has had buildings re-cycled into more intensive developments, but any re-valuation of devalued space is rare. Such behavior, of course, makes the development process in Houston much different than that in Philadelphia or Boston or Baltimore. Houston is neither a city of historic time nor historic place. Instead, Houston is a city where capital pushes the limits of hyperdevelopment.

Acknowledgements

Thanks to Debra L. Bilow for providing real estate data and maps.

Notes

1. We are not claiming that this is true only of Houston, but rather that the image we have described is central to the ideological perception of Houston. Such unabashed entrepreneurialism is not currently true of all U.S. cities.

2. A number of sources were consulted in the preparation of this historical sketch: Buchanan 1975; Feagin 1988, 1985a, 1984b; Kaplan 1983; Platt 1983; and Writers' Program 1942.

3. Houston's developmental pattern can neither be described as zonal, made up of concentric rings, nor sectoral, but is best labeled multinodal or multinucleated; that is, characterized by roughly evenly distributed, relatively large, high-density developments against a background pattern of low-density sprawl.

4. Of the total metropolitan population over five years of age in 1980 who had migrated from a different state, 18.0 percent came from the Northeast, 25.6 percent from the north central region, 39.5 percent from the South, and 16.9 percent from the West. The corresponding percentages for 1970 were 10.5, 20.3, 47.8, and 21.4. Data are from the U.S. Department of Commerce, *Detailed Population Characteristics* (Washington, D.C.) for selected years.

5. See Table 5.3 below.

6. Data were taken from the U.S. Department of Commerce, *Census of Manufactures* (Washington, D.C.) for 1958 and 1982.

7. See Economic Division, Texas Commerce Bancshares, *Texas Facts and Figures* (Houston: Texas Commerce Bancshares, 1982), 24–45; and "Houston Leads U.S. Gulf Ports in Cotton Exports," *Port of Houston Magazine* (October, 1986): 4–6.

8. Unless otherwise noted, data in the text have been taken from decennial Bureau of the Census documents for various years: *General Population Characteristics, Detailed Population Characteristics,* and *Social and Economic Characteristics.*

9. These data refer to market areas, not to office complexes as do the data in the above paragraph.

10. Data on retail space in the CBD are not readily available. Sale and employment data come from U.S. Department of Commerce, *Census of Retail Trade* (Washington, D.C.).

11. See Bank of the Southwest, "Industrial Map of Metropolitan Houston," 10th edition; and Houston City Planning Commission, "Houston Year 2000 Map," October 1980.

12. More precisely, 52.2 percent of city residents were renters in 1980, and 25.6 percent of non-central city metropolitan residents. See U.S. Department of Commerce, *Metropolitan Housing Characteristics* (Washington, D.C.), for Houston in 1980.

13. See Perrenod (1984:3–31); and Rice Center, *Annexation and Houston: Research Summary* (Houston: Rice Center, 1979), 1–3.

14. Only one oil entrepreneur was part of the business elite at this time, and he was not in the core group.

15. For an historical analysis of this perspective for the United States, see Christine Boyer (1983). A more theoretical interpretation is provided by David Harvey (1985:1–31).

16. See Warren, Gorham, and Lamont, "The Mortgage and Real Estate Report," September 15, 1982, 1–3.

17. The December 8, 1986, issue of *Fortune* magazine, in an article entitled "Agony and Ecstasy in Family Castles," reported on a Standard Oil project manager whose house in River Oaks had a $600,000 value in 1981 and a $410,000 value in 1986. Land prices have also fallen. Well-located land for office construction in the CBD which sold for $450 or even $600 a square foot in the early 1980s could be obtained in 1987 for $250 per square foot (Laventhol and Horwath 1987).

18. For further discussion of the depression in Houston's economy, see Feagin (1987); Hill and Feagin (1987); and Hooper (1986).

19. During its boom, land prices in downtown Houston exceeded $450/square foot, and in the bust are quoted around $250. In Philadelphia, however, $300/square foot is the top of the market, and prices range much lower.

CHAPTER 6

The Spatial Transformation of Postwar Philadelphia

Robert A. Beauregard

City Hall sits at the intersection of the two major streets in downtown Philadelphia, Market and Broad. Poised atop its tower is a statue of William Penn. Prior to late 1986, no building in the city exceeded the height of 548 feet, the top of Penn's hat, which a gentlemen's agreement between the City Planning Commission and office builders in the 1950s had established as development's limit. The agreement ensured that William Penn would always stand above the "greene County Towne" laid out in 1682, and that those who entered his city would thereby be reminded of its history.[1]

In 1984, the sanctity of Penn's hat was threatened. A local developer proposed two office buildings that would exceed the height limit, violate the gentlemen's agreement, and irreversibly realign the city's skyline. The seriousness of the proposal engendered a public debate. Opponents argued for the city's historical integrity, its reputation as a city of neighborhoods, and the Quaker values of consensus and harmony. Proponents wanted to move Philadelphia into the future, to establish it as a world-class city of finance and administration, and to set it in competition with other cities in the global economy. The walkable city of homes would become a city of skyscrapers; community and quality of life would be replaced by high finance and commercial values.

The debate was not only about how Philadelphia would be perceived but also about how it would develop. Could Philadelphia cling to its historically-rich physical environment amid an economy in profound flux? Was there a place in the urban hierarchy for a city of manageable scale, political consensus, and economic stability? If de-

195

Figure 6.1   City Hall and the Statue of William Penn.

velopment were not allowed free rein, would Philadelphia be rele-
gated to a path of economic, social, and physical decline? Philadelphians believed such questions could be answered, that the city's destiny
was within their control. To push pass Penn's hat, however, would
invite unknown and unresponsive forces. Eventually the existing scale
and fabric of the city would be rewoven; historical consciousness
would be displaced by a forward-looking amnesia.

The debate ignored existing variations in the urban landscape—
the slums of North Philadelphia and the affluence of Rittenhouse
Square—and the degree to which different social groups (Italians and
Eastern Europeans, English, Blacks, Hispanics, and Asians) participated in and recognized historic Philadelphia. More germane to this
chapter, both opponents and proponents ignored the history of the
city's built environment. Those who opposed violation of Penn's hat
seemed to have forgotten that City Hall was a relatively new building
which in 1901 had replaced the steeple of Christ Church on the
skyline, a landmark by which ship captains had navigated their way
up the Delaware River since 1754. The neighborhoods being de-
fended had been abandoned to manufacturing, warehousing, and
low-income renters, and only subsequently, in the 1960s and 1970s,
were recreated as affluent, historic districts.

As recently as the 1930s, Philadelphia was a "core city of poverty,
low skills, and low status surrounded by a ring of working-class and
middle-class homes" (Warner 1968a; 171) quite unlike its present
spatial configuration. Moreover, the low-rise office development of
the post-World War II period, which opponents found so acceptable
had its beginnings on the site of the Broad Street Station, one of the
grand edifices of the Penn Central Railroad and itself a powerful
symbol of Philadelphia's relation to earlier forces of economic transformation. In 1984, the prominence of Penn's hat was threatened,
and once again Philadelphians were made aware of the fragility of
the built environment and the unrelenting march of social change.

At issue is the sometimes blunt and sometimes subtle impact of
shifting socioeconomic and political forces upon the urban built
environment, that configuration of objects which constitutes the physical fabric of the city. The built environment is not simply the
cumulative layering of aesthetic inclinations acting to locate, shape,
and decorate houses, public buildings, parks, monuments, factories
and offices. Nor is it solely a product of changing technological
possibilities. The determinants of the spatial form and substance of a
city go beyond the creative and productive processes that culminate

in its buildings and artifacts. To the contrary, social, cultural, economic and political forces give those processes direction and simultaneously shape the form of the city.

Such generalities cannot stand alone, for while they set themes, they lack substance. My intent is to explore postwar Philadelphia's spatial transformations in the light of the ongoing restructuring of its economy, the changing composition of its citizens, the ever-shifting alignments of its politics, and the deceptive and revealing substance of symbols and ideology that explain and confound. The central theme is the transformation of the form of the city. The search is for those agents whose actions transmit the forces of change into the creation and destruction of the physical environment, and for the influences that the built environment, in turn, works upon those who would use and abuse it.

To organize this complex and potentially boundless search, the postwar era is divided into three periods. Intended primarily as a heuristic device, this periodization captures distinctly different spatial dynamics in Philadelphia's development after World War II. The immediate postwar years were ones of gradual but continued deterioration in the built environment along with the socioeconomic rearrangement of neighborhoods, isolated instances of large-scale development, and widespread public debate concerning the need for reinvestment in the city's physical development. From the middle of the 1950s to the middle of the 1970s, the second period, development was characterized by the suburbanization of the city's periphery, a multitude of large-scale redevelopment projects (mostly in Center City) subsidized by city, state, and federal funds, and the precipitous decline of the built environment of inner ring neighborhoods and industrial areas. Since then, during the third period, redevelopment has waned, the private sector has re-discovered Center City, and media and political claims of a resurgence are abundant. Yet as one strays outside the city's core, one enters the inner ring built environment, which, except for isolated instances of reinvestment, is ignored by developers and occupied by people all but discarded by society. Why did these transformations occur, and why at these times?

Erosion and Expansion in the Postwar Years

From the end of World War II in 1945 to the early 1950s, Philadelphia's built environment continued along a path of deterioration, a path whose origins can be found in the depression. Physical decline was particularly apparent in Center City and in adjacent residential and mixed-use districts. New growth was confined to institutions such as universities and hospitals, and to a northeastern section that once had been farmland. Large-scale development projects were extensively discussed, but few came to fruition. These were years of planning and reform; political power and investment capital needed to be coalesced before major development could take place.

Physical Deterioration

Prominent in the spatial transformation was the ongoing deterioration of the built environment. The depression of the 1930s and the war effort had minimized the maintenance and repair of the housing stock, factory buildings, and infrastructure. A lack of capital in the first instance and the redirection of capital to wartime production in the second had placed the built environment low on the list of investment options.

In the early 1940s, the Housing Association of Delaware Valley reported a severe housing shortage as defense workers poured into the metropolitan area (Pendzich, Miller, and Silverman 1976: 13). Construction experienced a brief spurt, but by 1944 building permits for private and public dwelling units had dropped to 160. While that number increased to 12,310 in 1950, it dropped once again to 5210 by 1954 (Shea and Grigsby 1957: 10). Overall, the number of housing units had increased during both the 1950s and 1960s.[2] Public pressure in the 1950s for a new housing code nonetheless reflected a deep dissatisfaction with the quality of housing. Government reports indicated that one-third of the housing units in the city required demolition or rehabilitation.

The deterioration of the residential environment was exacerbated by a changeover in the composition of the city's population. Even though overall population grew between 1940 and 1950 and declined only slightly in the 1950s, this relative stability masked a substitution of low-income, unskilled southern blacks for higher-income educated whites. From 1940 to 1950 the net increase in the black population approached 130,000 individuals. That number was exceeded in the following decade, when approximately 155,000 blacks were added. Black migrants found employment scarce, and when employed their incomes were not sufficient to make up for nearly two decades of disinvestment in the housing stock. Moreover, they were steered to those inner ring areas with the oldest and least desirable dwellings, mainly North Philadelphia and the traditional black enclave along South Street in South Philadelphia (see Figure 6.2).

The city was not faring as well as its suburbs. In the 1940s, the metropolitan population grew by 2 percent, while Philadelphia's declined by 1 percent. In the 1950s, the metropolitan increase was 14.7 percent, and the city's, 7.3 percent. Relatively weak population growth, the influx of southern black families, and the spatial and racial bias of the FHA mortgage program had a depressing effect on the city's housing market, despite continued new construction.[3]

Disinvestment characterized the industrial and commercial areas of the city during the depression and World War II, and continued in the immediate postwar period. Claims were made that retail establishments and manufacturing firms were leaving the city (Philadelphia City Planning Commission 1960). Whether retail establishments were migrating or simply closing or merging, the number was certainly declining. From 1948 to 1954, the number of retail establishments diminished by 10.4 percent to 25,340.[4]

As for the decline of industrial operations, the aggregate employment data by industry (see Table 6.1) do not register any precipitous decline. While manufacture's share of total employment shrank from 1940 to 1950, it increased in absolute terms. A similar pattern existed for retail trade; for fire, insurance and real estate (FIRE); and for services. Even though the resident labor force expanded by 18.2 percent in the 1940s and declined in the 1950s, the employment shares of manufacturing, FIRE and services remained stable or increased either relatively or absolutely. Manufacturing employment did fall by 10.9 percent in the 1950s, however.

Without doubt, the physical environment experienced deterioration while overall employment figures continued to show strength. What probably occurred was a drastic falling-off of new industrial and commercial construction in the 1940s, with some spatial shifting of industrial and commercial activity both within the city and between the city and the suburbs. This conclusion is partly supported by evidence on new office construction and retail trade. In the 1930s, 1.9 million square feet were added to the city's inventory. Additions dropped to 30,000 square feet in the 1940s, but in the next decade jumped to 2.6 million square feet (Philadelphia City Planning Commission 1977). Moreover, while retail sales in the city rose by 16.2 percent between 1948 and 1954, those in the metropolitan area almost doubled that rate—30.0 percent. Both types of data suggest a

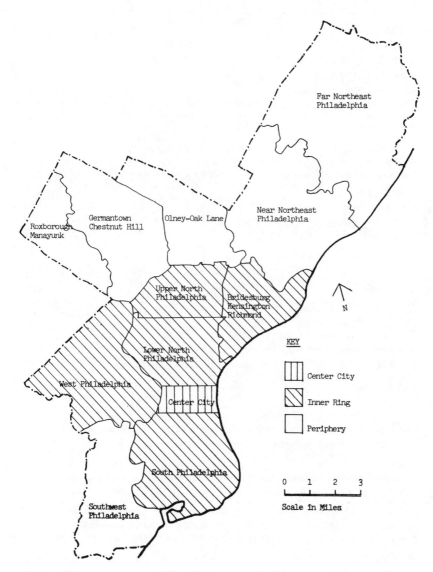

Figure 6.2   Map of the City of Philadelphia.

Table 6.1   Employment Shares by Industry, City of Philadelphia, 1940–1980

	1940[a]	1950[b]	1960[b]	1970[c]	1980[c]
Agriculture, forestry, fishing, and mining	0.3	0.3	0.3	0.5	0.3
Construction	4.9	5.7	4.5	4.6	3.7
Manufacturing	36.1	35.7	35.3	28.2	20.9
Transportation, communication, and public utilities	7.5	8.5	7.2	6.5	7.7
Wholesale trade	2.9	3.9	3.9	4.4	4.2
Retail trade	19.1	17.8	16.2	15.7	14.9
Finance, insurance and real estate	4.5	4.4	4.8	5.7	7.3
Services	20.6	18.6	21.3	26.4	32.7
Government (or public administration)	4.2	5.0	6.5	8.0	8.3
Total[d]	100.1	99.9	100.0	100.0	100.0
Absolute total[d]	688,291	813,317	741,560	763,520	624,706

[a]Except employment on emergency work.
[b]For employed persons 14 years or older.
[c]For employed persons 16 years or older.
[d]Excludes "industry not reported" for 1940, 1950, and 1960.

Source: U. S. Department of Commerce, Bureau of the Census, *General Social and Economic Characteristics, Pennsylvania,* selected years.

stagnant, but not contracting, economy in the 1940s and growth in the 1950s, but a growth neither substantially above that of the 1930s (a period of depression) nor robust relative to the suburbs.

Data on the occupation of the resident labor force also reflect the scale and restructuring of the local economy. The postwar stereotype is a diminution of well-paid skilled jobs such as craft and precision production workers and operatives, with an expansion in professional, managerial, and service occupations (Stanback and Noyelle 1982). As Table 6.2 shows, this is only partly true for Philadelphia. Within the context of a significant expansion of total employment during the 1940s, professionals and managers as well as craft and precision production workers grew in numbers both relatively and absolutely. Service workers experienced relative but not absolute decline, and clerical and sales workers increased in actual numbers

Table 6.2   Employment Shares by Occupation, City of Philadelphia, 1940–1980

	1940[a]	1950[b]	1960[b]	1970[c]	1980[c]
Professionals, semi-professionals and technicians	7.7	8.5	10.0	12.8	15.5
Proprietors, managers and officials (including farm)	8.3	8.3	6.5	5.7	8.0
Clerical and sales	23.0	23.9	27.2	29.2	30.9
Craft, precision production, foremen, and repair	14.7	15.6	13.7	12.5	7.5
Operatives	25.7	25.1	23.7	20.3	17.1
Laborers (including farm)	5.8	5.9	4.9	4.7	5.2
Service, private household, and protective service workers	14.8	12.7	13.9	14.8	15.7
Total[d]	100.0	100.0	100.0	100.0	99.9
Absolute total[d]	697,830	816,748	735,346	763,520	624,604[e]

[a]Except persons employed on emergency work.
[b]For persons 14 years or older.
[c]For persons 16 years or older.
[d]Excludes "occupation not reported" for 1940, 1950, and 1960.
[e]This number is less than that reported in the Census document by 102 workers, a difference of 0.01 percent.

Source: U. S. Department of Commerce, Bureau of the Census, *General Social and Economic Characteristics*, selected years.

and employment shares. The postwar stereotype does not fit Philadelphia well in this early period. Moreover, the data also suggest numerous employment opportunities for new workers migrating to the region. Whether blacks took these jobs or lost out in competition to commuters is difficult to ascertain. Nonetheless, the evidence of physical deterioration in residential, industrial, and commercial buildings is not reflected clearly in the city's economy or workforce.

The infrastructure of roadways, bridges, and public buildings, in fact, had been poorly maintained from the 1930s through the early postwar period. The local government was relatively passive in its approach to the built environment, and public services were of low quality. Philadelphia's per capita expenditures for municipal services in the 1950s, for example, were low relative to other major cities. The gap was wide: 83 percent of Detroit's per capita expenditures, 62 percent of New York's and 56 percent of Boston's (Vigman 1955:114). The sorry state of infrastructure and housing stock, the accusation of industrial and commercial decline and out-migration, and the in-migration of an economically insecure population were reflected in the economic worth of Philadelphia's built environment. Between 1945 and 1955 the dollar value of taxable property in the city fell 17.2 percent, from $4.88 billion to $4.03 billion in 1958 dollars (Tait 1976).

Although the market value of private buildings fell, new construction and additions and alterations to existing buildings were still evident. From 1945 to 1954, the value of building permits increased fourfold.[5] The value of additions and alterations doubled over that timespan, residential and commercial building increased by approximately 600 and 800 percent, respectively, and industrial construction grew by slightly less than 100 percent. The remaining building activity, involving hospitals, schools, churches, municipal buildings, and other miscellaneous structures expanded by more than 2000 percent. Despite a shared perception of deterioration, the physical fabric of the city was being maintained, and new building construction was underway.

Political Restructuring

The deterioration of the built environment was not being neglected by the government nor by community leaders who supported more robust development. In 1947, the Better Philadelphia Exposition was held at Gimbels department store. Its centerpiece display was a model of the existing buildings and roads in Center city, with movable parts which substituted redeveloped sites for those blighted and obsolete (Lowe 1967:322–24). Here was the City Planning Commission's vision of what Philadelphia would be like if private investors and local government concerted their efforts. In that same year, a Redevelopment Authority, one of the first in the country, was appointed. Any full-scale attack on a decade and a half of neglect, however, would have to await a political restructuring of the local government.

For years the city government had been controlled by a Republican machine that had earned for Philadelphia a reputation as a corrupt and sleepy, unprogressive city (Clark and Clark 1982: 650–57; Tink-com 1982:619–28; Urban Land Institute 1969:15). Business interests in the city, moreover, believed in a Jeffersonian government that would provide basic services, avoid intrusion in the local economy (particularly the property market), and maintain low taxes (Klen-iewski 1984; Lowe 1967). Adding to Philadelphia's woes was a city charter that severely limited governmental actions. Property interests, finance capital, and those involved with legal, administrative and business service industries organized to articulate a new vision of local government and urban development. Profitable investments, they reasoned, depended upon quality infrastructure and lack of blight. While taxes would have to increase to pay for such services, the return would be more than justified, and business would ultimately thrive (Petshek 1973).

For the vision to be realized, the Republican machine, which wasted tax dollars on graft and corruption, would have to be replaced by a reform government with pro-development leanings. By 1951, this new coalition of business interests had merged with political reform-ers to defeat the Republicans at the polls and to pass a new city charter. In January 1952, Joseph S. Clark became mayor. His succes-sor, Richardson Dilworth, who served from 1956 to 1964, continued the earlier agenda of political reform and aggressive governmental involvement in physical redevelopment.

With these events, the motives and commitment were in place for a serious and large-scale attack on the city's continuing deterioration. A Redevelopment Authority was operating, a Housing Authority had already been established in 1937 and Edmund Bacon, a guiding force in the city's redevelopment, became executive director of the City Planning Commission (Barnett and Miller 1983). Planning began on a number of major projects: the Triangle northwest of City Hall, a blighted area of mixed land uses; a major office complex adjacent to City Hall; the development of the Independence Mall National Park; and various public housing projects (see Figure 6.3)

Before the middle of the 1950s, preliminary work had begun on many significant redevelopment projects. The Broad Street Station and the "Chinese Wall" of railroad tracks leading to it were demol-ished in 1953, and the site of that railroad station became Penn Center, the city's first major office construction since before the depression. The Market Street Elevated was dismantled in West Phil-adelphia to facilitate the expansion of Drexel University and later the University City Science Center (a consortium of universities and

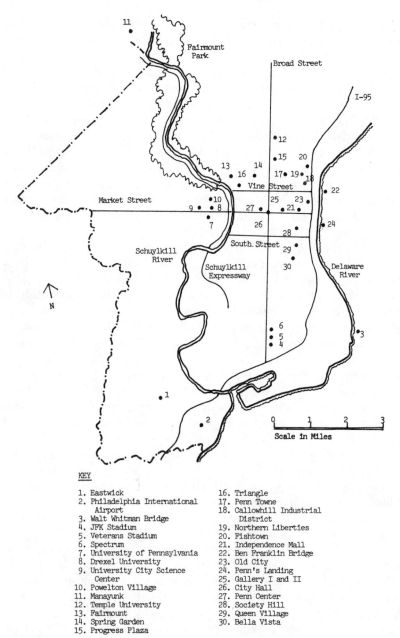

KEY

1. Eastwick
2. Philadelphia International
   Airport
3. Walt Whitman Bridge
4. JFK Stadium
5. Veterans Stadium
6. Spectrum
7. University of Pennsylvania
8. Drexel University
9. University City Science
   Center
10. Powelton Village
11. Manayunk
12. Temple University
13. Fairmount
14. Spring Garden
15. Progress Plaza

16. Triangle
17. Penn Towne
18. Callowhill Industrial
    District
19. Northern Liberties
20. Fishtown
21. Independence Mall
22. Ben Franklin Bridge
23. Old City
24. Penn's Landing
25. Gallery I and II
26. City Hall
27. Penn Center
28. Society Hill
29. Queen Village
30. Bella Vista

Figure 6.3 Postwar Development Projects, Gentrifying Neighborhoods, and Selected
Places of Significance.

businesses involved in science and technology). The clearance of warehouses, deteriorated houses and blighted factories began on the site of Independence Mall.[6] Almost all these development projects were clustered in Center City or West Philadelphia. Outside these areas, other projects were begun. Philadelphia International Airport expanded in 1953 with the addition of a new terminal building. The Walt Whitman Bridge in the southern portion of the city was placed under construction, and one of the country's first postwar public housing projects—Penn Towne—was completed in the Poplar neighborhood just north of Center City. Compared with the period to follow, however, large-scale development projects were few and not at all indicative of the dominant mode of physical change.

New Growth

While the background was deterioration, the foreground was incipient redevelopment projects and private construction on the periphery. Almost 4000 gross acres of residential development took place during this period, the bulk in the northeast portion of the city between the Tacony and Frankford creeks and Cottman Avenue, what came to be known as the Near Northeast (see Figure 6.2). Rather than flee to the expanding suburbs, numerous white households from the inner ring preferred to stay in Philadelphia but wanted lower-density development and new housing (Infield 1985; Mallowe 1985). Rowhouses were still the norm, but now they had yards in the front and the back, more than the minimum 144 square feet of unoccupied lot that had been required of rowhouses at the turn of the century (Boyer 1983: 103). The Near Northeast, once farmland, was the ideal solution. The new households were soon followed by retail activities and manufacturing firms. This "sub-urban" development, in turn, siphoned capital investment from Center City and the inner ring and contributed to their deterioration (Mallowe 1985; Muller, Meyer, and Cybriwsky 1976).

New construction was also occurring in the older areas of the city, almost solely the expansion of institutions, hospitals, and universities. In West Philadelphia, Drexel University and the University of Pennsylvania expanded in response to the return of veterans and the subsidies provided by the G.I. Bill. The city used its eminent domain power to acquire properties and thereby smooth the way for private sector development. Hospitals also expanded. Like the universities, they had postponed development during the 1930s and 1940s and were now ready to up-date their facilities and to absorb the rising demand for health care. The federal government, through the Hill-Burton Act of 1946, made expansion easier by subsidizing facility construction. In West Philadelphia and around Thomas Jefferson Hospital and the Graduate Hospital in Center City, new construction took place.

Overall, while the built environment deteriorated in Center City and adjacent areas, new development occurred in the Near Northeast and less so in Southwest and West Philadelphia. On balance, the city continued to grow. All major types of land use increased between 1944 and 1954: institutional by 20.1 percent, residential by 11.5 percent, industrial by 6.5 percent, and commercial by 3.7 percent. As a result, undeveloped land declined by 24.6 percent. Yet, most commentators fixed on the poor quality of the housing stock, closing stores, and abandoned factory buildings.

Compared to suburban areas, Philadelphia's growth was not dramatic. Within the four metropolitan counties in Pennsylvania, gross residential land use expanded by 95.3 percent, and gross industrial land use by 200 percent over the same time period. Population increased by an estimated 12 percent in Philadelphia from 1940 to 1954, but the corresponding expansion in the four-county area was 53 percent (Philadelphia City Planning Commission n.d.). In absolute terms, investment in Philadelphia's built environment was growing, and contradicting any conclusion of massive decline; the city remained desirable to many existing and new households. A relative perspective, however, sketches a quite different picture: much more rapid development in the suburbs.

The spatial transformations between the mid-1940s and the mid-1950s, then, involved a mix of continued deterioration of the built environment and new construction, each linked to the ending of two cataclysmic events: the depression and World War II. At the beginning of this period, Philadelphia "still physically reflected the forms and achievement of the Victorian Age" (Clark and Clark 1982: 649). By the middle of the 1950s, the built environment of the inner city (Center City and the inner ring) was shabbier and less valuable, and that of the Near Northeast and of parts of West and Southwest Philadelphia were new or renewed. Although the Near Northeast represented an addition to the built environment, the diminution of open space, and a major infusion of capital; this development was isolated from the vast land area of the city that persisted along its path of devaluation. In the subsequent twenty or so years, deterioration and decline would accelerate to breathless speeds and exacerbate white flight to the city's northeast and beyond. The local government responded with massive redevelopment.

Precipitous Decline, Redevelopment, and Peripheral Investment

From the mid-1950s and for approximately the next two decades, major efforts were undertaken by the local government to counteract the accelerated deterioration of the built environment and to stem the outflow of households, businesses, and investment capital. The institution of a pro-development reform government, the realignment of business interests toward aggressive governmental support of private investment, the establishment of redevelopment and public housing agencies, and the passage of the 1949 and 1954 federal housing acts coalesced to produce a supportive political environment for large-scale development and redevelopment projects.

Such efforts were confined to Center City and the inner ring, while in the northeast periphery the private sector led a massive transformation from open farmland to compact, residential, commercial, and industrial development. The interrelationship was obvious. As the older portions of the city deteriorated and became occupied by low-income minorities, white residents fled to the periphery and to the suburbs. Governmental efforts to halt decline, particularly demolition and clearance, only exacerbated both trends. By the end of the second period, the inner ring was even more blighted.

Urban Redevelopment

Projects that had been under consideration were now implemented (see Figure 6.3). After the demolition of the Broad Street Station and the wall of railroad tracks in 1953, land near City Hall was now available for the development of six high-rise office towers, Penn Center (Barnett and Miller 1983; Lowe 1967:331–32). The entire project was privately funded on private land. The city, through Edmund Bacon, the director of the City Planning Commission, and Mayor Joseph Clark, encouraged the developer to provide underground shopping linked with the subway system and to create public spaces at street level. Otherwise, the city's role was minimal.

The Independence Mall project also moved substantially forward in this period. In the early 1950s, three blocks of densely packed and blighted commercial, industrial, and residential buildings were acquired, through the eminent domain procedures of the Commonwealth of Pennsylvania, and demolished. These actions created a large expanse of open space focusing on Independence Hall, the building in which the Declaration of Independence and the Constitution had been debated and signed. A park was constructed on the site, along with an underground parking garage. The Liberty Bell was placed in a small structure fronting Independence Hall. By 1967 the project was essentially complete, having been carried out mainly by the federal government. The two projects served as catalysts for two areas of Center City: Penn Center anchored office development west of City Hall and Independence Mall served as a focal point for office development to the east. Neither was initiated or implemented by the local government.

Many locally initiated renewal projects came to fruition during this twenty-year period. The northern portion of the 200-acre Triangle was developed in 1959 with 971 units of housing in four high-rise buildings (Urban Land Institute 1969:29). Public subsidies were used to purchase and clear the site and finance the new construction, including the middle-income apartments. The renewal of Society Hill, a mid-1960s project and one of the city's most famous, recaptured an historic but run-down area of the city occupied by a food distribution market and a low-income population, and turned it into an enclave of upper-income households living in historically renovated Federal-style buildings (Lowe 1967; Petshek 1973:183–92, 222–28). Work on Society Hill required the relocation of the food distribution function to a site in the southern portion of the city, the public subsidy of three residential towers and adjacent low-rise townhouses, and the area's designation as an historic district. The federal government provided part of the funding through Urban Renewal and also through various mortgage subsidy programs (Smith 1979). Ultimately Society Hill became one of the city's most-affluent residential areas. For civic boosters, it became a symbol of Philadelphia's renascence.

The Redevelopment Authority also engaged in institutional expansion in West Philadelphia (Petshek 1973:243–55). Drexel University and the University of Pennsylvania continued to expand, as did the Philadelphia General Hospital and the Hospital of the University of Pennsylvania.[7] The University City Science Center became a quasi-public corporation in 1964, and soon thereafter became a major developer of existing and new office and research space. All these institutions utilized the area's urban renewal designation to facilitate the purchase and clearance of sites. Temple University, approximately two miles north of City Hall, also grew during this period, adding numerous buildings to its campus—quadrupling its physical plant in ten years—and doing so with the assistance of the government's redevelopment tools (Lowe 1967:375–76).

The most striking and devastating transformation of the city's built environment emanated from the urban renewal program: the virtual gutting of the housing stock in North Philadelphia, an area occupied by black low-income households (Kleniewski 1986a and 1986b). From 1950 to 1962, 10,126 dwelling units were demolished in this area. The Redevelopment Authority had declared North Philadelphia blighted, and the strategy was to remove dilapidated buildings in order to create land for new private development and public housing and also to stifle the blighting effect many existing dwellings were having on adjacent properties. Between 1950 and 1980, North Philadelphia lost 35,196 dwelling units—32 percent of the total—as a result of public demolition, private abandonment and arson. The population fell by 54 percent as the non-white population, while not increasing in absolute terms, went from 45 percent to 83 percent of the total population. Although deterioration had eaten away the physical structure, redevelopment brought about a vast change in form. With clearance came numerous high-density public housing projects, but almost no new private construction.

Many of the residents displaced by the demolitions in North Philadelphia were relocated to a "new town in town"—Eastwick—in the southwest portion of the city, an area of low-lying land and low-density, poor quality housing (Petshek 1973:165–66; Kleniewski 1986a). Approximately 2000 dwelling units were to be demolished, eighty-five hundred people displaced, and 5000 dwelling units constructed. Whereas its original purpose was to serve as a destination for displacees from North Philadelphia, black families resisted the move, and Eastwick eventually became an integrated middle-income development. While the project represented significant new construction, it was not a statement about the desirability of investment in Philadelphia, but rather an attempt by the government to rehouse the many people displaced by a massive transformation of North Philadelphia.

Public housing increasingly became a new element in the city's landscape. Relatively large, usually high-density projects were constructed in inner ring neighborhoods where the housing stock was old and blighted, and where blacks were concentrated (Goldstein and Yancey 1986). North Philadelphia was a prime location. South and West Philadelphia received fewer projects, and the northwest and northeast hardly any. Before the end of the war, four public housing projects with 3248 units were constructed, and another eleven projects of an additional 4000 units were proposed or under construction (Philadelphia Housing Authority n.d.).[8] By the later years of this period, some had become locations of high crime, welfare dependency, and additional physical blight. At best, neighborhoods with such projects were areas of social tension and unstable property values. At worst, they were areas of increasing abandonment.

During this period, urban renewal and public housing were not the sole focus of large-scale, subsidized development projects. The city also became involved in industrial development in order to provide alternative sites and buildings for firms, particularly manufacturing firms, that might otherwise leave the city. Industrial parks were established on undeveloped land in the southwest near the airport and in the northeast. Built-up areas of the city were also targeted. Smaller industrial areas utilizing existing structures were established in the eastern portion of the city and along American Street in North Philadelphia in the late 1970s.

The Callowhill district, just blocks north of Center City, was transformed from an area of high-density factory buildings, residences, narrow streets, and little off-street parking to the industrial counterpart of a suburban housing tract (see Figure 6.3). Buildings were thinned out, large parking lots were created, roads were eliminated to create larger land parcels, and sites were cleared for new construction. Not until 1986, however, was this area fully developed.[9] In general, as the former industrial districts of the city were abandoned and factories within neighborhoods lay empty, new industrial space was being created either on the fringes of the city or by transforming the fabric of older districts.

Industrial development projects directly confronted the spatial dilemmas created by the city's economic transformation. Between 1950 and 1970, manufacturing's employment share fell precipitously in the context of an overall decline in the job generating capacity of the economy (see Table 6.1). The number of manufacturing firms in the city declined by 52.0 percent between 1953 and 1977, and the total number of business establishments fell by 31.9 percent (see Table 6.3). One result was the deterioration of older industrial districts in Center City and the inner ring, along with the concomitant decline of the neighborhoods that abutted and overlapped these districts. On the other hand, employment in government, FIRE, services, and wholesale trade was expanding between 1950 and 1970. The new and expanding businesses were not likely to locate in inner ring industrial space, but to search for Center City or peripheral locations. Thus while the city wished to retain and attract manufacturing employment, it also faced a shift away from traditional manufacturing plants to office and commercial buildings less interested in existing industrial structures and locations.

At the same time, the occupational composition of Philadelphia's residents was changing. Fewer skilled, craft, and precision production workers and operatives were being employed, fewer low-skilled laborers and, surprisingly, fewer proprietors and managers (see Table 6.2). The traditional blue-collar jobs were disappearing. In their place between 1950 and 1970, low-skill, low-paid service, clerical, and sales persons increased in number, and the number of professionals and semi-professionals grew. The consequences fell not only on housing, as will be discussed below, but on the types of redevelopment activities undertaken.

On the one hand, as we have seen, the city attempted to lessen the loss of manufacturing through industrial park development, to encourage nonmanufacturing firms in Center City with new office buildings (for example Penn Center), and to combat deterioration caused by declining household incomes and population loss in inner ring neighborhoods. In addition, the changing economic structure of the city, operating through occupational and household incomes, had consequences for retail activity. Between 1954 and 1977, Philadelphia lost nearly 12,000 retail establishments, and its retail sales fell from 57.0 percent of the metropolitan area's retail sales to 24.6 percent.

A number of city-subsidized retail projects were undertaken during the two decades to counter these trends. Progress Plaza in North Philadelphia, designed in the format of a suburban shopping area, was built in 1968. Chestnut Street in Center City was transformed in the late 1970s into a pedestrian mall, where only public transit was allowed to move along its ten blocks during shopping hours. The major retail project was Gallery I on a portion of Market Street east of City Hall, a product of the Center City Plan published in 1963 which had envisaged eastern Market Street as an integrated complex of mass transit, retail development, and office structures meant to revitalized the CBD (Beauregard 1986a; Cybriwsky and Western 1982). Gallery I opened in 1977. Covering three city blocks, the mall linked the existing Strawbridge and Clothier department store with a new Gimbels department store, the first major retail facility constructed in the city since 1931 (Teaford 1986:151). Gallery I contained approximately 125 stores and numerous food establishments. The north side of Market Street was totally transformed by the structure and the multilevel parking garages that lined it along the back. The subways ran underneath and connected Gallery I to the city's mass-transit network.

Making all these publicly subsidized projects possible, and helping to facilitate such private sector, inner-city projects as Penn Center, was a local government committed to reform and development. The 1952–1972 mayoral administrations of Joseph S. Clark, Richardson Dilworth and James H. J. Tate, were each, in its own way, supportive of redevelopment activities and inclined to support private investment with expanded public utilities and services. The mayors' visions of the growth potential of Philadelphia were essentially alike. With the election of Frank Rizzo in 1971, the general policy of the local government toward new private investment remained, even though certain public investment projects became embroiled in racial controversy. At issue was public housing, particularly in white working class neighborhoods that were the bastion of Mayor Rizzo's electoral strength. In response to the intrasigence of the Rizzo administration, the federal government in the late 1970s temporarily declared Philadelphia ineligible for Urban Development Action Grants, public subsidies for large-scale redevelopment projects.

By the end of this second period the political consensus that drove redevelopment activity began to unravel. Mayor Rizzo's policies were often divisive, and the business community, after more than two decades of friendly and mutually beneficial relations with city government, became less willing to work closely with the city. While the local growth coalition was under strain, national politics were dismantling the urban renewal program. At the beginning of the third postwar period, the major actor in the development of Philadelphia—the Urban Renewal Authority—was playing only a cameo role.

Transportation Development

Some of the most expensive, publicly funded construction projects during this period, ones that had major impacts upon the built environment, were transportation projects (see Figure 6.3). Between 1950 and 1973, Philadelphia acquired many miles of interstate highways, although the center of the city remained unscathed. In the late 1950s and early 1960s, the Schuylkill Expressway linking the northwest and the southeast to Center City was opened. For the most part, it was tucked between the Schuylkill River and the bluffs adjacent to it, thus passing mainly through open space or Fairmount Park. Interstate 95, however, running from the northeast along the eastern portions of the city and then turning west to pass by the airport, had a more dramatic effect. It sliced through many of the river wards causing the taking and demolition of large numbers of buildings and dividing neighborhoods physically. Moreover, it cut off Center City from the waterfront. The Walt Whitman Bridge had opened in 1959 to connect the southeastern portion of the city to New Jersey. With the completion of I-95 throughout this area, the bridge permitted north-south travelers to bypass much of Philadelphia. By the end of the period, the southern portion of the city was a virtual tangle of interstate highways, access roads, and bridge ramps.

Just as Interstate 95 enabled residents of the northeast to commute to Center City for work and return to their new neighborhoods at night, Roosevelt Boulevard, originally opened through farmland in the 1920s, improved accessibility for this expanding northeast portion of the city. With these new highways came opportunities for large-scale retail development. Two downtown department stores, Gimbels and Lit Brothers, located branch stores along Cottman Avenue in the late 1950s, the Ashton Shopping Center became reality in 1961, and Roosevelt Mall, the area's largest, opened in 1964 (Muller, Meyer, and Cybriwsky 1976).

Residents and business to the south of Center City also benefited from I-95 and from the extension of the Broad Street subway. The reason was the construction of two sports facilities: the Spectrum for basketball and hockey in 1967 and Veterans Stadium for baseball and football in 1971. These were publicly subsidized projects located north of JFK Stadium, previously named Municipal Stadium. The other addition to the subway network was the opening of the Lindenwold Line in 1969, which linked Philadelphia with communities in southern New Jersey. While a mass-transit line had crossed the Benjamin Franklin Bridge between Philadelphia and Camden since 1926, the Lindenwold Line represented an upgrading and extension of that line into the reaches of suburbia. Unlike Interstate 95, the Lindenwold Line had little direct physical impact on the city. Still, it contributed to the ability of workers to live outside the city in the rapidly expanding suburbs, just as the Schuylkill and Interstate 95 facilitated residential and retail development of the city's periphery and beyond. In 1960, 23.6 percent of the jobs in Philadelphia were held by commuters, by 1970 that figure had increased to 29.1 percent, and by 1980 commuters held 32.1 percent of the jobs in the city.[10]

Peripheral Development

While the built environment of Center City and the surrounding inner ring were being transformed, and the city was integrated more tightly into the metropolitan area with transportation projects, the northeast was experiencing new construction on unimproved land.[11] In the earlier postwar period, development had reached up to Cottman Avenue. Now it pushed beyond that point to the northern boundaries of Philadelphia—the Far Northeast (Mallowe 1986).

New residential development was given a boost by the construction of limited-access highways and the opening of shopping malls. Earlier patterns of development continued. Housing took the form primarily of rowhouses, but at lower densities than existed in the inner ring neighborhoods from which the new residents had migrated. From 1961 to 1977, the Far Northeast had a net gain of 36,424 housing units, while the Near Northeast experienced a net gain of 8933. Together they accounted for 102.1 percent of the city's net additions in this period. Unlike what existed in the older neighborhoods, commercial strips emerged to dominate retail activity and to foster automobile usage. Moreover, commercial businesses located along commercial strips and manufacturing firms in industrial parks, rather than intermingling with residential development, as was the case historically in Center City and the inner ring.

By the end of this period, the northeast was near fully developed, with few large tracts of open space available. Its built environment was only vaguely reminiscent of the inner-city agglomeration of residential, commercial, and industrial areas. Moreover, the composition of the population was strikingly different. Increasingly, the occupants of inner ring neighborhoods were predominantly black and Hispanic, of low income and with minimal job skills. Center City residents were mostly white and affluent. The occupants of the northeast were predominantly white, of middle income and employed in both blue-collar and white-collar occupations. Ethnic identity was not abandoned in the migration. Households continued to locate near those of similar national and religious backgrounds. While the city as a whole lost population, the northeast experienced major growth.

The northeast, in essence, represented Philadelphia's internal counterpart to suburbanization. Simultaneously, it was the city's defense. On the one hand, the large amount of unimproved land in the northeast enabled those households wishing to leave the inner ring to settle in a suburban (that is, low density) setting but to remain within the city. This became especially important when fire, police, and other city personnel were required to reside in Philadelphia. On the other hand, without such available land Philadelphia would probably have lost even more population than it did, and the additions to its housing stock would have been fewer. In effect, the northeast allowed Philadelphia to capture part of the suburbanization phenomenon within its boundaries.[12]

. Without the Far Northeast, the city's 18.5 percent population loss between 1950 and 1980 would have likely been greater, and the decline in the city's share of the metropolitan population—from 56 percent to 36 percent over this time—even steeper (see Table 6.3). The metropolitan population was growing in this second period, despite a slight decline in the late 1970s, and Philadelphia's was in absolute and relative decline. Due mainly to the development of the northeast, the number of year-round housing units in the city actually increased between 1950 and 1980, even though its share of the metropolitan housing stock plummeted.[13] The much greater population growth in the suburbs simply pushed housing construction to much higher levels than what could be sustained by the redistribution of the population in Philadelphia.

Other parts of the city were going from open space to developed land, but at a scale much below that of the northeast. The southern portion of the city was developed with sports stadia, interstate highways, new airport construction, and related warehousing and hotels. The southwestern portion received the Eastwick development. Along City Line Avenue in the lower northwest, an area adjacent to relatively affluent suburbs, new office construction occurred. Nonetheless, the northeast with its primarily private sector and mainly residential new development gave Philadelphia a strong sense of bifurcation.[14]

In the inner city, changes in the built environment took the form of clearance of obsolete structures and slums and their replacement by publicly subsidized projects. Residential area densities were reduced in some instances and increased, with high-rise public housing, in others. Office development in Center City was substantial, with almost 40 percent of the 1974 inventory added between 1950 and that date (Philadelphia City Planning Commission 1977). In contrast,

Table 6.3   Selected Characteristics for Three Periods in
Philadelphia's Postwar Development

	Period I	Period II	Period III
Average ten-year population growth rate (percent)[a]	7.3 (1940–50)	−6.5 (1950–80)	−6.9 (1980–82)
Average annualized change in employment[b]	17,317 (1946–53)	−7,532 (1953–77)	−2,238 (1977–84)
Average annualized change in business establishments[b]	782 (1946–53)	−550 (1953–77)	−1,761 (1977–84)
Average five-year change in city to SMSA retail sales (percent)[c]	−10.0 (1948–54)	−15.2 (1954–77)	4.9 (1977–82)
Average annualized increase in new office space (millions of square feet)[d]	0.01 (1940–49)	0.63 (1950–76)	0.71 (1977–84)
Average number of new housing units constructed[e]	7,248 (1946–53)	5,383 (1954–77)	2,206 (1977–85)
Average annual change in investment in building adtivity[f]	3.49 (1946–53)	−2.09 (1953–77)	10.3 (1977–84)
Average annualized change in estimated market value of real property[g]	163.8 (1944–54)	45.8 (1954–77)	194.4 (1977–86)

[a]Population data were taken from the decennial reports of the Bureau of the Census.
[b]Data on private sector employment and business establishments are from *County Business Patterns* (Washington, DC), selected years.
[c]Retail sales data are from *Census of Retail Trade* (Washington, DC), selected years.
[d]Data on office construction are from the Philadelphia City Planning Commission.
[e]The number of new housing units constructed comes from Shea and Grigsby (1957) and from building permit data from Department of Licenses and Inspections.
[f]Data based on the value of building permits issued by the Philadelphia Department of Licenses and Inspections and were deflated using the GNP implicit price deflator with 1958 as the base year.
[g]Data from various issues of the *Bulletin Almanac* published by The Philadelphia Evening Bulletin and from the Philadelphia Board of Revision of Taxes.

retail development, with the exception of Gallery I, was minimal. Between 1954 and 1977 Center City lost 31.9 percent of its retail establishments while the city as a whole lost 47.1 percent. With the exception of Penn Center, much Center City development was publicly subsidized. This was not the case in the northeast, with the exception of highways and support facilities such as infrastructure, schools, and fire and police stations. The private sector was the major actor. Moreover, even though the physical landscape of the northeast mimicked inner city neighborhoods, the densities were lower and the architecture clearly a hybrid of inner-city rowhousing and suburban tract housing. The social consequences completed the bifurcation: low-income black households concentrated in inner-city areas with the northeast virtually devoid of minorities and the poor. No wonder that in later years, the northeast advocated secession from the city.

Precipitous Decline

Motivating the spate of urban renewal projects in Center City and the inner ring and contributing to the bifurcation of the city was the precipitous deterioration of the inner-city built environment. While the number of year-round housing units throughout the city increased from 1950 to 1970, the number of occupied units did not grow proportionately, which indicated major housing abandonment. The city estimated that in 1972 there were more than 36,000 long-term vacancies, about 5 percent of the total housing stock. Industrial buildings were also being abandoned. With the demise of the textile industry, numerous factories in Kensington, for example, became empty, later to become prime candidates for arson. In neighborhoods, an unoccupied or abandoned factory also spread its blight to the surrounding housing.

At the same time, retail activity in both Center City and in neighborhood commercial areas was in decline. Retail sales in the city almost doubled in current dollars, but in constant dollars fell by 23.9 percent. By the mid-1970s, Market Street East had only three of its original group of seven major department stores, and only the construction of Gallery I prevented Gimbels from abandoning its Center City site. Many neighborhood shopping districts, in fact most of those in rapidly deteriorating neighborhoods in North Philadelphia, experienced empty storefronts and a decline of merchandise quality. In lower North Philadelphia, Marshall Street, once an area of numerous Jewish and other eastern European stores and restaurants, virtually disappeared, and eventually received urban renewal funding to provide a new one-story building, barely occupied in 1988, and to demolish structures to create parking lots. The activity of earlier years was not recaptured, though Asian and Hispanic storeowners appeared to serve the low-income population of the neighborhood. This scenario was repeated throughout the inner city.

With overall population and job loss characterizing the aggregate fate of Philadelphia between the mid-1950s and the mid-1970s, the city took its place among large, old industrial cities in decline. Philadelphia increasingly developed a reputation as a city to avoid, and households and capital disproportionately went to the suburban periphery. As a result, Philadelphia's suburbs in both Pennsylvania and New Jersey experienced rapid growth, and more and more of the city's labor force commuted from outside the city's boundaries. Had it not been for the fortuitous availability of open land in the northeast, those households and businesses—and the capital—that had rejected the inner-city environment, might well have fled to suburban municipalities, and Philadelphia's decline would have been even more precipitous. Still, it was difficult to be sanguine: during this second period, from 1956 to 1977, the market value of the city's taxable real property fell 22.6 percent.[15]

Stabilization, Resurgence and Distress

By the late 1970s the aggregate loss of people, businesses and jobs was much less pronounced. While precipitous decline in the built environment was no longer as great as it was in the preceding period, some sections of the city, such as North Philadelphia, remained deteriorated and distressed. The rate of population loss slowed considerably, and the population even seemed to be stabilizing. The employment base, although still weak, was more aptly described as stagnant, and the number of business establishments actually grew between 1982 and 1984.[16]

To a great extent, the years of rapid decline of population and employment seemed to have passed. Commentators often stated that people and businesses who were likely to flee the city as a result of suburbanization and decentralization of production had already done so. Those who remained truly wanted or truly needed a Philadelphia location. On this base, the city could ostensibly begin its resurgence. Resurgence of investment and activity, however, would have to occur without the massive infusion of federal and city funds that had characterized the earlier period. The recession of 1973–75, coupled with the ascendency of the Carter and the Reagan administrations' lack of concern for urban problems and their reliance on national economic growth to spur local economies, resulted in the virtual evisceration of the urban renewal and other programs that had subsidized large-scale redevelopment projects (Fainstein, et al., 1986 ed:1–26,283–88). Urban Development Action Grants (UDAGs) and Community Development Block Grants, supplemented by various industrial development and industrial revenue bonds, took their place, but the funding was not nearly as great. Moreover, community groups were more critical of large development projects in Center City, particularly given the precarious fiscal condition of the city government in the late 1970s and early 1980s, the rising wage and property taxes confronting city residents, and the continued deterioration of neighborhoods. Public housing projects were no longer in favor; their dream had too often become a nightmare.

The spatial transformations of the third period were not driven by publicly subsidized investment in the core and private investment on the periphery. Rather, Center City experienced unprecedented investment in office construction in the 1980s, along with the continued gentrification of Center City and even certain inner ring neighborhoods. While public actions and funds were evident, the initiative and the bulk of the financing were private. Simultaneously the periphery of the city, specifically the northeast, stabilized as the inventory of unimproved land was depleted. The flow of capital and the subsequent development underwent a spatial shift.

Large-Scale Redevelopment

Under these conditions, the number of large-scale redevelopment projects diminished but did not wholly disappear. By late 1983, Gallery I had been extended two blocks above a newly constructed tunnel linking the city's two regional train systems. This mall extension included another department store and numerous retail and food establishments, many along the concourse of the new train station, Market Street East. At the same time, a large office tower, One Reading Center was built adjacent to the headhouse of the old Reading Terminal. It was partly subsidized through a city lease commitment, and represented only the second office tower completed along the eastern portion of Market Street since the 1930s. The other was 1234 Market Street, part of the urban renewal program of the second postwar period, which by the mid-1980s was wholly occupied by city agencies. In 1986, the city began the reconstruction of the portion of Market Street that extended east from City Hall to Independence Mall, repaving the roadway and adding landscaping.

The Delaware waterfront also was being redeveloped. Philadelphia had once been a major port, but by the 1970s its national position had all but evaporated. The city government wished to emulate the waterfronts of such cities as Baltimore (Harborplace), San Francisco (Ghiradelli Square), and New York (South Street Seaport) and thus began to invest in Penn's Landing, the waterfront east of Center City (see Figure 6.3). In preparation for the 1976 bicentennial celebration, a promenade was constructed along with the Port of History museum. From then through to the early 1980s, however, the city was unable either to interest developers in the site, or the developers, if they were interested, were unable to produce viable development projects. In 1986, in an attempt to spur and anchor development, the city-funded Great Plaza was opened. With the reception in that same year of a UDAG for a commercial and office complex, and with the creation of a marina and the adaptive reuse of one of the piers for an apartment complex, both just north of Penn's Landing, development seemed to be imminent. Other developers began proposing residential and commercial projects, including a hotel.

The city still had to solve the problem of access and parking. The construction of Interstate 95 had not only severed the waterfront from Center City and Old City (an area undergoing a transition from warehouses, wholesale firms and small factories to apartments, lofts, restaurants and retail outlets), but had itself taken up much of the acreage near the water. Moreover, few exit and entry ramps for I-95 had been built near Center City. The task was not easy. Adjacent neighborhoods undergoing revitalization or having been revitalized were disinclined to endure the burden of increased traffic. By late 1986, nonetheless, construction had resumed on the Vine Street Expressway linking the Ben Franklin Bridge and I-95 to the Schuylkill Expressway to the west.

For the most part the city government no longer took the lead in designating and clearing sites for redevelopment. Governmental subsidies continued but with fewer land write-downs and more financial grants and low-interest loans, tax abatements, lease guarantees, infrastructural improvements, and applications of eminent domain. Indicative of the diminished role of governmentally funded large-scale development projects in Center City was the proposal in the early 1980s for a major convention center to be built behind the Reading Terminal headhouse. The initial idea was that the convention center would be built by the Reading Company and then be leased to the city. In effect, the private sector would take the lead, and the city would guarantee the success of the project, eventually purchasing the building.

The convention center proposal represented the diminished governmental influence over the built environment in another way. The project proceeded in fits and starts. Opposition was quick to form, not only that of community groups and businesses in the area designated for clearance but also political opposition in the state legislature and City Council. Large-scale redevelopment projects had not simply lost favor. Such projects also were seen increasingly as a source of jobs and profits to be reaped by those groups who could gain control. The dark specter of blight and deterioration no longer motivated commitment and consensus.

An important force in the creation of uncertainty, which made problematic the quick realization of the convention center, was the racial tone of city politics, both the voice of minority groups in the City Council and the racial concerns of councilmembers themselves. Of the many issues surrounding the financing and construction of the convention center, two stand out in this regard. One was the concern that the city control the project and not have its influence over the awarding of contracts and the allocation of revenues diluted by State representation on the governing board. The center was perceived as a lucrative financial and political opportunity, particularly by minority councilmembers who had been elected within the last decade.

The other salient issue was the concern for affirmative action. The State, in return for its financial assistance, wanted affirmative action to be voluntary and not dictated by local ordinances. Local elected officials (with the exception of the mayor) and community groups were adamant in their position that a fixed percentage of subcontracts and jobs be set aside for minorities. This argument was possible only because of the access of minorities to the City Council and the presence of a black mayor (Bennetts 1981; Eisner 1985; Kilbanoff 1984). Moreover, affirmative action increasingly dominated the development and implementation of other large-scale, publicly aided construction projects (Beauregard 1988b). Gallery I and II, for example, involved agreements with the developer, Rouse Associates, to include minority-owned retail outlets, and with the contractors to hire minority workers.

Gentrification

As urban decline lessened, the need for government-funded redevelopment no longer seemed as urgent. Moreover, private investment capital was now, after the recession of 1973–1975, moving·into the inner city. The development of the northeast was virtually complete by 1987. For this and other reasons, the inner-city built environment began to undergo up-grading and transformation. The transformation was two-pronged: gentrification and office development.

While Society Hill had experienced redevelopment in the late 1960s and early 1970s, not until the late 1970s and thereafter did other inner-city neighborhoods begin to receive an influx of households able to buy and rehabilitate relatively inexpensive housing (Levy and Cybriwsky 1980; Weiler 1980). The result in many instances was displacement of the existing less-affluent population, either as a direct result of the purchase of single-family rowhouses and the conversion of small apartment buildings or as an indirect result of rising property tax assessments. Gentrified neighborhoods, by definition, experienced a turn-over in population, usually from lower to higher income and often including the diminution of the non-white population. In the early 1980s, Queen Village just south of Society Hill was added to the list of gentrified neighborhoods, and was joined by Bella Vista in the mid-1980s. Fairmount (or "Behind the Art Museum" as it was often labeled in real estate advertisements) was gentrified in the early years of this period (Cybriwsky 1978; DeGiovanni 1983), and in the mid-1980s, the adjacent Spring Garden neighborhood experienced instances of massive displacement and large-scale residential redevelopment.

Much private residential renovation activity seemed centered on Society Hill, and diffused from there to the south, to the west into the hospital area, and north to Old City. Old City, in fact, represented a different instance of this spatial phenomenon. Rather than being a residential area, Old City was the city's traditional warehouse and factory space, interspersed with some significant colonial houses, particularly Elfreth's Alley. In the 1980s, new commercial retail establishments (such as hair salons, convenience food stores, and art galleries) began to locate there, loft buildings were converted to apartments, and restaurants began to appear. Almost no new structures were built. Rather, the strategy was one of adaptive reuse. Moreover, as was true in a number of other gentrified neighborhoods (such as Bella Vista), blight was not rampant. The extant built environment was simply vulnerable to reinvestment.

By the mid-1980s, neighborhoods farther away from Center City were gentrifying. Northern Liberties, just north of Center City, was increasingly the home of many artists who purchased small empty factories or rehabilitated occupied or abandoned buildings. Fishtown just northwest of this neighborhood also had some evidence of gentrification. The areas around the universities in West Philadelphia were experiencing reinvestment. Powelton Village, once the home the city's university-based counterculture, became a hot real estate market. Farther northwest, Manayunk, a stable and solid working-class neighborhood, found itself the recepient of up-scale restaurants and middle-class households.

During this period, the city experienced what came to be called a "restaurant renaissance." Numerous small restaurants catering to affluent urbanites sprouted up in Center City and the surrounding gentrified or gentrifying neighborhoods, but not, of course, in the still-dilapidated areas of North Philadelphia and West Philadelphia. The restaurants generated further commercial investment and attracted additional residential developers and gentrifiers. South Street between Society Hill and Queen Village epitomized this trend. It went from delicatessens and wholesale outlets to up-scale restaurants, expensive clothing stores, nightclubs, and specialty shops. Gentrification was not simply residential, but involved commercial reinvestment as well. The result was to increase the market value of these areas, renew the built environment, and change the composition of the neighborhood's inhabitants.

Center City Office Redevelopment

The 1980s were also a time of office development. Like many other cities and certain suburban areas around the country, Philadelphia experienced an office boom. West of City Hall, new office construction exceeded in scale any office development that had previously occurred (Mallowe 1984). Low-rise commercial buildings were purchased for exorbitant prices and replaced by high-rise offices. From 1976 to 1984, approximately 8.5 million square feet of office space was added to the city's stock, 29 percent of the 1976 inventory. Almost all this space was located in Center City. An area of three- to six-story buildings was being replaced by twenty- to thirty-story structures, including a competition to dominate the skyline and at least equal the height of One Liberty Place, the tower that set off the Penn's hat controversy. Traffic congestion rose, and the streets were darker during the day as Philadelphia, for the first time, began to experience the canyon effect that had existed for decades in Manhattan. Through 1987, the office development boom did not abate, and high-rise construction continued to move west along Market Street.

As new towers came on line in early 1987, some industry analysts were warning of an office glut (Cohn 1987). They pointed not only to the 36.2 million square feet planned but not yet built, but also to the 8.1 percent vacancy rate and the intense pursuit of a few "lead tenants" in the city. Just months before its completion in late 1987, One Liberty Place had leased only 20 percent of its 1.2 million square feet. While new office space was appearing, older office space was being vacated by firms taking advantage of developers' desperate quest for tenants. This portended more problems for older office space. The owner of the renovated Curtis Center near Independence Hall claimed only a 25 percent occupancy rate. Most commentators reveled in this supposed building boom in Center City, but doubters were beginning to appear. The firms that were supposed to be attracted into Philadelphia to absorb the vacancies, thus taking advantage of relatively inexpensive urban office space, were not forthcoming.

At the same time, suburban office development was booming, although suburban vacancy rates in the 1980s were higher than in the city. King of Prussia, Pennsylvania, and Cherry Hill, New Jersey, were undergoing massive capital investment in office buildings, shopping malls, and residential complexes. Office space was being added throughout the metropolitan area. Rental rates for prime suburban office space, moreover, were generally lower than comparable space in Center City, and accessibility by automobiles better. While office development was robust in Center City, Philadelphia was once again being out-distanced by its suburbs.

This spatial competition is important to an understanding of the nature of Philadelphia's overall economic stabilization, and thus its attractiveness to middle-income households in this period. Philadelphia had been experiencing the shift of employment out of manufacturing and into services. Manufacturing and FIRE establishments were decreasing in number, while service establishments were increasing. FIRE establishments were also fewer in 1984 than 1977, but employment in this sector had expanded (see Tables 6.1 and 6.3). The development competition was not for new industrial space, but for new commercial space, particularly office space. While Center City office development was substantial, it was still less in relation to its less-centralized suburban counterparts. The city's economic dominance of manufacturing and retail services had been undermined during the first two postwar periods. Now, in the third postwar period, business services were being threatened.

One way Philadelphia could compete was in terms of its accessibility to other regions and countries via the airport. The city and the business community took the position that a vibrant downtown and a major international airport were necessary for Philadelphia to be a national and even international city. As a result, the city went forward with the construction of an international terminal, worked with the Southeastern Pennsylvania Transportation Authority (SEPTA) to implement train service to the airport from Center City, and successfully encouraged the Commonwealth of Pennsylvania to complete and resolve highway access to the airport, a long-term problem plaguing airport operations. These projects were not those of a city placing its hopes in a renewed manufacturing sector: the targets were business and financial services in a larger than regional context.

The industrial transformation was also, through its impact on the city's occupational structure, integral to gentrification. As can be seen in Table 6.2, employed professionals since the postwar period had experienced the greatest relative growth of all the major occupational categories. These individuals were increasingly finding employment in the new Center City office towers, and although the number of commuters continued to grow and many professionals opted not to become gentrifiers or to reside outside the city, enough stayed in the city to make a significant impact on Center City and certain inner ring neighborhoods. Gentrification and office development were not independent of the underlying restructuring of the local economy.

Periphery

While Center City seemed to be booming with new office towers, rehabilitated apartment buildings, new restaurants and renovated rowhouses, the robust development activity that had characterized the city's periphery in the previous period dissipated. The northeast was almost fully developed, with the exception of the 288 acre Liberty Bell Race Track site. After its purchase in 1986, the developer by early 1987 had negotiated an agreement with neighborhood groups to provide community improvements in return for city approval on a zoning change. On the site would be office buildings, a retail mall and a hotel. Residents adjacent to the site were not pro-development. Rather, recognizing the degree to which the northeast was saturated with development, they were concerned about traffic congestion. No demands for additional residential development emerged. The residents wanted a new senior citizens' center and recreational facilities for youngsters. These are not the demands of an area experiencing an influx of young households, major new construction and expansion, but rather of an area that had aged and had little space within which to grow. In turn, the governmental renewal subsidies that characterized earlier periods were lacking. The project reflected the forces operating in Philadelphia in this third postwar period.

Admittedly, open space still existed in the city in early 1988, much of it forest or swampland. Few large, developable, unimproved parcels were in evidence, with the exception of the site discussed above. The present and future were not witnessing and were unlikely to witness any major internal accretions to the built environment of the city. Any growth would probably take the form of intensification rather than expansion. The most-recent available land-use data reflected this condition (Delaware Valley Regional Planning Commission 1984). From 1970 to 1980, no major land-use category showed any growth. In each case, with the exception of mining which went from nine to ten acres, there was no change or only a one-acre increase. At its greatest, that one acre increase represented a relative change of 0.06 percent. Such stability was in stark contrast to land-use change in the metropolitan region. There, manufacturing land uses increased by 26.7 percent, transportation by 21.7 percent, residential by 16.5 percent, and commercial by 4.6 percent.[17] New construction on large unimproved sites was an unlikely future event in Philadelphia, but a common occurrence in the suburbs.

The need to compete with the suburbs, and the pressure to encourage development with subsidies and other assistance while protecting the city against large claims on its budget, led to numerous conflicts between Philadelphia and its surrounding suburban municipalities. The conflicts played themselves out in the arena of state legislative politics. Three issues are illustrative. One was the control of SEPTA, the regional transportation authority. The city, despite its residents' greater use of and need for mass transit, has fewer votes on the governing board than the suburbs. As fares rose to the highest in the country in 1986—$1.25 for a token—tensions increased. The existence of lower costs for suburbanites was the irritant.

A second issue involved the city's wage tax. Both residents of Philadelphia and those who reside outside but work within the city must pay a tax on wages earned. In the mid-1980s, the tax rate was higher for city residents (4.96 percent) than for commuters (4.31 percent), and a State court subsequently declared the unequal tax rates to be unconstitutional. Suburban legislators wanted a reduction; the city claimed that it could not afford any fall in revenues. The difference of opinion spread to the Convention Center controversy, the third issue, with suburban State legislators angling for a trade: their support in return for a tax decrease on wages. By early 1987, all these issues were still unresolved. From the city's perspective, its location within an expanding suburban ring that was gaining political strength had direct implications for Philadelphia's developmental potential, particularly in the face of sharply diminished new growth.

The saturation of land with development did not mean that new construction came to a halt. From 1977 to 1985, overall yearly investment in building construction averaged $418.1 million in current dollars. This represented the highest yearly average in any previous postwar nine-year period, even when expressed in constant dollars. Spatially, the inner ring received the highest proportion of construction investment. Center City and the northeast (including the Olney-Oak Lane section) received similar but much smaller proportions, approximately two-thirds of the inner ring share. Such aggregate data thus capture the slow-down of the northeast and the gentrification and institutional expansion in the inner ring, but do not reflect the recent surge in office construction in Center City.

Decline and Distress

Despite the resurgence of Center City, the gentrification of neighborhoods within the inner ring, and the stabilization of employment and population; many of the city's households were still living a precarious existence. Areas of North Philadelphia, West Philadelphia, and South Philadelphia occupied by blacks and Hispanics remained areas of poverty, high unemployment, and crime. Moreover, the flow of housing and commercial investment into these areas was a virtual trickle. At the same time, many white, working- and lower-class areas in the inner ring increasingly suffered similar problems (Mallowe 1986). The loss of entry-level jobs in manufacturing and the shift of entry-level jobs into the service sector, with its bias for low-paid female employment, meant that the traditional path toward stable working-class status was unavailable. Neighborhoods such as Kensington and Bridesburg continued to decline, and social and economic distress was pervasive.

No new public housing units were built during this period, housing abandonment (and the concomitant need for demolition) persisted and, overall, low-income neighborhoods lacked an adequate supply of quality housing. In some parts of North Philadelphia, the built environment had the proverbial quality of a bombed-out area. Most of the factory buildings that had contributed to Philadelphia's industrial prominence remained empty, and many of those had been further destroyed by arson or vandalism. Retail and personal services in these neighborhoods were also lacking. The distress embodied in the physical fabric was also woven in the social fabric. Drugs became a major problem in North and West Philadelphia and crime maintained its high profile. Many households were on welfare, and unemployment rates were higher here than elsewhere in the city. Stabilization and resurgence—and decline—were spatially confined.

The surge of office construction and the gentrification of specific inner city neighborhoods represented, for some, the rediscovery of Philadelphia by the middle class. The public discourse of this third postwar period thus had a different coloration than previous discourses. Since the end of World War II, Philadelphians had been struggling with the city's deterioration. In the immediate postwar years, public discourse focused on defining the problem and planning a response. The resultant magnitude of the deterioration, however, led many not only to abandon the optimism of the first postwar period but to abandon the city itself. This occurred despite the government's commitment to redevelopment and private sector investment in the northeast. After the recession of 1973–1975 had passed, Philadelphia experienced an expansion, one confined spatially and sectorally. Optimism reemerged. Philadelphia's built environment would be, many thought, redeveloped, up-graded, and preserved; resurgence was underway. The bottom of the trajectory had been reached; no longer would disinvestment and its extreme, abandonment, be the problems. The viewpoint, however, was narrow. In areas of North Philadelphia, the river wards, and South Philadelphia, poverty and deterioration had not lost their hold on the people or on the built environment.

Conclusions

Forty-some years is not a long span of time for exploring the spatial restructuring of a city. Yet these were not normal times. Philadelphia entered the depression as a giant among industrial producers, and the third largest U.S. city. After World War II, Philadelphia joined other industrial cities along the path of decline. By the mid-1980s, with the worst population and employment losses seemingly over, the transformations of the previous forty years seemed to bode more health than ill. Breaking the height limit imposed by Penn's hat was, for some, only one of many positive signs.

Because the spatial transformation was so rapid, many elements of capitalist urban development were condensed within a relatively short span of years. The spatial switching of investment is one of the most prominent. The uneven spatial development of Philadelphia, however, cannot be separated from its temporal uneven development, the historical layering of investment opportunities and obstacles. The interaction of space and time, nonetheless, does not occur in a vacuum. Also illustrated has been the role of various agents and structural trends in shaping the spatial-temporal transformation. We now turn to these three themes.

Spatial Switching

The spatial transformation of postwar Philadelphia and its metropolitan area was profoundly uneven. Investment, population, and the value of the built environment exhibited sharp variations across residential and commercial areas. Within the city, the first postwar period witnessed a spatial switch of investment and population from inner ring neighborhoods to the Near Northeast, a migration that accelerated in the second period. In the third postwar period, investment switched back to Center City from the periphery and, to a lesser extent, to the inner ring in the form of gentrification. Overlaid upon this intracity uneven development was a city-surburban switch of capital and people, which peaked in the second period but served as a backdrop throughout the years after World War II. Regional shifts were also apparent: black migration from the South just after the war, and later the in-migration of Hispanics from outside the country. The switching was not only of capital but also of people, and not only of private capital but also of public investment.[18]

The movement of capital and people was expressed vividly in the value of the built environment. Center City and the inner ring declined in the first two periods, despite, and sometimes because of, the infusion of renewal investments. At the same time, the periphery was increasing in value. In the third period Center City and certain places within the inner ring became revalued. Thus, it was not just that certain areas of the city became affluent, well-maintained, and valuable, but that areas which once had been so could relatively quickly become devalued, only to have disinvestment switch to reinvestment in a subsequent period. Spatial switching is by its nature a temporal process whereby areas see-saw, to use Smith's phrase (1984), among various degrees of market value and use value.

Just as important, spatial switching is not simply a temporal process whereby individual places independently undergo qualitative changes. The devaluation of certain places is linked functionally with the increased valuation of others. The lack of investment in the built environment of the inner ring as a result of the depression and the war contributed to its attractiveness for low-income migrants. For example, as North Philadelphia was being devalued, the white outmigrants who were contributing to its devaluation were developing the northeast. When the northeast became overvalued and fully developed, capital switched back to Center City. Economic and social transformations spurred this uneven development and generated complex relations among various areas within the city.

Historical Layering

The switching of capital, people and value from one place to another is intrinsically linked to the historical nature of spatial transformations. The legacy of earlier periods looms large in the following ones, setting constraints and opportunities that contribute to decisions to invest and relocate. As a result, the built environment can be viewed metaphorically as a layering of rounds of development or decline (Harvey 1985:15–25; Massey, 1984:117–20). Each subsequent layer is erected upon previous ones, which shape the type, speed, and extent of new capital and the activities and people who will be attracted to or deposited in that place.

The development of Society Hill, for example, required investors and the local government to probe down through many layers into the colonial period. There they found the architectural elements and urban fabric that would make the neighborhood attractive to middle-income households in the 1960s and enable its ultimate gentrification.

The years of farming in the northeast maintained a large stock of unimproved land, which eventually absorbed inner-city residents looking for a suburban environment in Philadelphia. Office development in the 1980s was transforming the western portion of Center City, but was unable to penetrate the decades of neglect and retail abandonment to the east. The attempt to integrate the metropolitan region with the nation and to solve problems of traffic congestion contributed to the construction of Interstate 95, which by the 1980s had itself become a barrier to the recycling of the waterfront from shipping and warehousing to marinas, apartments, and commercial development.

Such historical layering of development activity is inseparable from the spatial switching of capital, people, and value. Temporal and spatial uneven development are one. They are the underlying themes of the postwar transformation of Philadelphia's built environment. The story is not simply one of cumulative causation whereby the loss of population and capital is reflected directly in a decline of the built environment. Neither is spatial transformation a matter of temporal and spatial equilibrium whereby, over time, different areas of the city become equally desirable to developmental pressures. Philadelphia has had a long time to reach this equilibrium, and never has.

Contingency and Complexity

What also stands out in this brief historical account is the contingency and complexity of the development process. No simple, one-to-one correlation existed between the industrial and occupational restructuring of the city and changes in the city's built environment; the local government was not able to control decline and never has been able to generate growth; and various social changes were influential, while others were not. One cannot simply read spatial transformations as wholly derivative from the economy, the state or civil society.

Office development in the third period, for example, was clearly linked to a restructuring toward services and away from manufacturing. New office space in considerable amounts, moreover, was also added in the second period before the restructuring had peaked and when the city's economy was undergoing precipitous decline. The deterioration of the built environment, particularly in the inner ring, had its roots not in economic restructuring per se, but in the economic stagnation of the depression and the redirection of capital to war mobilization. Last, gentrification is difficult to explain simply as a function of a manufacturing-to-service shift (Beauregard 1986b). In other instances, such as the abandonment of factories in North Philadelphia or the closing of stores on the eastern portion of Market Street, the link between economic change and spatial transformations is clearly tied to a decline in economic demand.

The rise of service employment, moreover, did not compensate blacks for the loss of manufacturing jobs, a condition that had important implications for the deterioration of black neighborhoods. Race is an important component of the decline of North Philadelphia and areas of South Philadelphia. Economic restructuring undermined the manufacturing job base in which blacks might have found employment, but an equally likely scenario would have whites staying in the city to take up those new manufacturing jobs and blacks still left under-employed and locked into ghettos. A long distance exists between economic restructuring, the types of individuals slotted into well-paid and poorly-paid jobs, and the resultant investment or disinvestment in the built environment. Economic restructuring, to reiterate, hardly explains the development of the periphery by white inner ring residents.

Nor does economic restructuring fully explain the flow of capital into the built environment. Governmental investment in the second period was clearly linked to federal subsidies, which emanated from national economic prosperity, and local subsidies for private development necessitated by the atmosphere of decline. None of that would have occurred to the same degree without a supportive, pro-development local government. The later withdrawal of the federal government from redevelopment and economic development activities, hindering local government in the third period, had little to do with the economic restructuring of Philadelphia. Economic restructuring, in addition, does not explain why overall investment in the built environment has been rising ever since the end of the war.

Profitable investment opportunities in the built environment, it seems, are neither tied simply to economic restructuring nor are a direct function of local governmental incentive. In fact, the local government is generally unable to create profitable investment opportunities where none existed before. It can support development where demand already exists, as it did with infrastructural investments in the northeast or with eminent domain and transportation projects around universities and hospitals in West Philadelphia. Certain governmental projects might eventually serve as anchors for later private investment, as happened at Independence Mall, Society Hill, and Penn's Landing. Market Street East, on the other hand, has languished despite more than two decades of governmental attention and investment.

The government was capable of contributing to the deterioration and restructuring of areas through the demolition and clearance provisions of urban renewal. That strategy is no longer available. Still, the government continues to subsidize the work of private investors. One Liberty Place, in fact, sits on land obtained through the city's eminent domain powers. Local elected officials and administrators also contribute to expectations about development, providing a supposed unbiased appraisal of the communitywide benefits of convention centers and hotels, waterfront development, office development and gentrification.[19] To the extent that private development is partly built on a financial foundation of expectations, this function of local government is not to be dismissed. Without federal assistance, however, the local government plays primarily a passive role.

Of course finance capital, property capital, and the local government do not operate in a passive social environment. Neither the suburbanization of the northeast nor the transformation of North Philadelphia to a black ghetto was wholly in the control of investors and elected officials. Even gentrification is a phenomenon that would lack momentum if developers and elected officials only were in charge. This is not to say that uneven development primarily follows changes in sociocultural attitudes and ways of living. Rather, such changes are reinforced and even, at times, spurred on by finance and property capital, with the government almost always trailing behind. At other times, social forces can hinder the development desired by capital and the state. The convention center project stalled in 1987 partly because the racial make-up of the city and its reflection in local politics made affirmative action an issue. The building of a crosstown expressway along South Street in the 1960s was halted by neighborhood activists. Speculation and gentrification frequently meet neighborhood opposition. Development is not simply imposed upon people.

This suggests that the controversy surrounding the construction of One Liberty Place and the violation of the gentlemen's agreement was less subtle than the postwar transformations of Philadelphia allow. Office development west of City Hall could not assure Philadelphia's national status, considering the unevenness of development throughout the region and the historical presence of spatial switching. Neither could the opposition expect that historic neighborhoods and the image of Philadelphia as a city of homes was of pivotal importance within the forces of spatial development. No simple story can be told about Philadelphia's spatial transformation, and no future is guaranteed.

Acknowledgments

Roman Cybriwsky, Joe Feagin, Tim Fluck, Nancy Kleniewski, and Robert Lake provided comments on earlier versions of this chapter and their mention here is public acknowledgment of my debt to them. I would also like to thank the Institute for Public Policy Studies at Temple University for giving me the opportunity to present my arguments at one of their colloquia.

Notes

1. There is disagreement about the heights to be respected. The top of the statue is 548 feet above street level, but the limit has also been claimed to be 491 feet. All material for the description of the controversy was taken from numerous articles in *The Philadelphia Inquirer* beginning in May 1984.

2. The percentage increase was 12.4 percent between 1940 and 1950, and 8.3 percent from 1950 to 1960. Unless otherwise noted, all data are from the decennial reports of the U.S. Bureau of the Census.

3. A yearly average of 5819 housing units was added to the city's stock between 1944 and 1954 (Shea and Grigsby, 1957). From 1940 to 1950, year-round dwelling units in the metropolitan area expanded by 29.9 percent, while comparable city growth was 12.4 percent. Philadelphia's share of metropolitan dwelling units fell from 65.8 percent to 57.0 percent.

4. All retail data are from various years of the Department of Commerce's *Census of Retail Trade* (Washington, D.C.).

5. In 1958 dollars the value went from $31.8 million to $137.5 million. All building and construction investment data were collected from the City's Department of Licenses and Inspections.

6. This and subsequent listings and descriptions of projects were derived from a variety of sources including but not confined to, Cybriwsky and Western (1982), Foundation for Architecture (1984), Lowe (1967), Petshek

(1973), Tait (1976), Urban Land Institute (1969), and Wurman and Gallery (1972).

7. From 1952 to the mid-1970s, the University of Pennsylvania built approximately 121 projects at a total cost of $251 million (Tait 1976).

8. As of 1966, only 9 percent of the housing units built on Redevelopment Authority land or with Redevelopment Authority agreements were low-rent units, and 75 percent were for middle-income families. (See *Issues*, a newsletter published by the Philadelphia Housing Authority in December 1966.)

9. By 1987, buildings in the Callowhill district were being purchased from manufacturing firms and converted to inexpensive office space, primarily as a result of a robust office market in Center City.

10. Data are from *Journey to Work*, a supplementary report of the U.S. Department of Commerce, Bureau of the Census.

11. The Philadelphia Housing Authority in April 1943 reported that 12.3 percent, or 10,660 acres, of the city's area was occupied by 239 farms. Most of this farmland was in the northeast. See Housing Association of Delaware Valley, Urban Archives, Temple University, Urb 3, Box 335.

12. In contrast, all the vacant land within Detroit's city limits was developed by 1900 (Zunz 1982: 94) and Boston started to experience a shortage of land as early as the 1830s (Warner 1962: 18).

13. The relevant figures are 599,495 housing units to 685,131 housing units over these three decades, and a fall in the metropolitan share of 57.0 percent to 32.5 percent.

14. The amount of land in residential use declined between 1960 and 1970 in Center City and in a number of inner ring areas, whereas in the northeast and the southwest it increased. In the Far Northeast, the area receiving almost all of the new development in this period, residential land increased by 53 percent, and in Southwest Philadelphia it increased by 10.8 percent (Philadelphia City Planning Commission 1975).

15. In dollar figures the decline was from $6.359 billion to $4.921 billion in constant dollars. See Department of Commerce, Commonwealth of Pennsylvania, *Pennsylvania Abstracts*, for the relevant years.

16. The total population had dropped 1.34 percent on average each year in the 1970s. From 1980 to 1984 the yearly rate was significantly less at 0.62 percent. From 1978 to 1984, total nonagricultural employment fell by 5.9 percent, much less of a fall than in the previous two periods (see Table 6.3). From 1982 to 1984, total nongovernmental employment virtually stabilized.

17. Agricultural land declined by 4.8 percent and undeveloped land by 5.5 percent.

18. I do not mean to imply that there was a fixed amount of capital, people, and value to be shifted spatially within Philadelphia, so that if one area were depopulated, another *had* to be populated. Rather, spatial switching is relative and influenced by opportunities and obstacles outside the city and its region.

19. Local governments tend to support most development projects, and thus provide the ideological pronouncements that help developers to obtain financing, even though certain governmental agencies (such as city planning) might voice reservations. Of course, since government serves as a conduit for community protest, its ideological support can be weakened.

CHAPTER 7

Urban Restructuring in Comparative Perspective

Robert A. Beauregard

One cannot read the preceding five case studies without gaining an appreciation not only of the similarities but also of acute and significant dissimilarities. These are cities of advanced capitalism, of a joining of political economy and culture unique to the United States, and of a common location atop the urban hierarchy. Parallel processes and events are to be expected. Yet Los Angeles is so different from Philadelphia, Houston is close kin neither to New York nor to Chicago, and Philadelphia and Chicago, probably the best match of any pair, cannot claim equal stature with New York City. What are we to make of the consistencies and divergences that characterize postwar urban development in this common, historical, spatial, and political economic setting?

The general purpose of this final chapter is to reflect upon the five cities as part of a single, admittedly chaotic category. More specifically, its goal is a comparative analysis of the scope and scale of the spatial transformations each of the cities has experienced. In what ways have these cities—of different size, at incommensurate but contiguous positions in the urban hierarchy, and with quite dissimilar trajectories of postwar development—responded to economic, political, and social forces operating at regional, national, and international scales? How have spatial arrangements of activities and buildings, landscapes of value, and the social use and cultural identification of place adapted to, resisted, ignored or themselves shaped the economic and social restructuring of the postwar United States?

Such questions necessitate the use of comparative analysis, a search for generalizations and abstractions. Generalizations tap traits that the cities have in common, while abstractions explore the essential processes that drive capitalist development, but that appear in quite different forms at various spatial scales.[1] Specifically, the analysis focuses on what Charles Tilly (1984:82–83, 125–43) calls encompassing comparisons, comparisons that identify the variations of instances within, and their relationship to, a "system." The use of encompassing comparisons requires a good sense of the system before one explores fully the parts that constitute it. Such comparisons, certainly, can easily degenerate into functionalism, a tendency to interpret each specific instance as beneficial to the system if it persists, or as dysfunctional and harmful if it does not. This creates a conservative, theoretical bias; a defense of the system as currently constituted and thus of the extant distribution of power, privilege, and resources as well as the system's underlying structure.

Neither of these problems is debilitating or a reason to reject encompassing comparisons. The comparative analysis herein is driven by a particular system, that of advanced capitalism as viewed with a Marxist lens. The belief in the necessary, abstract logic of advanced capitalism, nonetheless, is tempered by an awareness of the contingent nature of the practical consequences of that logic as contradictions emerge. The events and processes being investigated are not determined by the system but have the capacity to respond to the tendencies of capitalism in unique ways (not always simply by being overwhelmed) and, at times, to mobilize, almost independently, new permutations of that logic (Williams 1977:75–89). Such theoretical values make encompassing comparisons much less susceptible to an uncritical functionalism. Interpretive flexibility thereby absolves the theorist of a preestablished, full-blown theory. One embarks with a theoretical map for exploring an ill-defined terrain.

In addition to understanding how each of these cities has responded similarly or dissimilarly to the restructuring of capitalism, we also wish to examine in detail the variations among those responses, to make what Tilly (1984:116–24) labels variation-finding comparisons. The two types, of course, are interrelated; encompassing comparisons "will often lead to alternative explanations of structures and processes that seem to yield to variation-finding" (ibid.: 146). In this way, the fixity of the initial theoretical scheme encounters the conjunctures of reality. The Marxist perspective is open to evidence but never abrogates its pivotal role in interpreting systemic relations and cross-variations (Harvey 1987).

The presence of theory further facilitates our endeavor by suggesting a number of comparative trajectories (Urry 1986:241) with which to structure the analysis. At the base of this project has been a concern with the spatial consequences of economic restructuring, a sometimes tacit and sometimes explicit adherence to the importance of production in the spatial development of cities. Our first comparative trajectory is thus the relation of local restructuring to the industrial restructuring of the national economy and of the cities' regional economies. These spatially-encompassing economies function as the systems for the encompassing comparisons. Then, attention turns to the primary issue—spatial transformations. The comparative base now is local, regional, and national. The issue is how each city's development path unfolded given the spatial configuration and physical form of each at the onset of the postwar period, and the relation of that path to the country's overall spatial trends as described in Chapter 1. The spatial comparative trajectory is cast broadly: "It includes distance, and differences in the measurement, connotations and appreciation of distance. It includes movement. It includes geographical differentiation, the notion of place and specificity, and of differences between places. And it includes symbolism and meaning which in different societies, and in different parts of given societies, attach to all of these things" (Massey 1984:5).

The third comparative trajectory links the first two: spatial transformations with economic restructuring. The linkage takes the form of the agents—investment firms, developers, corporate executives, elected officials, community groups, and households—who translate the opportunities and tribulations of economic and social growth and decline into transformations of the built environment. Given a matrix of potential spatial shifts and modifications in capital investment, labor consumption, and reproduction and political control; which agents mobilize the capital and political support to actualize that potential? The trajectory thus leads to another: the degree to which local groups resist the spatial transformations put into motion by capital and its agents. The system, of course, is not defined simply by its movers and shakers, but by the nature of the contradictions and the struggles that are engendered.

As each comparative trajectory is explored in an encompassing fashion, variations are also considered. The encompassing comparisons permit a sense of structure to define the analysis, and the variation-finding comparisons force consideration of the particularities of place. Specificity, however, does not displace the background logic of capitalism. Each of these cities is not unique, although each demonstrates uniqueness, and their development does not proceed independent of the constraints laid down by capitalism's historical presence. At root here is a search for the structure of advanced capitalism, and the ways it, as a social formation, penetrates the nooks and crannies of American society and maintains its identity despite being flexible and heterogeneous. Only by exploring the spatial agenda of capitalism in many instances, in comparative fashion and at various spatial scales, will such structure be revealed.

Comparative Trajectories

The prime suspect in our investigation of spatial transformations is economic restructuring. The rearrangement of capital and labor, and the places and structures that contain them, to increase profits and forestall crisis is a major force mobilizing the capitalist, social formation. Most of the attributes of capitalist societies can be traced to this base. It is not all-encompassing and fully determinative. Neither does it stand as proximate cause to all that we might observe. Rather, to the extent to which households must turn to the economy and to the capitalist State, or to their families, philanthropic organizations, or churches, for the wherewithal to survive; their consumption and reproduction, the policies of civil society and the quest for knowledge, all have roots, no matter how slender, in the sphere of production.

Industrial Restructuring

As discussed in almost every chapter, the postwar period was one of unprecedented national prosperity, followed by a period in the 1970s of abrupt restructuring and retrenchment. Production processes were reorganized to facilitate flexible accumulation, the social relations of production became a spatial division of labor, global production linkages proliferated, and large, multinational corporations overrode the political and economic constraints of nations (see Peet 1987; Scott and Storper 1986). At the urban scale, the issue has been one of a restructuring of the economic base away from a reliance on manufacturing for employment and exports. The now-dominant sector is services, a melange of activities providing personal care and attention, information, advice, and support to the agents who circulate and accumulate capital. In most declining cities, service employment has not compensated for manufacturing job loss, but in some

(New York and Boston are good examples), financial, business, and information services have led a resurgence of the local economy. In growing cities, the picture is less clear: while all have traveled the path of an increased emphasis on services, many have also gained manufacturing employment. Whether these changes represent a sharp disjuncture in the history of capitalism or, as some have argued (Fainstein and Fainstein, 1988), merely a gradual transition only now recognized after the economic hard times of the 1970s, is an issue that cannot be resolved here. Regardless of timing, in comparison to the United States of the late 19th century, a restructured economy is now evident.

Table 1.2, showing the employment shares by industrial sector for the United States from 1950 to 1984, illustrates the decline of manufacturing and the dramatic expansion of services. Other shifts reinforce the general sense of a movement away from goods production: a relative expansion of retail trade, FIRE, and government and a relative decline of transportation, communication and public utilities. Agricultural employment, as a percent of overall employment, has also been falling for many more decades. To what extent have the five cities changed in comparable ways? More precisely, is urban industrial restructuring unfolding in parallel with national industrial restructuring?

Comparing each of the cities to the national pattern yields an interesting result. Despite the difference among the cities—for example, New York, Los Angeles, and Houston lay claim to global status; the cities achieved their lofty positions during different centuries— the restructuring of all five cities is comparable to the nation in the postwar period.[2] While Houston and Los Angeles do have patterns of temporal shifts in employment shares at variance with the national pattern, the differences are not significant enough to earn status as anomalous cases. The five cities have had a relative decline (or stagnation in the case of Los Angeles) in manufacturing employment and a relative rise in service employment. Houston and Los Angeles displayed this pattern despite a near 300 percent and 200 percent respectively increase in resident manufacturing employment since 1940. Outweighing and equaling these changes, however, were expansions in services of more than 700 percent and 180 percent, respectively, during the same four decades.

The fact that rapidly growing Houston and Los Angeles, and New York, Chicago, and Philadelphia which have suffered through significant postwar decline, have all moved parallel to national economic trends in relative employment shares is strong evidence to support the pervasiveness of national industrial restructuring and its ability to overcome spatial differences and to penetrate local economies. Weakening this somewhat unequivocal conclusion, however, is the fact that Los Angeles's regional economy, not the city economy, has changed contrary to the nation. Since 1962 there has been an absolute *and* relative growth in manufacturing employment, and an absolute growth but relative decline in services, trade, FIRE, government, transportation, and public utilities. Within this fast-growing regional economy, manufacturing has continued to be robust. Even within the city, resident manufacturing employment expanded in absolute terms from 1950 to 1980, although its relative share of total resident nonagricultural employment remained stable: 23.5 percent to 23.3 percent. That the Houston region did not produce a similar counterfactual trend provides evidence that even rapid growth is insufficient to overcome national trends.

As we know, there are specific differences among these cities' economies, and these differences make it difficult for us to accept readily the local correspondence with national restructuring. Houston's economy is built on shipping, chemicals and petroleum products, and oil-drilling and -processing equipment. Los Angeles's economy features technology-based industries functionally related to aerospace and defense, along with labor-intensive apparel and service industries. Shipping is important too, but energy is not the pivotal element, and defense expenditures are much more important, although not absent from the Houston economy. Philadelphia has a very diverse economy with roots in fabricated metals, machinery, and other producer goods. It harbors a regional service industry, but its port functions have atrophied, and aerospace and defense, with the exception of the Navy yard and ship repairing, are hardly significant. New York's service sector has global overtones and is dominated by corporate headquarters, financial and professional services, and the hospitality and tourism industry, with the manufacturing sector focused around apparel and printing. In Chicago, electrical machinery is pivotal, along with printing, toolmaking, and food and kindred products. These are very different economies now, as they were in the past, yet each exhibits the national shift from manufacturing to services.

Of course, the correspondence across employment shares between each city and the nation is not perfect. Significant, albeit small-scale, variations exist. As mentioned above, Los Angeles's manufacturing share has not declined. New York and Houston have had a more robust construction sector than the United States, while New York has had stronger growth in trade, public utilities, transportation, and communications. Houston shows a relative stabilization in governmental employment, a trend not shared with the rest of the cities. Los Angeles has experienced an expansion of peripheralized manufacturing (such as apparel), FIRE, and government, but a decline in the resident employment share in construction. Chicago's construction sector has also declined, as has its (and Los Angeles's) retail trade sector, both relative changes contradictory to national trends. Last, Philadelphia has had a similar postwar history to Chicago in construction and retail trade, a stable employment share in transportation, communications, and public utilities, and an increase in wholesale trade, whereas that for the whole country declined.

These sectoral variations also have a temporal dimension. The timing of the restructuring has been slightly different from one city to the next. Philadelphia and Los Angeles encountered serious losses in manufacturing share in the 1960s, whereas between 1940 and 1969, New York basically maintained a balance between manufacturing and services. Chicago lost the largest portion of its manufacturing share in the 1970s (the greatest five-year absolute decline in manufacturing jobs occurred between 1967 and 1972), and gained the largest portion of its service share in the 1960s. While Chicago's manufacturing sector was struggling during the 1970s, Houston was enjoying its largest absolute increase in this sector and in services, construction, retail, and finance, insurance, and real estate. Los Angeles had its largest jump in total resident employment—228,787—during the same decade, but the manufacturing employment share declined while the service employment share had its largest increase between 1970 and 1980. Thus, despite the general correspondence between the sectoral shifts in these five cities and the nation, sectoral and temporal variations exist to distinguish one city's economy from the next and to suggest an uneven spatial pattern in the diffusion of industrial restructuring.

The uneven spatial pattern, however, is not that pronounced. In fact, if measured in terms of shifting employment shares, it is relatively mild when compared to absolute changes in resident employment by industrial sector (see Table 7.1). On that measure, the contrast between the growing cities of Los Angeles and Houston and the other three cities is stark. Neither of the former lost any resident employment in any industrial sector, while New York City, Chicago,

Table 7.1 Absolute Change in Nonagricultural Resident Employment, 1950–1980 (in thousands)

	USA	New York	Los Angeles	Chicago	Houston	Philadelphia
Mining	−178.0	0.6	0.5	0.5	33.4	0.1
Construction	3,532.0	−65.4	3.7	−28.5	52.3	−23.4
Manufacturing	5,432.0	−409.8	138.5	−264.1	88.4	−160.3
Transportation, communications, and public utilities	1,417.0	−17.9	29.3	−59.1	39.2	−21.2
Wholesale trade	3,079.0	−58.8	20.2	−20.4	37.7	−5.8
Retail trade	10,028.0	−169.9	66.1	−93.2	81.1	−51.5
Finance, insurance, real estate	3,783.0	106.3	66.6	20.7	45.8	9.5
Services	17,313.0	330.9	271.6	80.2	182.1	53.2
Government	10,215.0	−16.7	4.1	4.5	14.6	11.0
Total	54,621.0	−300.7	600.6	−359.4	574.6[a]	−188.4

[a]There is a discrepancy of 1700 workers between Total change and the sectoral totals.

Source: U.S. Department of Commerce, *Statistical Abstract of the United States* and *Social and Economic Characteristics*, selected states and years.

and Philadelphia together lost employment in all but FIRE and services. New York City even had an absolute decline in government employment, although Chicago and Philadelphia experienced growth. Thus, only Los Angeles and Houston match the national trends overall. The remaining cities show little correspondence and exhibit countertrends in construction, manufacturing, wholesale and retail trade, and transportation, communication, and public utilities. While postwar shifts in employment shares result in a general conclusion that national trends overwhelm the particularities of local economies, absolute changes in employment by sector make that conclusion much less tenable.

To elaborate on this theme of interrelated spatial scales, we might compare these cities with the larger regions in which they are located (Sternlieb and Hughes 1978). The manufacturing-service shift was most pronounced in the Northeast between 1960 and 1975, and both New York and Philadelphia followed this pattern. Chicago imitated a similar restructuring in its East North Central Division. Both the West South Central Division and the Pacific Division, locales for Houston and Los Angeles, respectively, experienced absolute growth in both manufacturing and nonmanufacturing employment, and both of those cities paralleled the regional changes. In terms of the industrial restructuring of these five cities, then, the regional correspondence seems just as tight as the national correspondence. The regional comparison, it should be noted, utilizes absolute changes in employment by sector and thus is more sensitive to overall growth and decline in employment. To that extent, a city-region correspondence is at odds with a region-nation correspondence; the nation was growing, while the Northeast and Midwest were declining.[3]

Overall, it seems clear that cities with very different growth trajectories, such as Los Angeles and Chicago, mimic national industrial restructuring, if by structure we mean the relative sectoral distribution of employment. In absolute terms, and both for cities and their regions, this correspondence does not hold. In effect, growing cities are both restructuring and experiencing the benefits of a prosperous national and regional economy, while declining cities are similarly restructuring, but that restructuring is placing it in opposition to national economic prosperity. Such a spatial division, of course, is at the root of the notion of a new spatial formation. The declining central cities are the outmoded cities of industrial capitalism, the postwar suburbs and Sunbelt cities, with their expanding geopolitical boundaries, the new "anit-cities" (Louv 1983), are the post-industrial cities of advanced capitalism. That ideological gloss, however, is tarnished by the fact that growth, the phenomenon of progress, is not a sufficient condition for a purging of manufacturing activity, an "old" production process.[4] Growth may include, as Los Angeles and Houston demonstrate, an expansion of the manufacturing sector. Thus, the uneven spatial and temporal development of the economy is such as to cast doubt on any bold claim to a post-industrial information society reaching throughout the spatial interstices of the United States. What is not in doubt is the spatial reach of restructuring.

Spatial Transformations

To prepare further for the theoretical integration of industrial restructuring and spatial transformations, the analysis now turns to an in-depth and comparative investigation of the postwar urban form and dynamics of the five cities. Encompassing comparisons in which each city is compared with a stable postwar urban form are inappropriate here. Although many urban theorists might readily agree that the macro form of the American city of the 1940s and early 1950s consisted of a central business district surrounded by low-rent industrial, commercial, and residential activities (the zone of transition) with more-affluent residential and commercial areas toward the city's periphery, they would readily concur that significant variations existed from one city to the next: Philadelphia, for example, contained some very affluent residential areas within the downtown.[5] Moreover, it would be neither a surprise nor a subject for debate that the macro form was soon transformed by rapid and massive suburbanization, and then changed once again in the late 1970s and early 1980s. In addition, Los Angeles did not correspond to the earlier pattern of urban development, since it lacked a dominant CBD, and Houston did not follow the typical central city to suburb growth path.

Thus, rather than positing a fixed postwar urban form by which to engage encompassing comparisons, we will instead submerge these comparisons within two others: the contrast of each city's present form to that which it had just after World War II, and a comparison of historical variations across the five cities. The former suggests the impacts of industrial restructuring. If it has fallen more or less equally on all cities in the country, a conclusion which is supported by the above analysis, and if economic forces are central to spatial transformations, a conclusion to be explored below, then the developmental paths would, one could hypothesize, be converging. The variation comparisons, then, enable differences between places to enter the analysis.

In general, Houston, and less so Los Angeles, displays a disjuncture between the form of the city in the early postwar period and its current developmental dynamics. The Houston of 1945 was still a city with one major commercial center, a single industrial zone along the ship channel, and residential and mixed-use areas arrayed around those two nodes in a relatively tight areal configuration. By the mid-1980s Houston was much different. The CBD was challenged for commercial dominance and new investment by two or three nodal office-retail complexes, and retail competition by these and other planned retail centers had overwhelmed the original CBD. While industrial activities were still clustered to the east around the ship channel, new industrial space was also arrayed to the southeast near the Johnson Spacecraft Center and to the north near the Houston International Airport. Moreover, Houston is no longer as compact. Spread over almost 600 square miles, its form is one of low-density sprawl linked by numerous radial and circumferential highways.

Los Angeles also displays this movement toward commercial and industrial nodes and corridors, and low-density sprawl surrounding high-density concentrations. Los Angeles, however, was not as compact just after the war, having begun its sprawl-like development in the 1920s with the advent of the automobile. Then the city also lacked a vibrant and centralized business district; Los Angeles was known for its lack of a downtown core. Since that time a requisite scaled core has emerged as a result of new office, retail, and residential construction. In addition, few of Los Angeles's nodal developments are within the city limits, whereas Houston's nodes are more city than suburban in location. Annexation and extraterritorial jurisdiction played a much stronger role in this Texas city than in the California city. In both cases, nonetheless, the urban form exhibits qualitative differences from that present in the immediate postwar period.

A deceptively equivalent statement can be made about the three declining cities in the northeastern part of the country: New York, Chicago, and Philadelphia. Viewed with a macro lens, these cities have experienced qualitative changes over the last four decades, although their spatial transformations deviate from those found in Los Angeles and Houston. In these cities the major shifts in urban form have involved a redefinition of the zone of transition, an adaptation of waterfront areas to a profoundly different economy, a rearticulation of the edges of the city, and a realignment of the hierarchy of the city's retail nodes. Simultaneously, aspects of the immediate postwar form were elaborated and reinforced. Of particular importance in this regard is the deconcentration and then reconcentration of administrative and other office activities in the CBD.

The office boom of the 1980s in these cities has mainly taken place in core areas, although Manhattan has historically had two cores (Midtown and Wall Street) with some office development in Brooklyn. In all three cases suburban office parks have appeared: Stamford, Connecticut, Route 287 in Westchester County, and New Jersey's Route 1 corridor outside New York City; the areas adjacent to O'Hare Airport and Tri-State—Northwest Tollway corridor in Chicago's suburbs; and Cherry Hill, New Jersey, and King of Prussia beyond Philadelphia's city limits. Office development within the city, however, has remained in its traditional locations, although these locations have spread horizontally and intensified vertically. As we will discuss in more depth below, inner-ring neighborhoods have often been gentrified, thus changing the socioeconomic and racial landscape, and older industrial districts have become decayed or adapted to new uses, for example along the waterfronts. Overall, however, we still find a single central core surrounded by residential and, less so, industrial districts in relatively concentrated form. A few low-density developments have occurred in the peripheries of New York and Philadelphia, but these have not been identical to suburban developments and are too small in scale to have shifted city form to any great extent. Regardless, New York, Chicago, and Philadelphia all exhibit the same qualitative transformations in their built environment. They are more like each other than they are like Los Angeles and Houston.

Such baseline comparisons still omit the variations within the two broad clusters. Certainly there are differences between Houston and Los Angeles, cities which have very different urban forms now than they had forty years earlier. The Los Angeles nodes are mainly outside the city limits. Los Angeles is approximately 100 square miles smaller in area than Houston, although still much larger than the other cities, and has virtually ceased annexation, whereas Houston has not. Otherwise, the present similarities seem to overwhelm the variations. Both have developed in a tight correspondence with highway networks and port and airport facilities. Both have a core area of comparable or greater scale than the nodes, but challenged by them for new capital investment. Both are cities with most land developed in low-density sprawl. Thus the differentiation of space by activity and value seems comparable, even to the degree that cities display extreme contrasts in socioeconomic characteristics of residential areas despite their prosperity. To this extent, both the dynamics and the form of property development in Los Angeles and Houston have been strikingly similar.

The spatial variations among New York, Chicago, and Philadelphia are also overwhelmed by the similarities. The anomaly here is that Chicago's growth spurt occurred in the mid-to-late 19th century, whereas by that time New York and Philadelphia had already reached their lofty position in the urban hierarchy. Such a major historical difference suggests the implantation of a much different spatial form. The latter two cities had a strong commercial developmental pattern untainted by industrial development before experiencing the great surge in manufacturing, whereas Chicago's expansion was simultaneous with the establishment of the great urban factories and the railroads. A close look at the original commercial areas of New York and Philadelphia, however, shows that they did not serve as barriers to the emergence of industrial districts nor were they of such a scale as to give these cities a unique spatial form that could not be overtaken by new spatial arrangements. In Philadelphia, for example, Old City with its warehouses, shipping offices, and maritime banks became the site for the location of small manufactures and is now experiencing residential and commercial gentrification. Its size, approximately a half-mile square, is insignificant in a city of roughly 136 square miles. Wall Street and the port area at the southern tip of Manhattan Island were adapted, absorbed, or demolished for other types of development and did not shape urban form beyond the years when commercial, shipping, and fishing activities were dominant.

In effect, the long-term historical transformations of New York and Philadelphia prior to World War II meant that all three cities entered the postwar period with relatively similar urban forms. Moreover, those forms, when viewed from afar, have changed in very similar ways over the last four decades. Still there are variations. New York and Philadelphia filled in undeveloped peripheral areas. In New York City, the northern portions of the Bronx adjacent to Westchester County went from low density development and unimproved land to apartments. Parts of Brooklyn along Long Island Sound became residential areas, while Staten Island, New York's inner city suburb, has recently been attracting high-density, urban development. In Philadelphia, the northeast area went from farmland and institutions to residential and commercial, and the southeast became a major airport complex. Peripheral development was less evident in Chicago.

The new development, however, did not shift the broad arrangement of land uses and value that had traditionally located more affluent residential areas on the periphery. On the other hand, the development of these areas, such as Philadelphia's Far Northeast with its highway-oriented commercial malls and New York's Co-op City, certainly occurred at different densities from and in different patterns than older areas of the city.

Otherwise the similarities, once again, seem more pervasive than the dissimilarities. New office development has not resulted in nodes within the city competing with the traditional CBD. Chicago has the O'Hare Airport area and New York Brooklyn, but neither rivals the CBD to any great extent. In Philadelphia, almost all office space is concentrated in Center City. Sharp disjunctures in investment and socioeconomic residential composition continue to exist between these cities and their surrounding suburban areas. The polarization across the metropolitan area is now matched by a similar spatial differentiation within the cities. Residential areas are generally characterized by racial and ethnic segregation and by a concomitant clustering of affluence and poverty. New York might be an extreme example. Its status as a world city and the tremendous inflation in the value of land and property in Manhattan mean that New York has some of the richest households in the country. At the same time, its locus as a destination for immigrants and its large minority populations also make it a city with some of the country's poorest and most destitute areas. Poor people and poor areas are found not only in the outer boroughs, but exist relatively close to the more-affluent areas in Manhattan. Harlem and the Upper West Side are not that distant from each other. A similar but less-extreme pattern is found in Philadelphia and Chicago.

Other comparisons—waterfront development, neighborhood retail corridors, and gentrification—reinforce the similarity among the three cities and highlight the postwar changes in urban form. In New York and Philadelphia, and Chicago less so, waterfront areas were once sites for shipping, fishing, and heavy manufacturing. They have been abandoned now or replaced by commercial, residential, and recreational complexes. The waterfront has been transformed from a place of work to one of leisure and consumption. This is true of the South Street Seaport and Battery Park in New York City and of Penn's Landing in Philadelphia. The phenomenon is less obvious in Chicago, where Daniel Burnham's 1909 plan for the city had designated much of the lakefront for parkland and where the downtown shore and

North Shore were the traditional locales for expensive housing, the Gold Coast. The industrial waterfront in Chicago was neither located close to the CBD nor to the adjacent gentrifying neighborhoods of the 1970s and 1980s, as it was in New York and Philadelphia. For these reasons, Chicago varies from the other two cities on this particular spatial dimension.

In New York and Philadelphia, the edges of the central business area have been restructured to cater to the middle and upper classes, and a mix of classes strolls the promenades, shops at the boutiques, and eats at the seafood restaurants. New York and Philadelphia lost their dominance in shipping, and the land that those activities occupied lay fallow for years until recycled by the 1980s surge of urban investment. By replacing industrial activities with condominiums, marinas, museums, and retail malls, the form of the city has been realigned. The notion of a working river and a port has been displaced by the notion of a scenic and recreational amenity. The fringe has been transformed. The rivers and their edges have a new meaning and a new function.

This transformation is not unrelated to the gentrification that New York, Chicago, and Philadelphia have experienced. Residential areas contiguous to the downtowns, or distant but with significant urban amenities (for example, areas of Brooklyn), have had through the 1970s and 1980s an influx of relatively affluent homebuyers who have purchased and renovated somewhat dilapidated housing, or an influx of developers who have purchased, rehabbed, and then sold or rented large buildings. In New York City, SoHo, Park Slope, and the Lower East Side qualify for this category, while Philadelphia has Queen Village, Old City, and Fairmount. In Chicago, the former warehouse and industrial area just north of the Loop is being transformed in this fashion. A significant number of households have opted to remain within the city and become homeowners, thus increasing the demand for middle-income housing and bringing pressure on lower-income areas, often repositioning them from one socioeconomic rung to another and from one level of property value to a higher one. These areas have also experienced commercial gentrification as shops and restaurants have arrived to cater to this relatively affluent category of urban residents.

In effect, mixed-use districts adjacent to the CBD, what had once been labeled the zone of transition, and working- and lower-class neighborhoods have been physically, socially, and economically transformed. The zone has been replaced increasingly by high-priced

residences, recreational spaces, and new commercial corridors. It has
become the zone of reinvestment (see Figure 7.1). Other middle- and
upper-income areas still exist scattered throughout these cities, but a
central core surrounded by industrial, low-level commercial and transient residential uses no longer exists. Rather, substituting for that
arrangement is a vibrant office core with a shrinking zone of transition and an expanding collar of relatively affluent residential areas.
Without doubt, this is a change in form from that of the city just after
World War II: Still, New York, Chicago, and Philadelphia have proceeded in tandem along this dimension of spatial change, and only
minor variations exist across the cities.

Last, each of the three cities has experienced a less pronounced
shift in the importance of neighborhood commercial, mostly retail,
districts. With the diminution of population across many residential
areas and the substitution of low-income in-migrants for middle
income out-migrants, New York, Chicago, and Philadelphia have
experienced both shrinking and expanding neighborhood retail activity. For certain neighborhoods, those with declining populations
and falling consumer spending power, and those adjacent to shopping centers just outside the city limits, neighborhood retail districts
have become less vital. Upper Darby, outside Philadelphia, and Cross-
County Shopping Center, outside New York, are good examples of
external draws. The former is located one block west of the city and
at the end of the Market-Frankford subway line; the latter is a short
bus ride north of the Bronx. On the other hand, new immigrant
neighborhoods have often reinvigorated existing neighborhood retail
areas. Philadelphia, moreover, experienced in the mid-1980s a rash
of commercial strips, usually not enclosed and not large by suburban
standards, within the city itself. The strips siphoned consumer dollars
from more traditional retail streets spatially integrated in the neighborhoods, and redirected them toward major highways.

The end result, with exceptions, is neighborhoods with less of a
social center, fewer places that give it a central identity and where
people can, in their daily lives, congregate and socialize. Certainly
many neighborhoods, even those of low income, still have such areas,
but they are neither as vibrant nor as economically healthy and
diverse as they were when the war ended. Of course, gentrifying
neighborhoods have developed such areas, and at a different scale of
consumer expenditure they replicate the lost neighborhood retail
areas, albeit without the ethnic identity. Again, this represents a

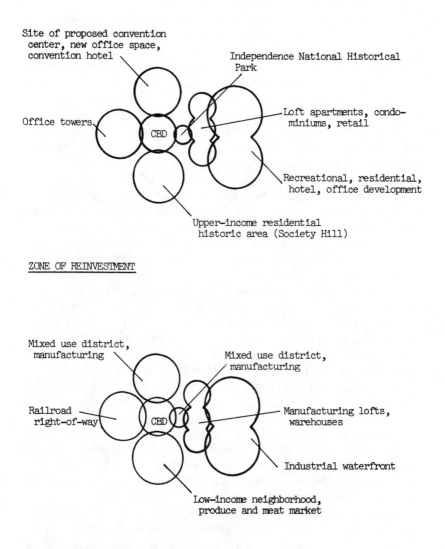

Site of proposed convention center, new office space, convention hotel

Independence National Historical Park

Office towers

CBD

Loft apartments, condominiums, retail

Recreational, residential, hotel, office development

Upper-income residential historic area (Society Hill)

ZONE OF REINVESTMENT

Mixed use district, manufacturing

Mixed use district, manufacturing

Railroad right-of-way

CBD

Manufacturing lofts, warehouses

Industrial waterfront

Low-income neighborhood, produce and meat market

ZONE OF TRANSITION

Figure 7.1 Zone of Transition to Zone of Reinvestment.

change in urban form, one which has unfolded to various degrees in Chicago, Philadelphia, and New York City.[6]

All these spatial transformations have engendered perceptual shifts.[7] New York, Chicago, and Philadelphia each went through most of the first three postwar decades carrying an image of a declining city losing population and jobs, and viewed generally as less desirable than suburbia as a location for investment. Minorities and the poor came to be seen as the typical urban residents, with the city increasingly thought of as a place where crime was rampant and the streets were dirty. As World War II ended, urban experts considered the industrial city as a place with troubles. For years the built environment had gone without maintenance and new construction. The housing stock had deteriorated. Supporters of postwar suburbanization exploited this image and worsened it. As minorities and unemployment filled the void left by the middle class and fleeing factories, the image isolated the central city from the suburbs. The riots of the 1960s exacerbated the external view as one of ghettos, industrial slums, and decaying downtowns. But by the mid-1980s this image had changed, not totally but significantly.

Large-scale office development, gentrification, waterfront reuse, fiscal stability and particularly the decline in the in-migration of blacks to New York and Philadelphia contributed to a more up-beat and positive image. Opportunities for interesting shopping, recreation and dynamic urban living were increasingly available within the cities, not in the sterile suburbs. Suburbanization did not abate greatly because of this, nor did population trends reverse and swing upward, but the change in the spatial dynamic and resultant form of these cities certainly led to a much different public perception. Of course, this was not true for all cities: Camden and Newark, New Jersey, still battle a very negative image. More important, this change in perception is not as true for or applicable to Houston and Los Angeles. Houston never was considered an urban wasteland. Los Angeles might have the Watts district, but its identification with the city has always been overshadowed by growth and prosperity and by Hollywood and Beverly Hills, and thus the deterioration of image is less pronounced. The point is that spatial changes have an ideological component that is important for our own perceptions—it affects our interpretations—and for the perceptions of investors and potential residents.

In sum, significant spatial changes have taken place in these five cities. Houston has probably had the greatest qualitative shift in its

form, with Los Angeles close behind. New York, Chicago, and Philadelphia have not transformed the earlier macro pattern of development to the same degree, but have altered it significantly within the
basic parameters set by a dominant CBD, industrial districts, and
outer rings of densely developed neighborhoods. Moreover, clear
differences exist between each of the cities within the two groups. We
can thus reject the generalization that the macro form of all large
cities has changed similarly during the postwar period. One must also
question the generalization that Sunbelt (or Snowbelt) cities have
changed similarly, particularly growing cities of the South and West.
The picture is much more complex. While it seems that history is not
destiny when expansion takes place, it is certainly an important spatial
constraint when boundaries are firm. To understand this further, we
need to look more closely at the agents and forces that have mediated
these spatial transformations.

Mediating Agents

Across and sometimes within the five cities, we have found opposing
phenomena: growth and decline, decentralization and centralization,
gentrification and neighborhood decline, sprawl and nodal concentration, large-scale redevelopments in previously built-up areas and
peripheral accretions, industrial abandonment and industrial development, and the repositioning, reemergence and even creation (as in
Los Angeles) of the CBD. The findings point not only to a profound
pattern of uneven development within these major cities and across
the United States but also to strong similarities between cities of much
different developmental trajectories. The existence of a basic structure for postwar urban development is credible but must be further
specified. This requires attention to the agents who have mediated
the spatial transformations and to the role played by the underlying
forces of economic restructuring.

For changes to occur in the built environment and the landscape of
value, individuals and organizations must make and implement decisions regarding investment and disinvestment. Land must be purchased, architects hired, construction loans obtained, contractors
mobilized, governmental regulatory powers applied, and the resultant
structures put into use. The demand for organized space must be
articulated, directed, and satisfied. The built environment does not
just happen but itself is the product of an industry, and like other

industries involves various social relations of production that determine output, financial viability, and its own restructuring (Feagin
1983; Smyth 1985). Here, however, we will concern ourselves solely
with those agents who mediate between the pressures for new construction, rehabilitation, or abandonment, and the construction industry that actually realizes those decisions. More specifically, the
focus is those who serve as developers, work with developers, or
oppose developers. Four broad groups will be considered: governments, property developers, local corporations, and community
groups.

Governments

In each city, the local, the federal, and to a lesser extent the state
governments have played a major role in shaping the built environment (see Stone and Saunders 1987). Houston's city government,
although passive regarding social services, residential infrastructure,
and land-use regulation, has been very active in promoting industrial
and commercial infrastructure (for example, the ship channel and
airport), while its absence from the property development arena has
facilitated low-density sprawl and large residential and commercial
ensembles. The city governments of New York and Philadelphia have
been more interventionist about the regulation of land use and
development and also the provision of infrastructure, although infrastructural development has had little impact upon urban form
because of the general lack of open space for new construction.[8]
Neither has regulation brought about qualitative changes in the form
of these cities; it is better interpreted as maintaining and preserving
existing patterns. Both cities have attempted to redirect CBD fixed-
capital investment, but neither has been entirely successful. Their
greatest impact on urban form stemmed from the federal Urban
Renewal program and took place between the early 1950s and the
mid-1970s. Philadelphia created Society Hill and preserved Market
Street East for retail activities, while New York created Lincoln Center
and numerous large-scale, middle-income residential projects. The
federally subsidized public housing program exacerbated the residential segregation of the minority population and concentrated
socioeconomic disparities. The direct consequences of urban renewal
and public housing for the macro form of the city were minor. Only
when joined with other forces of investment and disinvestment did

their impact extend beyond the microlevel and result in the redefinition of the zone of transition.

Chicago's postwar history presents us with a similar story of local government involvement: regulatory regarding land and property development, active in confronting blight and slums, and intrusive in its use of public housing projects. A comparable statement for Los Angeles is more problematic, not because that city has not engaged in urban renewal, built public housing, implanted infrastructure, or regulated development but because such local governmental interventions in Los Angeles's postwar development, with few exceptions such as the Bunker Hill project, have generally been overwhelmed by the rapid, new private investment. This city's local government seems much less active than the northern cities, but much more active than Houston, a city which has generally avoided governmental housing and community development programs (see Table 7.2). Los Angeles has not had to take a strong position on urban decay, but it has not been as aggressively pro-development as Houston. The Los Angeles government has not stood in the way of growth; neither have slow-growth and no-growth advocates been absent. During 1987, a citywide coalition emerged that was highly critical of the lack of interest in controlling growth and its consequences.

On the other hand, the federal government's impact on Los Angeles is much more pronounced and obvious. In all the cities, the interstate highway program was crucial to postwar suburbanization and, with the exception of Philadelphia, to the urban form itself. The Los Angeles freeways are world-renowned and have been extremely influential in its low-density nodal development, as freeways have been in Houston. The impact of these limited-access highways in New York and Chicago has been much different: vast swaths of property were cleared, and the relationships between areas were drastically altered. Only in Philadelphia, which halted all but one inner-city, limited-access highway, did most of the city remain unchanged by roadways.

Of course, interstate highways were not the only federal intervention that shaped urban form. In addition to urban renewal and public housing, more specific projects, such as the ship channel and the Johnson Spacecraft Center in Houston and less so Philadelphia's Independence Mall, also had an impact. Probably as important as the highways in Los Angeles and Houston has been federal support of different industries, support often linked to military objectives. The aerospace development in and around Los Angeles and Houston and shipbuilding in Houston helped to create major industrial districts

Table 7.2 Selected Development Characteristics for the Five Cities and Metropolitan Areas

	New York	Los Angeles	Chicago	Houston	Philadelphia
City					
Total 1983 governmental expenditures ($ millions) on housing and community development[a]	1,023.2	117.4	124.9	14.5	153.9
Per capita housing and community development expenditures, 1983[b]	142.8	37.9	41.7	8.5	93.4
Employed resident construction workers, 1980[c]	78,904	55,158	37,692	76,556	22,921
Total office space in millions of square feet, 1985[d]	492.2	282.0	178.5	87.1	102.4
Value of foreign investment in major office space ($ billions)[e]	7.65	2.60	1.20	1.37	NA
Primary Metropolitan Statistical Area					
Value of nonresidential construction ($ millions 1986)[f]	1,113.3	3,782.6	1,910.7	836.6	1,101.4
Total new residential units, 1986[g]	15,298	70,225	32,129	6,413	25,798

[a]Data from U.S. Department of Commerce, *Statistical Abstract of the United States.*
[b]Data from ibid., 1986.
[c]Data from U.S. Department of Commerce, *Social and Economic Characteristics.*
[d]MIT Center for Real Estate Development, "America's Office Needs: 1985–1995."
[e]Coldwell Banker (Boston) report titled "National Survey of International Investment Ownership of Major Office Buildings in 19 Largest United States Downtown Office Markets," 1987.
[f]Based on building permits. See U.S. Department of Commerce, *Construction Review* (May–June 1987).
[g]Data for 1986 for housekeeping units only and include both private and public construction. See *Construction Review* (May–June 1987).

and to attract additional investment and population. In all these instances, the federal government has been involved in a variety of activities that demolished areas, subsidized new construction, facilitated the shifting of land values, encouraged commuting, and rebuilt areas of the city. The point has been made often (Fainstein, et al. 1986 ed.) but bears repeating.

While governments, in conjunction with private investors, have been active in very substantial ways in shaping the urban form, they have also been influential ideologically. The best example, because it is so blatant, is Houston, although all city governments have and are, at least in the 1980s, seriously concerned with creating a good business climate. In Houston the ideology of development is shameless, whereas the other city governments temper their pro-development orientation with a concern for the social costs and community disruption that often accompany development. In the CBDs in particular, city governments offer minimal resistance to new investments. Despite outcries about traffic congestion, pollution, and overbuilding in New York and Philadelphia, for example, developers of office buildings have encountered little resistance from the city government. But the political debate intensifies and becomes more problematic when new developments (such as convention centers) move to the fringes of the CBD and beyond. Neighborhood groups in Chicago, New York, and Philadelphia are better able to push a different perspective and to erode the good business climate with civic obligations and neighborhood values. One does not have the same sense of governmental flexibility in Los Angeles and, certainly, in Houston. That does not mean that the social costs of development are any less, or that they are somehow mitigated by an automatic distributional mechanism that accompanies growth. Only recently have groups emerged in Los Angeles to question the endless sprawl and to lobby for growth controls. Such groups confront a developmental ideology with a long historic presence and, as groups in the three northeastern cities have done, must first establish their voice in the public arena.

Developers

Although governments have been active in shaping the postwar spatial transformations of these cities and in providing the justifications for private investment and disinvestment, governments themselves have more often than not simply been subordinate actors. Even when they have taken the initiative, as with the limited-access highways, the actual consequences of those highways for urban form have depended upon the decisions and actions of developers, real estate agents, financial institutions, and others involved in land and property development. The highway does not automatically cause a shopping mall or a suburban village to appear; they have to be built and occupants obtained. In fact, of the groups involved in urban development, developers, since they are lead agents in this process, are the most important.

In one sense, the importance of large developers in the postwar period has been widely recognized, although less deeply or widely researched (see Checkoway 1984; Feagin 1983). All urbanists know of Leavitt and his suburban communities, but knowledge frequently ends there. For the most part, developers have been associated with suburbanization (Jackson 1985; Weiss 1987). What we see in these case studies is the importance of large developers, not just for the suburbs but for the development of the city. The construction of office and apartment buildings requires big organizations with access to large amounts of capital and the ability to negotiate regulations, organize for implementation and attract tenants. Many of the largest developers—for example The Rouse Company, Trammell Crow—operate nationally. Gerald D. Hines Interests, for example, has developed buildings in Houston, New York, and Los Angeles. The capital for these massive investments also flows nationally and even internationally. The Prudential Insurance Company of Newark, New Jersey, has investments in most major cities, and a significant portion of property investments in Houston, New York, and Los Angeles are made by Japanese, Middle Eastern, and European investors (see Table 7.2). Cadillac-Fairview, for example, a Canadian developer, has been extremely active in the United States. The point is not only that large-scale property development requires large-scale developers and investors, a fairly obvious assertion, but that these agents are not confined to single cities or even to single countries. The spatial range of their activities contributes to the similarity of location and architecture and thereby contributes to similarities in urban form at both the macro and micro levels.

Of course, office tower development is not the only property sector where large-scale developers have proved important. While retail development is still dominated by commercial streets with many small retail investors, retail malls have gone from a purely suburban phenomenon in the 1950s and 1960s to an urban phenomenon. The Gallery in Philadelphia by the Rouse Company, the Galleria in Houston by Hines Interests, and Water Tower Place in Chicago are examples. Houston is probably the best illustration of the development of suburban malls within the city, and New York the worst. Mall-like complexes in the latter city are contained within office or residential towers and are not free-standing. Several reasons for the lesser role of large malls in New York, Chicago, and Philadelphia might be both the historical existence of neighborhood shopping areas and gentrification, with its deemphasis of mass-produced goods and franchise operations (Sassen-Koob 1986). Regardless, large developers are pivotal, and their actions shift the qualities of the microenvironment. Numerous small commercial developers have emerged to build retail strips in New York, Chicago, and Philadelphia, and their projects transformed earlier retail streets of the so-called walking city into automobile-dependent nodes.

One also sees the spatial implications of developer-driven property development in the industrial sector. All the cities have experienced a great deal of postwar industrial park development. Industrial firms now agglomerate in areas organized by local governments and developers. Land is purchased and cleared, infrastructure and even buildings are provided, and land and property marketed to industrial users. The resultant site is managed just like a suburban shopping mall. Industrial districts in the 1980s are less diffused, less integrated with other land uses, and operated in a more centralized fashion. Even in older cities such as New York and Philadelphia, industrial parks have emerged, although often toward the periphery.

In this and other areas of property development, large developers have played an important role in shaping the urban form. The evidence for this is most visible in Houston and Los Angeles. In the older industrial cities, developers have certainly had a high profile in the CBD with high-rise office towers, apartment buildings, and condominiums, but from a citywide perspective the previous high-density development, overall decline, and lack of available land for massive new construction has dampened their qualitative impacts. Along with government, large developers are the most important agents in the postwar spatial transformations of these cities.

Local Corporations

While corporate developers and large finance and property capital play a major role in the spatial transformations of these cities, local corporations are seldom directly or heavily involved, though exceptions such as Pittsburgh exist (Lowe 1967:110–63). Proponents of free enterprise point to the contribution that local corporations make to the community and, in such cases as Minneapolis, tout the civic responsibilities that they adopt. Large corporations are also seen by local governments to be central to the city's position as a regional or national center, to the image of the CBD, and to the city's labor market. In many medium-sized cities, such as Hartford, Connecticut, New Brunswick, New Jersey, and Wilmington, Delaware, large corporations have played central roles in local civic and social affairs, have shaped the local economy and, in turn, have had a major impact on spatial form (Beauregard and Holcomb 1979). On the other hand, one must not confuse the fixed-capital investment of these corporations with the spatial mobility of capital. In the later postwar period, corporations have decentralized operations, established a spatial division of labor in the production process, redirected retained earnings to mergers and take-overs, and more often than not avoided any commitment to the economic vitality of their host cities.

With the exception of Houston, corporations play a weak role in property development. In Houston, the oil and chemical corporations have been instrumental in creating industrial districts and their investments in office towers have affected the skyline and the development of commercial nodes. In addition, many oil corporations have established property development enterprises as part of a corporate diversification strategy and as an outlet for excess capital. Comparable relations are much less pervasive in the other cities, cities which lack the economic specialization of Houston and which have not experienced rapid growth of population and infusions of capital. Local corporations have built office towers that, like the buildings of Citicorp and AT & T in Manhattan, give definition to the skyline, but those corporations are seldom involved in commercial (or even residential) developments beyond their headquarters building, nor are they active via property development subsidiaries.

The prime influence of corporate elites on the built environment is channeled more through the political arena than through property development (Davis 1986). In all the cities, however, that influence is not exerted directly. Its general form is one in which corporate elites are consulted frequently about local fiscal issues (such as municipal bond sales) and the broad directions of economic development. The thrust of their advice is to facilitate private capital investment. The actual forms that investment takes, with the exception of convention centers, airports, and other major infrastructure projects, are left undefined. The general interest is directly represented by individuals deeply involved in property development, who sit on private-public partnerships and governmental boards that regulate and subsidize it. Corporate, finance, and property interests share a common concern with new investment in the built environment, but local corporations have participated in postwar spatial transformations from background positions.

Community Groups

More visible in property development are various community groups ranging from neighborhood associations to citywide tax lobbies and single-issue advocacy organizations. While more visible, their influence does not seem as great even as local corporations, although their numerous local successes—stopping an unwanted development or encouraging the government to construct a desirable one—is notable. Moreover, their impact on the form of the city is highly variable from one city to the next. Governments, developers, and corporations are much more pervasive and consistent across urban areas in wielding influence and provoking consequences. The particularities of place are patently obvious when one considers the role of community groups as agents mediating the formation and restructuring of the built environment. In part this is understandable: community groups are more likely to react to proposals than to initiate them, are more concerned with their immediate surroundings than with the larger city, are often more likely to lose than to win when faced with a major development project, and are usually small and without the capital to initiate projects or to buy in as co-developers.

The city which seems to have the most active community groups is New York. Not only does it have a history of ethnic and racial residential segregation, but it also has in place an institutional mechanism—community boards—through which such opposition and conflict can be channeled. Moreover, the high density of development, which dictates that almost any new project must disrupt existing residential, commercial, or industrial districts, further contributes to the active role of community groups in property development. Often these groups, when not stopping projects, are able to modify them and to gain concessions for the surrounding area and its people. The developers of the Javits Convention Center and of numerous office and residential projects have had to pay heed and respond accordingly to community concerns. A similar situation exists, although on a less-formalized basis, in Chicago and Philadelphia.

Community groups can be very influential in property development and can pose obstacles that can be overcome only through the modification of plans. Nonetheless, the actions of these groups do not add up to a major redirection of urban form. Concessions are obtained at the margins of the project; its negative impacts are mitigated or compensated, but it is still built. The inability of these groups to initiate projects is important in this regard. Such groups have had significant successes—the thwarting of plans for the West Side Highway in Manhattan is the best example—but most affect the microenvironment and leave the overall form and direction of urban development unchanged.

The influence of community groups declines in the CBDs where the bulk of new construction has taken place, and is less momentous in Houston and Los Angeles. The negative consequences of CBD projects are seldom focused on a clearly defined group that is also locally organized. Traffic congestion is borne by commuters from various suburbs, restaurant workers from lower-income neighborhoods, and corporate executives from affluent residential districts. Each can escape the problem at the end of the day. None of this, of course, speaks to the seeming lack of community organization in Houston and Los Angeles. The social costs of development in these cities has been documented and is unquestioned. Yet not as recognized is the active participation of community groups in property development controversies. Anecdotes are told of Houston property owners who banded together to discourage a certain type of activity from locating in their midst, and community groups do exist. The lack of formalized governmental channels for such oversight, the tradition of no zoning in Houston, large land areas, and rapid population growth only recently involving ethnic communities all contribute to the absence of community group involvement there.

Central to the inclusion or exclusion of community group participation is the structure of the local political arena. A pro-growth ideology is common to almost all the local governments, with few exceptions (Stone and Saunders 1987). Variations do exist: Houston is at one extreme; New York, Chicago, and Philadelphia city governments find their pro-growth sentiments tempered by local politics. As cities declined in the postwar period, thoughts of restricting growth go virtually unspoken. Within that context, however, growth is often channeled and modified to fit within historical constraints. In Chicago, for example, the administration of Mayor Harold Washington was more sensitive to the interests of neighborhoods than to those of corporations and investors in the CBD. Large-scale property development was viewed with skepticism; it detracts from neighborhood investment and bolsters the CBD at the expense of the community. Since it cannot be stopped, nor did the mayor want it stopped, the city then aggressively pursued spin-off benefits such as jobs, which can be targeted for city residents. In Philadelphia, while local politics is certainly built upon a pillar of property development, the local economy is less dependent upon property development than in Houston. Furthermore, race plays an important role in local politics to the extent to which new, subsidized CBD development becomes clothed in affirmative action goals, and development that impacts negatively on black communities is often averted. Local politics in Houston and New York seem much more preoccupied with and defined by property development interests.

Los Angeles seems to fall somewhere between these two extremes, although closer to Houston. Traditionally, local politics has been dominated by a pro-growth orientation, and few instances of community opposition are in evidence. Los Angeles has not been noted for its grass-roots organizations; the formal mechanisms for articulating such concerns are absent. On the other hand, in the last few years numerous communities in the Los Angeles region have opposed growth. Santa Monica is a prime example. Increasing amounts of development made it more and more difficult for residents to remain renters and homeowners. At one time the city government, to assess the direction of property investment, even imposed a moratorium on development. In other communities, such as Venice Beach, local groups have opposed the spread of condominiums and the inflation of property values. By the mid-1980s, a Los Angeles councilwoman was elected to office on a no-growth platform, and numerous people were speaking adversely of the traffic congestion, pollution, and unregulated development that was reducing the quality of life in the Los Angeles region. Such a political environment enhances the potential for more active community involvement.

While the social costs of growth might well create a new actor— community groups—on the development scene in Los Angeles and Houston, their presence is highly unlikely to shift the relative influence of major actors. Their presence has had only marginal impacts on urban form in the other three cities. Large developers, financiers, and real estate interests supported in numerous ways by local government, and in reaction, at times, to federal initiatives, hold the power and have had the greatest influence on postwar spatial transformations. Individual decisions made by thousands of sovereign households do not shape the built environment of a city. Those households are responding mainly to opportunities represented by developers and governments. Developers and governments amass the capital and focus it on single projects that bring about major shifts in spatial form. More important, the increasing concentration of capital in the development field and the desire, particularly on the part of governments in declining cities, for projects that provide a critical mass of investment sufficient to overcome previous disinvestment and attract other developers makes for a setting in which large-scale projects have replaced incremental additions to the built environment. Whether this is part of a larger process of industrial restructuring or is independent of those shifts needs to be carefully explored.

Economic Restructuring and Spatial Change[9]

In the postwar period, three types of spatial transformations were more or less indicative of all five cities under investigation. First was a simultaneous decentralization and, to a lesser extent, deconcentration of investment and people into suburban areas, investment which Houston and Los Angeles to a lesser degree were able to incorporate. Second was a reconcentration of investment in the city's core, exemplified by massive office development and gentrification. For New York, Chicago, and Philadelphia, this was preceded by disinvestment in these areas; in Los Angeles the downtown had been relatively undeveloped, and thus the investment of the 1980s was less a reconcentration than an initial concentration. Third, all of these cities have been the sites for an increasing residential polarization. While extremes of wealth and poverty had certainly existed for many, many decades, those extremes have diverged as the "middle" of solid, working-class and lower-middle-income neighborhoods has been eroded by gentrification, out-migration, and the spread of poverty areas. Two additional spatial transformations were more indicative of Los Angeles and Houston than of the other three cities, although the latter's suburbs evidence such changes. One is nodal development, the other is sprawl.

To what extent can these rearrangements of the built environment be attributed to the economic restructuring experienced by these cities and, concomitantly, to what extent must we look outside the sphere of production for directional forces? The decentralization and deconcentration of investment and people have frequently been traced to shifts in the organization of production and distribution (Ashton 1984; Walker 1978). Certainly the movement of manufacturing plants from central locations where railroad facilities and labor had been concentrated, the change in the technology of production processes, and the shift in the economy away from manufacturing has led to the decline of central city industrial districts and to the dispersion of manufacturing plants, a process underway since the 1920s.

The residential and commercial suburbanization processes of the postwar era are not as often understood in terms of changes in production and distribution. Land availability, deterioration of central-city housing, governmental mortgage insurance and highway programs, and the expansion of the middle class are the frequent components of an explanation. Many theorists do recognize that large-scale suburbanization depended upon the nature of housing production, but are not as ready to see this as part of the economic restructuring of the postwar period. The construction industry is not outside the economy. Its concentration, and thus ability to produce large numbers of units in single locations, enabled residential suburbanization, even if it was not a determinative factor. In part what enabled such houses to be built was governmental assistance, yet on the demand side more and more households were moving into relatively comfortable income categories, categories generated by the prosperity and restructuring of the postwar economy. Moreover, the decanting of the cities' retail sector was not simply a matter of retail services following their clients to the suburbs. Shopping malls and commercial strips were also dependent upon large developers to produce these commodities and, in addition, on the rise of franchises and branch stores. Reorganization of the social relations of production in retailing, in particular, were crucial to decentralization. Overall, decentralization and deconcentration were greatly affected by economic restructuring, although changes in social relations in the household and patterns of consumption also played a facilitative role (see Hayden 1984; Jackson 1985).

The central role of economic restructuring is repeated in the reconcentration of investment in the city centers during the 1980s. Office development and gentrification have strong roots in shifts in the composition of productive activities, the spatial divisions of labor within and between firms, and the impact of these changes on the occupational and wage structure of urban workers (Beauregard 1986b). Office development and gentrification, in certain neighborhoods, have also depended upon the existence of large developers and investors who could exploit economic and social changes with additions to the built environment. Moreover a tight correspondence exists between the one and the other development; the gentrifiers are likely to be workers in the new administrative towers. Nonetheless, gentrification requires more than changes in the spheres of production and circulation. Residential location is more than an economic decision. Issues of consumption and reproduction are also crucial and certainly cannot be ignored. Even those, however, cannot be dealt with separately from the restructurings of the labor market and the impact this has on gender relations (Rose 1986). One could also argue that the decision to work in administrative and business services in the CBD is partly a lifestyle decision over which the worker has some control; but if this is so, capital's control over such professional and managerial jobs overwhelms this supply-side occupational factor. The reconcentration of investment and people in the central-city core is mainly driven, as decentralization, by forces emanating in the economic sphere.

A similar line of evidence can be carried into the residential polarization of these cities. Gentrification is one element, as is the diminution in jobs for relatively skilled factory workers. The latter strikes at the working class and also removes a path of upward mobility for those who are poor, unskilled, and just entering the labor market. Unemployment, moreover, continues to be a structural problem. While by 1987 the unemployment rate had reached a low for the past two decades, the history of this statistic in the postwar period is still one of secular expansion. At the same time, the pool of unskilled, undereducated minorities and even whites in the central cities seems to be expanding. New waves of immigrants from Central and South America and Asia either join the ranks of the poor or quickly move beyond them, further increasing the relative distances in income and education across the population. For those with college educations and with professional, technical, and managerial skills, the economy offers opportunities. Well-paid working-class job opportunities for high school graduates, however, continue to be exported. Finally, residential polarization is solidified in the operations of the housing market as developers avoid high-quality, low-cost housing alternatives. Residential polarization is not simply a consequence of economic restructuring; racial discrimination and the failures of inner-city schools are also causes. Moreover, the economic forces are not confined to the sphere of production, but involve social reorganization of the circulation of capital and the distribution of commodities as well.

Nodal development and sprawl are spatial transformations that, unlike the above, are not so easily tied back into the productive sphere. The former seems dependent mainly on the hypermobility of capital, itself derived from the shift from production to service activities that freed capital for commercial and residential property development, and the emergence of large developers financed by the capital concentrations within banks, giant insurance companies, and large pension funds. In each instance, economic restructuring is in the background but still facilitative. The foreground, moreover, is only one of many possible manifestations of that restructuring. In addition, the existence of nodes, a phenomenon confined to Houston and less so to Los Angeles, is dependent upon the availability of large expanses of unimproved land and the development of a complex highway network. Sprawl has an almost equivalent relation to the economic base. The role of large developers, landowners, and transportation networks, combined with controlled patterns of residential consumption, occupies a position immediate to low-density development. Such factors as the decentralization of employment sit at a greater distance from this spatial transformation.

In sum, economic restructuring has played a significant albeit uneven role in the broad spatial transformations of these major American cities. In the instances of decentralization and reconcentration, its position has been dominant. In those of residential polarization, nodal development, and sprawl, however, economic restructuring moves increasingly to the background. At one extreme, the new economic structure is directly expressed in the urban form; at the other its consequences are mediated by forces of consumption and reproduction and by concomitant changes in the spheres of exchange, distribution and capital circulation. One can, in effect, read some of the spatial transformations directly from the economy, while others are so much more contingent that such a reading is highly erroneous. In either case, the reader would be capturing only the broad sweep of these changes.

As we have seen, residential polarization has different dynamics in different cities, and sprawl is created much differently in Houston, for instance, than it is in the suburbs of Philadelphia. Particularities of place do exist, and they do more than embellish macro changes in urban form. In addition, they are not confined only to the physical landscape but range into the local ideology of development, politics, patterns of consumption, and previous history. Economic restructuring might well be interpreted as a driving force in postwar spatial transformations, but it is a force that cannot make its mark unchallenged.

Conclusions

Four broad claims emerge from this analysis. First, the economic restructuring that has characterized the last few decades in the United States is a national phenomenon virtually unaffected by variations in the space economy. Its penetration of large, growing, and declining cities has been fairly uniform, with only minor distortions caused by local specializations in industrial structure. Second, postwar spatial transformations have somewhat less of a national and structural nature, although the difference is not strong enough to substantiate a claim that urban development is wholly place-specific. The macro form of development has unfolded much differently in ascending than descending cities, the former being newer and less tied to traditional manufacturing than the latter. Place is more influential, particularly when one looks to the micro form of the built environment. Still, one cannot but wonder whether New York, Chicago, and Philadelphia, if able to annex freely, would not have become cities similar in form to Houston and Los Angeles.

Encouraging a conclusion that postwar economic restructuring and spatial transformations are structural in nature are the pervasiveness and centrality of economic forces in the dynamics of urban development. The major and most common spatial shifts—decentralization and reconcentration—can be traced directly to economic restructuring, while other spatial shifts—nodal development, residential polarization, and sprawl—are indirectly linked to the economy. Political and social forces often mediate the latter, and historical forces of all types—that is, previous practices and events—have been influential. Capitalism has been able to overcome obstacles rooted in the past, but the cost to capital and the solutions devised often redirected development in unintended ways. Last, urban development within and across these cities is highly uneven spatially and temporally. Even in cities where expanses of unimproved land make continual accretion possible, values do not simply decline from the center to the periphery.

Neither have these cities experienced economic restructuring and spatial transformations in perfectly parallel sequences.

These claims assert the theoretical and practical importance of the capitalist economy in the large-scale, qualitative dynamics of urban form and development. There is no escaping the importance of investment in production of goods and services for the spatial organization of cities. Investment has a dominant role, not just a central one. At the same time, investment in the sphere of production does not determine urban form. Other economic realms, particularly the sphere of circulation, are important. In addition, all these forces require the mediation of developers, financiers, property owners and government before realization in the built environment. Although dominant, economic forces are not independent. The particularities of place, then, are best interpreted not simply as the physical landscape that each city must confront, although that is important, but more as the local configuration of mediating agents, with many of those mediating agents entering the largest cities from the outside. Their actions, more similar than not across the United States, determine whether economic restructuring manifests itself comparably in different cities. Thus the particularities of place are structural in one sense and spatially contingent in another.

These five cities, at one time or another, have been the locales for highly favorable configurations of mediating factors. Each rode one or more national economic waves to the top of the urban hierarchy. Despite aggregate decline, New York, Chicago, and Philadelphia are still able to capture major infusions of investment and, at least, to maintain the affluence of the CBD and certain neighborhoods. Thus Chicago and Philadelphia might slip in position, but their decline would be brief. Once on top, one's position is both problematic and assured; the capitalist economy is too dynamic and uneven to stabilize the rankings, and too enmeshed in past investments to disrupt them radically.

Notes

1. When doing comparative analysis, one must carefully distinguish between *common* attributes or processes and dissimilar attributes or processes generated by similar forces. The first is normally associated with large-scale empirical studies attempting generalization and the second with more theo-

retical endeavors in search of basic and dynamic laws of development, also known as abstractions (see Sayer 1985).

2. Unless otherwise noted, assertions about the five cities are taken from the case studies, and assertions about U.S. urban development from Chapter 1.

3. Of course, such encompassing comparisons, as we move down the spatial scale, have a not so insignificant statistical side. Within their regions, these are dominant cities, economically and demographically, and are also likely to dominate statistically, with the regional data heavily influenced by the city data. This certainly could contribute to an explanation for regional correspondences.

4. While manufacturing is considered to be a "sunset" sector, proponents of such a shift often hold a simultaneous preference for high-tech goods (such as microcomputers) and low-tech goods (for example automobiles) produced by high-tech processes (such as robotics).

5. By macro form I mean the large patterns of spatial differentiation in contrast to the "weave of small patterns" (Warner 1962) that occurs as one focuses on individual blocks and streets, what I term here the microenvironment.

6. Relatively little attention has been given to retail districts by urban political-economists, investigators opting to focus on office development and large public projects in the CBD and gentrifying residential areas. Even in the gentrification literature, the role of commercial gentrification is seldom highlighted.

7. Such a discussion, of course, is admittedly more speculative than scientific; the statements are a bit bold. A review of the popular and social science literature on cities in the United States since the 1930s, however, failed to uncover a contrary set of perspectives.

8. Of course, in peripheral areas within New York and Philadelphia where new construction took place, infrastructure (particularly highways) was important for the form of the developed landscape.

9. Throughout this chapter I have used the term industrial restructuring to refer to employment shifts across industrial sectors. Here, in concluding, I return to the more encompassing term economic restructuring.

Bibliography

Abbott, Edith. 1936. *The Tenements of Chicago, 1908–1935*. Chicago: University of Chicago Press.

Abrams, Charles. 1965. *The City Is the Frontier*. New York: Harper & Row.

Alcaly, Roger E., and David Mermelstein, eds. 1977. *The Fiscal Crisis of American Cities*. New York: Vintage Books.

Allswang, John M. 1986. *Bosses, Machines, and Urban Voters*. Baltimore: Johns Hopkins University Press.

Anderson, Martin. 1982. "Shake-Out in Detroit: New Technology, New Problems." *Technology Review*.

Ashton, Patrick J. 1984. "Urbanization and the Dynamics of Suburban Development Under Capitalism." In William Tabb and Larry Sawers, eds., *Marxism and the Metropolis*.

Babcock, Richard F. 1982. "Houston: Unzoned, Unfettered, and Mostly Unrepentent." *Planning* 48, no. 3 (March).

Baer, William. C. 1976. "On the Death of Cities." *The Public Interest* 45 (Fall).

Banfield, Edward C. 1961. *Political Influence*. Glencoe, Ill.: Free Press.

Barlett's Guide to Commercial Banking and Corporate Finance. 1979. Santa Monica: Barlett Publishing.

Barnett, Jonathan, and Nory Miller. 1983. "Edmund Bacon: A Retrospective." *Planning* 49, no. 11.

Barron, James. 1987. "TWA Relocates 500 to Westchester." *New York Times*, June 26: B1, 3.

Beauregard, Robert A. 1985. "Politics, Ideology and Theories of Gentrification." *Journal of Urban Affairs* 7, no. 4 (Fall).

———. 1986a. "Urban Form and the Redevelopment of Central Business Districts" *Journal of Architectural and Planning Research* 3.

———. 1986b. "The Chaos and Complexity of Gentrification." In Neil Smith and Peter Williams, eds., *The Gentrification of the City*.

———. 1988a. "In the Absence of Practice: The Locality Research Debate." *Antipode* 20, no. 1 (April).

———. 1988b. "Local Politics and the Employment Relation." In Robert A. Beauregard, ed., *Economic Restructuring and Political Response*. Newbury Park, Calif.: Sage Publications.

Beauregard, Robert A., and Briavel Holcomb. 1979. "Dominant Enterprises and Acquiescent Communities." *Urbanism Past and Present* 8 (Summer).

Beck, Melinda, and Ronald Henkoff. 1980. "A City's Growing Pains." *Newsweek*, January 14, 45.

Bender, Thomas, John Mollenkopf and Ira Katznelson. eds. 1988. *Power, Culture, and Place: Essays on the History of New York City*. New York: Russell Sage Foundation.

Bennett, Larry. 1986. "When Progressives Collide: Chicago's Save Our Neighborhoods/Save our City Coalition and the Washington Administration," paper presented at the annual meetings of the Association of Collegiate Schools of Planning, Milwaukee.

Bennetts, Leslie. 1981. "The Philadelphia Story, Updated." *The New York Times Magazine*, May 10, 56–63.

Bernard, Richard M., and Bradley R. Rice, eds. 1983. *Sunbelt Cities*. Austin: University of Texas Press.

Berry, Brian J. L. 1979. *The Open Housing Question*. Cambridge, Mass.: Ballinger.

Berry, Brian J. L. and Irving Cutler. 1976. *Chicago: Transformations of an Urban System*. Cambridge, Mass.: Ballinger.

Black, J. Thomas. 1980. "The Changing Economic Role of Central Cities and Suburbs." In Arthur P. Solomon, ed., *The Prospective City*. Cambridge, Mass.: The MIT Press.

Bluestone, Barry and Bennett Harrison. 1982. *The Deindustrialization of America*. New York: Basic Books.

———. 1986. "The Great American Job Machine." Paper prepared for Joint Economic Committee, U.S. Congress, (mimeographed).

Boast, Tom, and Eugene Keilin. 1980. "Debt and Capital Management." In Charles Brecher and Raymond Horton, eds., *Setting Municipal Priorities, 1981*.

Boyer, Christine. 1983. *Dreaming the Rational City*. Cambridge, Mass.: MIT Press.

Brecher, Charles and Raymond Horton, eds. 1980. *Setting Municipal Priorities, 1981*. Montclair, N.J.: Allanheld, Osmun.

———. eds. 1985. *Setting Municipal Priorities, 1986*. New York: New York University Press.

Brenner, Stephen W., Associates. 1987. Press Release Summarizing 1986 Annual Hotel Survey and Report.

Brilliant, Eleanor. 1975. *The Urban Development Corporation*. Lexington, Mass.: D. C. Heath.

Brownlee, W. Elliot. 1979. *Dynamics of Ascent*. New York: Alfred A. Knopf.

Brune, Tom, and Eduardo Camacho. 1983. *Race and Poverty in Chicago*. Chicago: Community Renewal Society.

Buchanan, James E. 1975. *Houston: A Chronological and Documentary History*. Dobbs Ferry, N.Y.: Oceana Publications.

Buder, Stanley. 1967. *Pullman: An Experiment in Industrial Order and Community Planning, 1880–1930*. New York: Oxford University Press.

Burnham, Daniel H., and Edward H. Bennett. 1909. *Plan of Chicago*. Chicago: Commercial Club.

"A California Business Magazine Economic Report: Orange County, 1982." 1982. *California Business,* pp. 1–30.

California Department of Industrial Relations. 1973–1979. Biannual Reports. *Union Labor in California*. Sacramento: Department of Industrial Relations.

California Employment Development Department. 1982. "Plant Closure Tables" (August). Sacramento: California Employment Development Department.

———. 1982–1983. *Annual Planning Information:* Los Angeles—Long Beach SMSA and Anaheim—Santa Ana—Garden Grove SMSA. Los Angeles: Southern California Employment Data and Research.

"California's Top 500 Corporations." 1982. *California Business* (May):96–118.

Caro, Robert. 1974. *The Power Broker*. New York: Alfred A. Knopf.

Castells, Manuel. 1985. "High-Technology, Economic Restructuring, and the Urban-Regional Process in the United States." In Castells, ed., *High Technology, Space, and Society*. Beverly Hills, CA: Sage Publications.

Chafe, William H. 1986. *The Unfinished Journey*. New York: Oxford University Press.

Checkoway, Barry. 1984. "Large Builders, Federal Housing Programs, and Postwar Suburbanization." In William Tabb and Larry Sawers, eds., *Marxism and the Metropolis*.

Checkoway, Barry, and Carl V. Patton, eds. 1985. *The Metropolitan Midwest*. Urbana: University of Illinois Press.

Chicago Central Area Committee. 1973. *Chicago 21 Plan*. Chicago: Chicago Central Area Committee.

Chicago Plan Commission. 1933. *The Chicago Plan in 1933: Twenty-Five Years of Accomplishment*. Chicago: Chicago Plan Commission.

————. 1941. *Rebuilding Old Chicago*. Chicago: Chicago Plan Commission.

————. 1942a. *Building New Neighborhoods: Subdivision Standards and Design*. Chicago: Chicago Plan Commission.

————. 1942b. *Industrial and Commercial Background for Planning Chicago*. Chicago: Chicago Plan Commission.

————. 1942c. *Population Facts for Planning Chicago*. Chicago: Chicago Plan Commission.

————. 1943. *Master Plan of Residential Land Use in Chicago*. Chicago: Chicago Plan Commission.

————. 1951. *West Central Area of Chicago*. Chicago: Chicago Plan Commission.

————. 1958. *Development Plan for the Central Area of Chicago*. Chicago: Chicago Plan Commission.

————. 1966. *Basic Policies for the Comprehensive Plan of Chicago*. Chicago: Chicago Plan Commission.

City of Chicago. 1984. *Chicago Development Plan*. Chicago: City of Chicago.

City of Chicago: Advisory Committee on Linked Development. 1985. "Draft Report." City of Chicago.

City of Chicago, Mayor's Task Force on Steel and Southeast Chicago. 1986. *Final Report: Building on the Basics*. Chicago: City of Chicago.

City-wide Council for Better Housing. 1957. *Slom Clearance Committee: A Critical Survey*. New York: City-wide Council for Better Housing.

Clark, Gordon L. 1986. "The Crisis of the Midwest Auto Industry." In Allen J. Scott and Michael Storper, eds., *Production, Work, Territory*.

————. 1988. "Pittsburgh in Transition." In Robert A. Beauregard, ed., *Economic Restructuring and Political Response*. Newbury Park, Calif.: Sage Publications.

Clark, Gordon L., Meric S. Gertler, and John Whiteman. 1986. *Regional Dynamics*. Boston: Allen & Unwin.

Clark, Joseph S., and Dennis J. Clark. 1982. "Rally and Relapse, 1946–1968." In Russell F. Weigley, ed., *Philadelphia: A 300-Year History*.

Clark, Rosanne. 1984. "High Tech On the Horizon." *Houston Magazine* 55 (May).

Cohn, Gary. 1987. "Fears of Vacancies Rise Along With Skyscrapers" *The Philadelphia Inquirer*, January 19, 1-A, 4-A.

Coldwell Banker. 1981. *Los Angeles County, 1981: The Commercial Real Estate Market*. Los Angeles: Coldwell Banker: Market Research Department.

————. 1986. "Real Estate Market Bulletin: Houston." Houston: Coldwell Banker (mimeographed).

————. 1987. "National Survey of International Investment Ownership of

Major Office Buildings in 19 Largest United States' Office Markets." Boston: Coldwell Banker (mimeographed).

Colean, Miles. 1953. *Renewing Our Cities.* New York: Twentieth Century Fund.

Collier, Peter, and David Horowitz. 1976. *The Rockefellers.* New York: Holt, Rinehart, & Winston.

Commercial Club of Chicago. 1984. "Make No Little Plans: Jobs for Metropolitan Chicago. Chicago: Commercial Club of Chicago.

Cooke, Phillip. 1987. "Clinical Inference and Geographic Theory." *Antipode* 19, no. 1 (April).

Cornelius, Wayne, Leo Chavez, and Jorge Castro. 1982. "Mexican Immigrants and Southern California: A Summary of Current Knowledge." *Working Papers in U.S.–Mexican Studies* 36. San Diego: University of California.

Crown, Judith. 1986. "HEDC Sets Goals for Growth by Year 2000." *Houston Chronicle*, April 2, 1–4.

Cutler, Irving. 1982. *Chicago: Metropolis of the Mid-Continent.* Dubuque, Iowa: Kendell/Hunt Publishing.

Cybriwsky, Roman. 1978. "Social Aspects of Neighborhood Change" *Annals of the Association of American Geographers* 68 (March).

Cybriwsky, Roman, and John Western. 1982. "Revitalizing Downtowns: By Whom and for Whom?" In D. T. Herbert and R. J. Johnston, eds., *Geography and the Urban Environment.* New York: John Wiley.

Danielson, Michael N., and James W. Doig. 1982. *New York: The Politics of Urban and Regional Development.* Berkeley: University of California Press.

Davies, J. Clarence, III. 1966. *Neighborhood Groups and Urban Renewal.* New York: Columbia University Press.

Davis, Perry, ed. 1986. *Public-Private Partnerships: Improving Urban Life.* New York: The Academy of Political Science.

DeGiovanni, Frank. 1983. "Patterns of Change in Housing Market Activity in Revitalizing Neighborhoods." *Journal of the American Planning Association* 49 (Winter).

Delaware Valley Regional Planning Commission. 1984. *Land Use in the Delaware Valley.* Philadelphia: Delaware Valley Regional Planning Commission.

Donovan, Robert J. 1977. *Conflict and Crisis.* New York: W. W. Norton.

Downs, Anthony. 1985. *The Revolution in Real Estate Finance.* Washington, D.C.: The Brookings Institution.

Ehrenhalt, Samuel. 1985. "Growth in the New York City Economy—Problems and Promise." In NY Council on Economic Education, *Proceedings of the Eighteenth Annual One-Day Institute.* New York: New York City Council on Economic Education.

Eisner, Jane. 1985. "Philadelphia's Emerging Black Power Structure." *The Philadelphia Inquirer Magazine*, January 13, 11–13, 19–23.

Fainstein, Norman I. and Susan S. Fainstein. 1974. *Urban Political Movements*. Englewood Cliffs, N.J.: Prentice-Hall.

———. 1983. "New Haven: The Limits of the Local State." In Fainstein, et al., *Restructuring the City*.

———. 1984. "Governing Regimes and the Political Economy of Redevelopment in New York City." Paper presented at the annual meeting of the American Sociological Association, San Antonio, Texas, August.

———. 1987. "Economic Restructuring and the Politics of Land Use Planning in New York City," *Journal of the American Planning Association* 53, no. 2 (Spring).

———. 1988. "Governing Regimes and the Political Economy of Redevelopment, New York City: 1945–1984." In Thomas Bender, John Mollenkopf and Ira Katznelson, eds., *Power, Culture, and Place*.

Fainstein, Susan S. 1985. "The Redevelopment of 42nd Street: Clashing Viewpoints." *City Almanac* 18 (Summer).

———. et al., eds. 1983. *Restructuring the City*. New York: Longman.

———. et al., eds. 1986 ed. *Restructuring the City*. New York: Longman.

Fainstein, Susan S., and Norman I. Fainstein. 1988. "Technology, the New International Division of Labor, and Location: Continuities and Disjuntures." In Robert A. Beauregard, ed., *Economic Restructuring and Political Response*. Newbury Park, Calif.: Sage Publications.

Fainstein, Susan S., Norman I. Fainstein and P. Jefferson Armistead. 1983. "San Francisco: Urban Transformation and the Local State." In Susan S. Fainstein, et al., *Restructuring the City*.

Feagin, Joe R. 1983. *The Urban Real Estate Game*. Englewood Cliffs, NJ: Prentice-Hall.

———. 1984a. "The Role of the State in Urban Development: The Case of Houston, Texas." *Society and Space* 2.

———. 1984b. "Sunbelt Metropolis and Development Capital." In Larry Sawers and William Tabb, eds., *Sunbelt/Snowbelt*.

———. 1985a. "The Global Context of Metropolitan Growth." *American Journal of Sociology* 90, no. 6 (May).

———. 1985b. "The Social Costs of Houston's Growth." *International Journal of Urban and Regional Research* 9, no. 2 (June).

———. 1987. "The Secondary Circuit of Capital: Construction in Houston, Texas." *International Journal of Urban and Regional Research* 11, no. 2 (June).

———. 1988. *Free Enterprise City: Houston in Political-Economic Perspective*. New Brunswick, N.J.: Rutgers University Press.

Feagin, Joe R., and Beth Anne Shelton. 1985. "Community Organizing in Houston." *Community Development Journal* 20, no. 2.

Fortune. 1982a. "The Fortune Directory of the Largest U.S. Corporations." May 3, 258–286.

————. 1982b. "The 50 Largest Private Industrial Companies." May 31, 108–114.

Foundation for Architecture. 1984. *Philadelphia Architecture.* Cambridge, Mass.: The MIT Press.

Fox, Clara. 1974. "Public Programs for Housing in New York." *City Almanac* 9 (February).

Fox, Kenneth. 1986. *Metropolitan American: Urban Life and Urban Policy in the United States. 1940–1980.* Jackson: University of Mississippi Press.

Fox, Stephen. 1985. "Planning in Houston: An Historic Overview." *Cite* (Fall).

Friedland, Roger. 1983. *Power and Crisis in the City.* New York: Schocken Books.

Friedmann, John, and Goetz Wolff. 1982. "World City Formation: An Agenda for Research and Action." *International Journal of Urban and Regional Research* 6.

Fusfeld, Daniel R., and Timothy Bates. 1984. *The Political Economy of the Black Ghetto.* Carbondale, Ill.: Southern Illinois University Press.

Gans, Herbert. 1968. "The Failure of Urban Renewal." In Gans, ed., *People and Plans.* New York: Basic Books.

Garn, Harvey A. and Larry C. Ledebur. 1980. "The Economic Performance and Prospects of Cities." In Arthur P. Solomon, ed., *The Prospective City.* Cambridge: The MIT Press.

Gelfand, Mark. 1975. *A Nation of Cities.* New York: Oxford University Press.

Gerard, Karen. 1972. "Headquarters Firms in New York Fortune Directory—1971." The Chase Manhattan Bank (unpublished).

Getis, Arthur. 1985. "Energy Costs and Land Use Patterns in Metropolitan Chicago." In Barry Checkoway and Carl Patton, eds., *The Metropolitan Midwest.*

Gibson, K. D., J. Graham, and D. Shakow. 1982. "A Theoretical Approach to Capital and Labor Restructuring." Clark University: Regional Development Unit (unpublished).

Ginzberg, Eli, and George J. Vojta. 1981. "The Service Sector of the U.S. Economy." *Scientific American* 244, no. 3 (March).

Goldberger, Paul. 1987. "When Suburban Sprawl Meets Upward Mobility," *The New York Times,* July 26, Entertainment section, 30.

Goldstein, Ira, and William Yancey. 1986. "Public Housing Projects, Blacks, and Public Policy." In John M. Goering, ed., *Housing Desegregation and Federal Policy.* Chapel Hill: University of North Carolina Press.

Gordon, David. 1984. "Capitalist Development and the History of American Cities." In William Tabb and Larry Sawers, eds., *Marxism and the Metropolis.*

Greenberg, Stephanie W. 1981. "Neighborhood Change, Racial Transition, and Work Location: A Case Study of an Industrial City, 1880–1930." *Journal of Urban History,* 7, no. 3 (May).

Gregory, Derek, and John Urry. 1985. *Social Relations and Spatial Structures.* New York: St. Martin's Press.

Hall, Peter. 1985. "The Geography of the Fifth Kondratieff." In Peter Hall and Ann Markusen, eds., *Silicon Landscapes.* Boston: Allen & Unwin.

Halliday, Fred. 1983. *The Making of the Second Cold War.* London: Verso.

Harrington, Michael. 1980. *Decade of Decision.* New York: Simon and Schuster.

Harrison, Bennett. 1981. *Rationalization, Restructuring, and Industrial Reorganization in Older Regions.* Cambridge, Mass.: Harvard-MIT Joint Center for Urban Studies.

———. 1984. "Regional Restructuring and Good Business Climates." In Larry Sawers and William Tabb, eds., *Sunbelt/Snowbelt.*

Hartman, James M. 1985. "Capital Resources." In Charles Brecher and Raymond Horton, *Setting Municipal Priorities.*

Harvey, David. 1985. *The Urbanization of Capital.* Baltimore: Johns Hopkins University Press.

———. 1987. "Three Myths in Search of a Reality in Urban Studies." *Society and Space* 5, no 4 (December).

Hawley, Amos. 1971. *Urban Society.* New York: Ronald Press.

Hayden, Dolores. 1985. *Redesigning the American Dream.* New York: W. W. Norton.

Hill, Richard Child. 1983. "Crisis in the Motor City." In Susan S. Fainstein, et al., *Restructuring the City.*

Hill, Richard Child, and Joe R. Feagin. 1987. "Detroit and Houston: Two Cities in Global Perspective." In Michael P. Smith and Joe R. Feagin, eds., *The Capitalist City.* London: Basil Blackwell.

Hinds, Michael deCourcy. 1987a. "421a:A Subsidy That Costs $551 Million." *New York Times,* March 24, Sect. B, 1, 20–21.

———. 1987b. "Financing Housing for Affordability." *New York Times,* (July 12), Sect. B, 1, 20.

Hirsch, Arnold R. 1983. *Making the Second Ghetto: Race and Housing in Chicago, 1940–1960.* Cambridge: Cambridge University Press.

Hoch, Charles. 1981. *City Limits: Municipal Boundary Formation and Class*

Segregation in Los Angeles Suburbs. Los Angeles: Ph.D. dissertation, UCLA School of Architecture and Urban Planning.

Holcomb, Briavel, and Robert A. Beauregard. 1981. *Revitalizing Cities*. Washington, D.C.: Association of American Geographers.

Holli, Melvin G. 1987. *The Mayors: The Chicago Political Tradition*. Carbondale, Ill.: Southern Illinois University Press.

Holli, Melvin G., and Paul M. Green, eds. 1984. *The Making of the Mayor: Chicago 1983*. Grand Rapids, Mich.: William B. Eerdmans.

Holli, Melvin G., and Peter d'A. Jones, eds. 1984. *Ethnic Chicago*. Grand Rapids, Mich.: William B. Eerdmans.

Hooper, Carl. 1986. "City Review: Houston." *National Real Estate Investor* (June).

Hoyt, Homer. 1933. *One Hundred Years of Land Values in Chicago*. Chicago: University of Chicago Press.

Infield, Tom. 1985. "In Frankford, Signs of Hope for a Renewal." *The Philadelphia Inquirer*, August 11, 1-B, 9-B.

Jackson, Anthony. 1976. "Where the Lindsay Reorganization Worked." *New York Affairs* 5, no. 3.

Jackson, Kenneth. 1975. "Urban Deconcentration in the Nineteenth Century." In Leo F. Schnore, ed., *The New Urban History*. Princeton, N.J.: Princeton University Press.

———. 1985. *Crabgrass Frontier*. New York: Oxford University Press.

Joravsky, Ben, and Eduardo Camacho. 1987. *Race and Politics in Chicago*. Chicago: Community Renewal Society.

Judd, Dennis R. 1983. "From Cowtown to Sunbelt City." In Susan S. Fainstein, et al., *Restructuring the City*.

Kaplan, Barry J. 1983. "Houston: The Golden Buckle of the Sunbelt." In Richard M. Bernard and Bradley R. Rice, eds., *Sunbelt Cities*. Austin: University of Texas Press.

Kilbanoff, Hank. 1984. "Joe Coleman's Quiet Revolution" *The Philadelphia Inquirer Magazine*, September, 16, 24–28, 30–33.

Kleniewski, Nancy. 1984. "From Industrial to Corporate City: The Role of Urban Renewal." In William Tabb and Larry Sawers, eds., *Marxism and the Metropolis*.

———. 1986a. "Triage and Urban Planning: A Case Study of Philadelphia." *International Journal of Urban and Regional Research* 10, no. 4 (December).

———. 1986b. "Race and Urban Renewal: North Philadelphi vs. Society Hill." Paper presented at annual meeting of the Association of Collegiate Schools of Planning, Atlanta.

Kleppner, Paul. 1985. *Chicago Divided: The Making of a Black Mayor.* Dekalb, Ill.: Northern Illinois University Press.

Kushner, James. 1981. *Apartheid in America.* Frederick, Md: Associated Faculty Press.

"L.A. Leads Area, State in Plant Closures, Jobs Lost." 1982. *Los Angeles Business Journal,* January 3.

Lambert, Bruce. 1987. "New York City Lacks Spaces for Increases of the Homeless." *New York Times,* May 28, B2.

Laska, Shirley, and Daphne Spain, eds. 1980. *Back to the City.* New York: Pergamon Press.

Laventhol and Horwath. 1987. "Houston Metropolitan Area." *Urban Land Institute Market Profiles.* Houston.

Lawrence, Robert Z. 1984. *Can America Compete?* Washington, D.C.: The Brookings Institution.

Lawson, Ronald. 1983. "Origins and Evolution of a Social Movement Strategy: The Rent Strike in New York City, 1904–1980." *Urban Affairs Quarterly* 18 (March).

———. 1986. "Tenant Responses to the Urban Housing Crisis, 1970–1984." In Lawson, ed., *The Tenant Movement in New York City, 1904–1984.* New Brunswick, NJ: Rutgers University Press.

Levy, Paul, and Roman Cybriwsky. 1980. "The Hidden Dimensions of Culture and Class: Philadelphia." In Shirley Laska and Daphne Spain, eds., *Back to the City.*

Little, Arthur D., Inc. 1985. *Feasibility and Benefits of the Chicago 1992 World Fair.* Chicago: Chicago World Fair 1992 Authority.

Leon, Carol Boyd. 1982. "Occupational Winners and Losers: Who Were They During 1972–1980?" *Monthly Labor Review* (June).

"Local Aerospace Hiring Boom is Some Time Off, Experts Say." 1982. *Los Angeles Business Journal,* September 27.

Louv, Richard. 1983. "Laissez-faire Lifestyle: The Anticity Unchained." *America II.* New York: Penguin Books.

Lowe, Jeanne R. 1967. *Cities in a Race With Time.* New York: Random House.

Ludgin, Mary K., and Louis H. Masotti. 1985. *Downtown Development: Chicago, 1979–1984.* Evanston, Ill: Northwestern University, Center for Urban Affairs and Policy Research.

Lyall, Sarah. 1987. "KLM Might Move Out of Manhattan." *New York Times,* June 23, B4.

Main, Thomas J. 1986. "The Homeless Families of New York." *The Public Interest* (Fall).

Mallowe, Mike. 1984. "Welcome to the Real Estate Wars." *The Philadelphia Magazine* 75, no. 1 (January).

———. 1985. "Corruption City." *The Philadelphia Magazine* 76, no. 1 (January).

———. 1986. "Notes From the White Ghetto." *The Philadelphia Magazine* 77, no. 12 (December).

Marcuse, Peter. 1986. "Abandonment, Gentrification, and Displacement." In Neil Smith and Peter Williams, eds., *Gentrification of the City.*

Markusen, Ann. 1985a. *Profit Cycles, Oligopoly, and Regional Development.* Cambridge, Mass.: The MIT Press.

———. 1985b. *Steel and Southeast Chicago.* Evanston, Ill.: Northwestern University, Center for Urban Affairs and Policy Research.

Markusen, Ann, and Robin Bloch. 1985. "Defensive Cities: Military Spending, High Technology, and Human Settlements." In Manuel Castells, ed., *High Technology, Space, and Society.* Beverly Hills, Calif.: Sage Publications.

Martin, Douglas. 1987. "Accounting Firm Plans to Leave New York." *New York Times,* June 19, B3.

Massey, Doreen. 1984. *Spatial Divisions of Labor.* New York: Methuen.

Massey, Doreen, and Richard Meegan. 1982a. "Industrial Restructuring versus the Cities." In Larry Bourne, ed., *Internal Structure of the City.* New York: Oxford University Press.

———. 1982b. *The Anatomy of Job Loss.* New York: Methuen.

Mayer, Harold M., and Richard C. Wade. 1969. *Chicago: Growth of a Metropolis.* Chicago: University of Chicago Press.

McCain, Mark. 1987. "Competition and Costs Moving Jobs to Suburbs." *New York Times,* May 3, R45.

McClelland, Peter, and Alan Magdovitz, 1981. *Crisis in the Making: The Political Economy of New York State Since 1945.* New York: Cambridge University Press.

McClory, Robert. 1986. *The Fall of the Fair.* Chicago: Chicago 1992 Committee.

McDonald, John F. 1984. *Employment Location and Industrial Land Use in Metropolitan Chicago.* Champaign, Ill.: Stripes.

Metzger, John T., and Marc A. Weiss, 1988. "The Role of Private Lending in Neighborhood Development: The Chicago Experience." Evanston, Illinois: Center for Urban Affairs and Policy Research, Northwestern University.

Meyerson, Martin, and Edward C. Banfield. 1955. *Politics, Planning and the Public Interest.* Glencoe, Ill.: Free Press.

Mier, Robert, Kari J. Moe, and Irene Sherr. 1986. "Strategic Planning and the Pursuit of Reform, Economic Development and Equity." *Journal of the American Planning Association* 52, no. 3.

Mollenkopf, John H. 1981. "Paths Toward the Post Industrial Service City." In Robert Burchell and David Listokin eds., *Cities Under Stress*. New Brunswick, N.J.: Center for Urban Policy Research.

————. 1983. *The Contested City*. Princeton, N.J.: Princeton University Press.

————. 1988. "The Post-Industrial Transformation of the Political Order in New York City." In Thomas Bender, John Mollenkopf and Ira Katznelson, eds., *Power, Culture, and Place*.

Monchow, Helen Corbin. 1939. *Seventy Years of Real Estate: Subdividing in the Region of Chicago*. Evanston, Ill.: Northwestern University Press.

Moody, Walter D. 1919. *What of the City?* Chicago: A. C. McClurg.

Morales, Rebecca. 1983. "Undocumented Workers in Manufacturing," Boston University: Institute for Employment Policy, (mimeograph).

Morales, Rebecca, Tania Azores, Richard Purkey and Suha Ulgen. 1982. *The Use of Shift-Share Analysis in Studying the Los Angeles Economy, 1962–1977*. Report 58. Los Angeles: UCLA Graduate School of Architecture and Urban Planning.

Morris, Charles R. 1980. *The Cost of Good Intentions*. New York: W. W. Norton.

Muller, Peter, Kenneth C. Meyer, and Roman Cybriwsky. 1976. *Metropolitan Philadelphia*. Cambridge, Mass.: Ballinger Publishing.

Murgatroyd, Linda, et al. 1985. *Localities, Class, and Gender*. London: Pion.

Murray, Richard. 1980. "Politics of a Boomtown." *Dissent*. 27 (Fall).

Narvaez, Alfonso A. 1987. "Brokerage to Move 600 Jobs From New York to Jersey City." *New York Times*, July 9, B3.

National Resources Planning Board. 1940. *The Economic Effects of Federal Public Works Expenditures, 1933–1938*. Washington, D.C.: Government Printing Office.

National Training and Information Center. 1983. "Preliminary Analysis of 1982 Aggregate Home Mortgage Disclosure Act Data," (mimeograph).

Nelson, K. 1986. "Labor Demand, Labor Supply, and the Suburbanization of Low-Wage Office Work." In Allen J. Scott and Michael Storper, eds., *Production, Work, Territory*.

Netzer, Dick. 1986. "State Tax Policy and Economic Development: What Should Governors Do When Economists Tell Them Nothing Is Wrong?" *New York Affairs* 9, no. 3.

New York City Council on Economic Education (NYCCEE). 1985. *1985–86 Fact Book on the New York Metropolitan Region*. New York: New York City Council on Economic Education.

New York City Planning Commission. 1960. *The Administration of Robert F. Wagner* (mimeograph).

————. 1965. *New York City's Renewal Strategy/1965*. New York: New York City Planning Commission.

————. 1969. *Plan for New York City: Critical Issues*. Volume 1. New York: New York City Planning Commission.

New York City Public Development Corporation (NYCPDC). n.d. *1984/85 Development Projects*. New York: Public Development Corporation.

"Now Is the Time to Stop the Bleeding." 1987. *Crain's New New York Business*, May 11.

Noyelle, Thierry J. 1983. "The Rise of Advanced Services" *Journal of the American Planning Association* 49, no. 3, (Summer).

Noyelle, Thierry J., and Thomas M. Stanback, Jr. 1984. *The Economic Transformation of American Cities*. Totowa, N.J.: Rowman & Allanheld.

Olstein, Andrea. 1982. "Park Slope: The Warren Street Balancing Act." *New York Affairs* 7, no. 2.

Panuch, J. Anthony. 1960. "Mayor's Independent Survey on Housing and Urban Renewal, Building a Better New York." Final Report to Mayor Robert F. Wagner, New York.

Parson, Donald. 1982. "The Development of Redevelopment: Public Housing and Urban Renewal in Los Angeles." *International Journal of Urban and Regional Research* 6.

Peet, Richard, ed. 1987. *International Capitalism and Industrial Restructuring*. Boston: Allen & Unwin.

Peltz, Michael and Marc A. Weiss. 1984. "State and Local Government Roles in Industrial Innovation." *Journal of the American Planning Association* 50, no. 3 (Summer).

Pendzich, Sheryl Dams, Fredric Miller, and Peter Silverman. 1976. *Housing Association of Delaware Valley: A Guide to the Collection*. Philadelphia: Temple University, Urban Archives.

Perrenod, Virginia M. 1984. *Special Districts, Special Purposes*. College Station: Texas A & M Press.

Perry, Louis B., and Richard S. Perry. 1963. *A History of the Los Angeles Labor Movement, 1911–1941*. Berkeley: University of California Press.

Petshek, Kirk R. 1973. *The Challenge of Urban Reform*. Philadelphia: Temple University Press.

Philadelphia City Planning Commission. 1960. *Comprehensive Plan for City of Philadelphia*. Philadelphia: City Planning Commission.

————. 1975. "1975 Land Use File." Philadelphia: City Planning Commission (computer printout).

————. 1977. *Philadelphia Center City Office Space*. Philadelphia: City Planning Commission.

————. n.d. *Land Use in Philadelphia 1944–1954*. Philadelphia: City Planning Commission.

Philadelphia Housing Authority. n.d. *A Guide to Philadelphia's Public Housing Program*. Philadelphia: Housing Authority.

Philpott, Thomas L. 1978. *The Slum and the Ghetto: Neighborhood Deterioration and Middle-Class Reform, Chicago, 1880–1930*. New York: Oxford University Press.

Platt, Harold L. 1983. *City Building in the New South*. Philadelphia: Temple University Press.

Port Authority of New York and New Jersey. 1985. *Airport Statistics 1985*.

Pushkarev, Boris. 1980. "The Future of Manhattan." In Benjamin Hebaner, ed., *New York City's Changing Economic Base*. New York: Pica Press.

Puth, Robert C. 1982. *American Economic History*. Chicago: Dryden Press.

Rakove, Milton. 1975. *Don't Make No Waves, Don't Back No Losers: An Insider's Analysis of the Daley Machine*. Bloomington: Indiana University Press.

Real Estate Board of New York. 1952. *Office Building Construction, Manhattan 1901–1953*. New York: Real Estate Board of New York.

————. 1985a. *Rebuilding Manhattan*. New York: Real Estate Board of New York.

————. 1985b. *Fact Book 1985*. New York: Real Estate Board of New York.

Reps, John W. 1981. *The Forgotten Frontier*. Columbia: University of Missouri Press.

Robbins, Tom. 1983. "Banking the Unbankable." *City Limits* 8 (March).

Robinson, Maynard T. 1976. *Rebuilding Lower Manhattan: 1955–1974*. Ph.D. dissertation, City University of New York.

Roistacher, Elizabeth, and Emanual Tobier. 1980. "Housing Policy." In Charles Brecher and Raymond Horton, eds., *Setting Municipal Priorities, 1981*.

Rose, Damaris. 1986. "The Changing Conditions of Female Single Parenthood in Montreal's Inner City and Suburban Neighborhoods." *Urban Resources* 3, no. 2.

Rosenwaike, L. C. 1972. *Population History of New York City*. Syracuse, N.Y.: Syracuse University Press.

Royko, Mike. 1971. *Boss: Richard J. Daley of Chicago*. New York: E. P. Dutton.

Sale, Kirkpatrick. 1977. "Six Pillars of the Southern Rim." In Roger E. Alcaly and David Mermelstein, eds., *The Fiscal Crisis of American Cities*.

Salisbury, Robert H. 1964. "Urban Politics: The New Convergence of Power." *Journal of Politics* 26 (November).

Sassen-Koob, Saskia. 1986. "New York City: Economic Restructuring and Immigration." *Development and Change* 17.

Sawers, Larry. 1975. "Urban Form and the Mode of Production." *Review of Radical Political Economics* 7 (Spring).

Sawers, Larry, and William Tabb, eds. 1984. *Sunbelt/Snowbelt: Urban Development and Regional Restructuring.* New York: Oxford University Press.

Saxenian, AnnaLee. 1984. "The Urban Contradictions of Silicon Valley." In Larry Sawers and William Tabb, eds., *Sunbelt/Snowbelt.*

Sayer, Andrew. 1985. *Method in Social Science.* London: Hutchinson Publishing Group Ltd.

Schnore, Leo. 1975. *The New Urban History.* Princeton, N.J.: Princeton University Press.

Schwartz, A. R. 1982. "Stumping for State Land Use Controls, or Why I Took on the Good Ol' Boys," *Planning* 48, no. 3 (March).

Schwartz, Gail Garfield. 1979. "The Office Pattern in New York City." In P. W. Daniels, ed., *Spatial Patterns of Office Growth and Location.* New York: John Wiley.

Scott, Allen J. 1982. "Production System Dynamics and Metropolitan Development." *Annals of the American Association of Geographers* 72, no. 2.

———. 1986. "Industrialization and Urbanization: A Georgraphic Agenda." *Annals of the Association of American Geographers* 76, no. 1.

Scott, Allen J. and Michael Storper, eds. 1986. *Production, Work, Territory.* Boston: Allen & Unwin.

Scott, Mel. 1969. *American City Planning.* Berkeley: University of California Press.

Security Pacific National Bank. 1981a. *The Sixty Mile Circle: The Economy of the Greater Los Angeles Area.* Los Angeles: Security Pacific National Bank.

———. 1981b. *Statistical Supplement to the 60-Mile Circle.* Los Angeles: Security Pacific National Bank.

Shea, Thomas W., and William Grisgby. 1957. *Major Statistical Indicators of the Philadelphia Housing Market.* Philadelphia: University of Pennsylvania, Institute for Urban Studies.

Shefter, Martin. 1985. *Political Crisis/Fiscal Crisis: The Collapse and Revival of New York City.* New York: Basic Books.

Siegan, Bernard H. 1972. *Land Use Without Planning.* Lexington, Mass.: Heath-Lexington Books.

Smith, Michael Peter, and Marlene Keller. 1983. " 'Managed Growth' and the Politics of Uneven Development in New Orleans." In Susan S. Fainstein, et al., *Restructuring the City.*

Smith, Neil. 1979. "Gentrification and Capital: Practice and Ideology in Society Hill." *Antipode* 11, no. 3.

————. 1984. *Uneven Development.* New York: Basil Blackwell.

————. 1987. "Dangers of the Empirical Turn: The CURS Initiative." *Antipode* 19, no. 1 (April).

Smith, Neil, and Peter Williams, eds. 1986. *Gentrification of the City.* Boston: Allen & Unwin.

Smyth, Hedley. 1985. *Property Companies and the Construction Industry in Britain.* Cambridge: Cambridge University Press.

Soja, Edward W. 1986. "Taking Los Angeles Apart: Some Fragments of a Critical Human Geography." *Society and Space* 4, no. 3 (September).

Soja, Edward W., Allan D. Heskins, and Marco Cenzatti. 1985. "Los Angeles: Through the Kaleidoscope of Urban Restructuring." Los Angeles: University of California, Graduate School of Architecture and Urban Planning (pamphlet).

Soja, Edward, Rebecca Morales, and Goetz Wolff. 1983. "Urban Restructuring: An Analysis of Social and Spatial Change in Los Angeles" *Economic Geography* 59, no. 2 (April).

South Side Planning Board. 1983. *Development Study Report,* Chicago: Perkins & Will.

Spear, Allan H. 1967. *Black Chicago: The Making of a Negro Ghetto, 1890–1920.* Chicago: University of Chicago Press.

Squires, Gregory D., Larry Bennett, Kathleen McCourt, and Phillip Nyden. 1987. *Chicago: Race, Class, and the Response to Urban Decline.* Philadelphia: Temple University Press.

Stanback, Thomas, and Thierry Noyelle. 1982. *Cities in Transition.* Totowa, N.J.: Rowman & Allanheld.

Starr, Roger. 1970. "Housing: Prospects for New Construction." In Lyle Fitch and Annemarie Walsh, eds. *Agenda for a City.* Beverly Hills, Calif.: Sage Publications.

Stegman, Michael. 1985. *Housing in New York.* New Brunswick, N.J.: Center for Urban Policy Research.

Stein, Abraham. 1980. *The Port Authority of New York and New Jersey and the 1962 PATH-World Trade Center Project.* Ph.D. dissertation, New York University.

Sternlieb, George. 1971. "The City as Sandbox." *The Public Interest* 25 (Fall).

Sternlieb, George and James W. Hughes. 1976. *Housing and Economic Reality: New York 1976.* New Brunswick, N.J.: Center for Urban Policy Research.

————, eds. 1978. *Revitalizing the Northeast.* New Brunswick, N.J.: Center for Urban Policy Research.

Sternlieb, George, and David Listokin. 1985. "Housing." In Charles Brecher and Raymond Horton, eds., *Setting Municipal Priorities*.

Stone, Clarence N. 1981. "Complexity and the Changing Character of Executive Leadership: An Interpretation of the Lindsay Administration in New York City." Paper presented at the annual meeting of the American Political Science Association.

Stone, Clarence N., and Heywood T. Sanders, eds., 1987. *The Politics of Urban Development*. Lawrence: University Press of Kansas.

Storper, Michael, and Richard Walker. 1983. "The Spatial Division of Labor: Labor and the Location of Industries." In William Tabb and Larry Sawers, eds., *Marxism and the Metropolis*.

"Strange Recovery of 1983–1984." 1985. *Monthly Review* 37, no. 5.

Tabb, William K. 1982. *The Long Default*. New York: Monthly Review.

————. 1984. "Urban Development and Regional Restructuring." In Larry Sawers and William Tabb, eds., *Sunbelt/Snowbelt*.

————, and Larry Sawers, eds., 1984. *Marxism and the Metropolis*. New York: Oxford University Press.

Tait, Adam, ed. 1976. *The Bulletin Almanac*. Philadelphia: The Journal Bulletin.

Teaford, Jon. 1986. *The Twentieth-Century City*. Baltimore: Johns Hopkins University Press.

Temporary Commission on City Finances. 1976. "The Effects of Taxation on Manufacturing in New York City." Ninth Interim Report to the Mayor.

————. 1977. "Economic and Demographic Trends in New York City: The Outlook for the Future." Thirteenth Interim Report to the Mayor.

Tilly, Charles. 1984. *Big Structures, Large Processes, Huge Comparisons*. New York: Russell Sage Foundation.

Tinkcom, Margaret B. 1982. "Depression and War, 1929–1946." In Russell F. Weigley, ed., *Philadelphia: A 300-Year History*.

Tobier, Emanuel. 1984. *The Changing Face of Poverty*. New York: Community Service Society of New York.

Tobier, Emanuel, and Walter Stafford. 1985. "People and Income." In Charles Brecher and Raymond Horton, eds., *Setting Municipal Priorities, 1986*.

Travis, Dempsey J. 1987. *An Autobiogaphy of Black Politics*. Chicago: Urban Research Press.

Urban Land Institute. 1969. "Philadelphia." *Nine Cities—The Anatomy of Downtown Renewal*. Washington, D.C.: The Urban Land Institute.

U.S. Bureau of the Census. 1975. *Historical Statistics of the United States, Colonial Times to 1970*. Washington, D.C.: Government Printing Office.

———. 1986. *State and Metropolitan Area Data Book, 1986.* Washington, D.C.: Government Printing Office.

U.S. Bureau of Labor Statistics (USBLS). 1973–1982. *Analysis of Work Stoppages.* Bulletins 1777, 1813, 1877, 1902, 1940, 1996, 2066, 2092, 2120. Washington, D.C.: Government Printing Office.

———. 1974–1986. "Establishment Data, State and Area Employment." *Employment and Earnings.* May 1974; September 1977; May 1980; May 1981; May 1986.

———. 1979. *Employment, Hours and Earnings, States and Areas, 1939–1978.* Bulletin 1370-13. Washington, D.C.: Government Printing Office.

———. 1982. *Supplement to Employment, Hours and Earnings, States and Areas, 1980–82.* Bulletin 1270-16. Washington, D.C.: Government Printing Office.

———. 1983. *Handbook of Labor Statistics.* Washington, D.C.: Government Printing Office.

U.S. Congress, House Committee on Ways and Means, Subcommittee on Trade. 1976. *Special Duty Treatment or Repeal of Articles Assembled or Fabricated Abroad.* Hearings, 94th Congress, 2nd Session, March 24 and 25.

U.S. Department of Commerce. 1966. *Housing Construction Statistics 1889 to 1964.* Washington, D.C.: Department of Commerce.

———. 1987. *Statistical Abstract of the United States.* Washington, D.C.: Government Printing Office.

U.S. Department of Housing and Urban Development. 1974. *Urban Renewal Directory.*

U.S. Department of Labor. 1976. *Employment and Training Report of the President.* Washington, D.C.: Government Printing Office.

U.S. Housing and Home Finance Agency. 1962. *Urban Renewal Project Characteristics.*

Urry, John. 1986. "Locality Research: The Case of Lancaster." *Regional Studies* 20, no. 3 (June).

Vigman, Fred K. 1955. *Crisis of the Cities.* Washington, D.C.: Public Affairs Press.

Vogel, David. 1986. "The Future of New York City as a Financial Center: An International Perspective." Paper prepared for the Workshop on Metropolitan Dominance, Committee on New York City, Social Science Research Council, New York.

Vrazo, Fawn. 1987. "Houston's Weather Is Fine, If You Don't Go Out." *The Philadelphia Inquirer,* July 25, 1-A, 4-A.

Wachter, Michael L., and Susan M. Wachter., eds. 1981. *Toward a New U.S. Industrial Policy?* Philadelphia: University of Pennsylvania Press.

Walker, Richard A. 1978. "The Transformation of Urban Structure in the Nineteenth Century and the Beginnings of Suburbanization." In K. Cox, ed. *Urbanization and Conflict in Market Societies*. Chicago: Maaroufa Press.

Walker, Robert A. 1950. *The Planning Function in Urban Government*. Chicago: University of Chicago Press.

Warner, Sam Bass. 1962. *Streetcar Suburbs*. Cambridge, Mass.: Harvard University Press.

———. 1968a. *The Private City*. Philadelphia: The University of Pennsylvania Press.

———. 1968b. "If All the World Were Philadelphia: A Scaffolding for Urban History, 1774–1930." *The American Historical Review* 74, no. 1 (October).

———. 1972. *The Urban Wilderness*. New York: Harper & Row.

Webber, M. J. 1986. "Regional Production and the Production of Regions." In Allen J. Scott and Michael Storper, eds., *Production, Work, Territory*.

Weigley, Russell F., ed. 1982. *Philadelphia: A 300-Year History*. New York: W. W. Norton & Company.

Weiler, Conrad. 1980. "The Neighborhood's Role in Optimizing Reinvestment: Philadelphia." In Shirley Laska and Daphne Spain, eds., *Back to the City*.

Weiss, Marc A. 1981. "The Origins and Legacy of Urban Renewal." In Pierre Clavel, et al., eds., *Urban and Regional Planning in an Age of Austerity*. New York: Pergamon.

———. 1987. *The Rise of the Community Builders*. New York: Columbia University Press.

Weiss, Marc A., and John T. Metzger. 1987. "Technology Development, Neighborhood Planning, and Negotiated Partnerships," *Journal of the American Planning Association* 53, no. 4.

———. 1988. "Neighborhood Lending Agreements: Negotiating and Financing Community Development." Cambridge, Mass.: Lincoln Institute of Land Policy.

Western Economic Research Company. 1982a. *1980 All Races and Ethnic Data by ZIP Codes in California, Los Angeles 5 County Area*. Sherman Oaks: Western Economic Research Company.

———. 1982b. *Hi-Rise Office Buildings in the Los Angeles-Orange County Region*. Sherman Oaks: Western Economic Research Company.

———. 1982c. *Manufacturing Statistics in the Los Angeles 5 County Area*. Sherman Oaks: Western Economic Research Company.

Williams, Raymond. 1977. *Marxism and Literature*. New York: Oxford University Press.

Winkleman, Michael. 1980. "Why the Apple Beckons: The Return of Tourism." *New York Affairs* 6, no. 2.

Wiseman, Carter. 1981. "Power to the People." *New York* 14 (October 4).

Wolin, Merle Linda, 1981. "Sweatshops: Undercover in the Garment Industry." *The Los Angeles Herald Examiner*, 16-part series beginning January 14.

Wolinsky, Leo C. 1982. "Latinos Assail Illegal Alien Study." *Los Angeles Times*,
April 9, Sect. II, 1, 4.

Writers' Program, WPA. 1942. *Houston: A History and Guide*. Houston: The
Anson Jones Press. Republ. 1975: St. Clair Shores, Mich.: Scholarly Press.

Wurman, Richard S., and John A. Gallery. 1972. *Man-Made Philadelphia*.
Cambridge, Mass.: The MIT Press.

Yates, Douglas. 1974. "The Urban Jigsaw Puzzle: New York Under Lindsay."
New York Affairs 2 (Winter).

Zukin, Sharon. 1982. *Loft Living*. Baltimore: Johns Hopkins University Press.

Zukin, Sharon, and Gilda Zwerman. 1985. "Housing the Working Poor: A
Historical View of Jews and Blacks in Brownsville." *New York Affairs* 8, no. 2.

Zunz, Olivier. 1982. *The Changing Face of Inequality*. Chicago: The University
of Chicago Press.

Index

agriculture, 7, 8, 25
aerospace, xiii, xix, 92, 97–103
aircraft industry, xiv, 12, 92–93, 111
Alinsky, Saul, 143
Allen, John and Augustus, 155, 184
anti-cities, 247
architects, 77
Asia, 68
Atlanta, 93
automobile, 4, 5, 18
automotive industry, xix, 12, 28–29,
    33, 38, 39, 91, 103

Bacon, Edmund, 205, 209
Baltimore, 4, 22, 72, 222
banks, 112
barrio, 108, 116
Beame, Abraham, 64, 81
Bedford-Stuyvesant, 26, 59
bedroom suburbs, 16
Beirut, xvii
Bennett, Edward, 125
Berlin airlift, 26
Better Philadelphia Exposition, 204
Beverly Hills, 256
Bilandic, Michael, 137
blacks, 7; and central cities, 16, 25;
    migration, 7, 8, 18, 25, 126; see
    Negroes
blight, 9, 21, 22, 126, 134
boosterism, 154

Boston, xvi, xviii, 4, 6, 22, 35, 36, 39,
    40, 72, 106, 153, 171, 172, 180,
    204, 243
Bronx, 47, 50, 51, 61, 70, 80, 254
Brooklyn, 26, 47, 50, 51, 66, 70, 80
Brown and Root, 167
Buffalo, 20
building activity, 5, 10, 34; housing,
    7; see individual cities
built environment, xiv, xv, xviii, 7,
    160–161, 197, 268, 273; see in-
    dividual cities
Burnham, Daniel, 124, 125, 127,
    133, 252
Byrne, Jane, 137

capital mobility, 32, 36, 89, 264
capitalism, xv, 88–91, 117–119,
    153–155, 189–192, 240, 242,
    247, 273
Cadillac-Fairview, 262
Camden (NJ), 7, 12, 256
Camp Kilmer, 12
Carribean, 68
Carter, Jimmy, 32, 221
CBD redevelopment, 22–23; see ur-
    ban renewal
central city, 16, 18, 20, 23, 24, 25,
    164
Charlestown (Indiana), 10
Cherry Hill (New Jersey), 20, 226,
    250

Chester (Pennsylvania), 7
Chicago, xiii, xviii, xix, 4, 8, 19, 21, 22, 25, 32, 36, 43, 114, 153, 172, 239, 243–273; airport, 131; blight, 126; central business district, 133; commercial development, 136, 138; community groups, 128, 143–146; decline, 126; economic development, 146–147; employment, 123–124, 133; ethnic groups, 131; fire, 123; housing, 134–135; inner zone, 140–147; land use, 143; manufacturing, 129–132, 140–141; neighborhoods, 126, 136, 142–143; population, 123–124, 131; suburban ring, 147–151; transportation, 125–126; urban planning, 124, 151; urban redevelopment, 126
City Beautiful movement, 125
city biographies, xv
city studies, see locality studies
Civil War, 129
Civilian Conservation Corps, 9
Clark, Joseph S., 205, 209, 214
Cleveland, 4, 34, 35, 180
Cold War, xvii, 27
Commercial Club, 125, 127, 128, 133
commercial development, 23, 42; see individual cities
Community Development Block Grants, 74, 138, 221
community groups, 265–268
Community Reinvestment Act, 145
company towns, xiv
comparative analysis, 239–242
comparative trajectories, 241–242
computers, xiii, 40
Conservation of Human Resources Project, xvi
construction investment (see building activity)

corporations, 75–76, 104, 116, 263–265
Cross-Bronx Expressway, 54
Cuban Missile Crisis, 26

Daley, Richard, 127, 134, 135, 137
Dallas, xvii, xviii, 39, 93
decentralization, 18, 19, 268, 270
decline; urban, 21–24, 34; regional, 24–26
deconcentration, 268
deindustrialization, xvi, 63–67, 89
Denver, xv, 114
Depression, 3, 7–9, 21, 92, 123–124, 199
Detroit, xv, xvii, 4, 10, 25, 34, 88, 96, 106, 171, 180, 204
developers, 41, 179, 261–263
developing countries, 27–29
Dilworth, Richardson, 205, 214
discrimination, racial, 25
disorganic development, xvi
Dominican Republic, 26

economic development, 40; see individual cities
Economic Recovery and Tax Act of 1981, 36
economic restructuring, see restructuring, economic
electronics, xvii, 28, 29, 97–103, 106
Emergency Financial Control Board, 65
employment, 30, 87; military, 15; shifts, 31; see individual cities
enterprise zones, 97
Europe, 2, 4, 9, 10, 14, 28, 202
Evanston (Illinois), 20
exports, 4
extra-territorial jurisdiction, 161–162, 249

federal expenditures, 11, 32; military, 4, 9, 11, 27, 38, 39, 114

finance, xix, 51, 68, 77
fiscal crisis, 34, 63–67, 90
foreign investment, 112, 118
French Quarter, 153
functionalism, 240

Galveston, 155, 157–158
Gary (Indiana), xiv
gentrification, xv, 41–42, 79, 137, 210, 224–225, 227, 253–254, 269–270; see individual cities
ghetto, 25, 26, 108
Ghiradelli Square, 222
G. I. Bill, 207
global city, xiv, 46, 67, 88, 112, 116, 118
government intervention, 258–261
Great Lakes, 7
greenbelt towns, 9
Greenway Plaza, 175
Greenwich (Connecticut), 19
Grenada, 38

Hamilton, Ontario, xvii
Harborplace, 222
Harlem, 53, 80, 252
Hartford, 39, 264
high technology, xiv, 39–40, 79, 90, 96, 97–103, 115
highway construction, 5, 16, 174–175, 214–215; see individual cities
Hines, Gerald D., 86, 262
historical layering, 232–233
Hollywood, 256
Home Mortgage Disclosure Act, 145
Hong Kong, 97
housing, public, 22, 92; new units, 37; see individual cities
Houston, xiii, xv, xviii, xix, 4, 8, 9, 10, 11, 12, 16, 20, 21, 22, 33, 35, 39, 43, 88, 93, 96, 100, 106, 153–194, 239, 243–273; annexation, 161–163, 170, 184; built environment, 160; CBD, 174–177; city building, 157; developers, 179, 186; economic base, 103–106, 155–160, 163–166; economic development, 188; employment, 167–171, 187–189; government, 166–167; ideology, 189–190; income, 171, 172; industrial development, 177; intergovernmental relations, 185–186; land use, 159, 173–174, 184; local politics, 181–185; manufacturing, 157, 158, 165, 171–172; migrants, 163; minorities, 172; NASA, 185–186; nodes, 179–180; office development, 175; oil companies, 158; oil industry, 159, 187; population, 157, 160, 161; property development, 153, 186–187; residential development, 158, 178; retail development, 175–177; spatial patterns, 171–180; sprawl, 172; transportation, 161, 174; zoning, 173
Hoyt, Homer, 126, 127

ideology, 18–19, 154, 189–190
immigration, 7, 68, 111; see individual cities
In rem properties, 74–75
Independence Mall, 205, 207, 209
Indianapolis, 25
industrial development, 263; structure, 243
industrial policy, 35
industrial restructuring; see restructuring, industrial
international restructuring, xvii, 2, 28–29; competition, 29, 38
internationalization, 89, 104

Jacob Javits Convention Center, 72
Japan, 10, 14, 28–29, 112, 115, 164, 262

Johnson, Lyndon Baines, 30, 166
Johnson Spacecraft Center, 166,
    186, 259

K-Marting, 106
Kennedy, Robert, 59
King, Jr., Martin Luther, 143
King of Prussia (Pennsylvania), 42,
    226, 250
Koch, Edward, 74, 81, 83
Korean conflict, 21, 27, 28, 92

labor market, 15; see employment
labor market segmentation, 90
LaGuardia, Fiorello, 52, 55
Latin America, 68
Lebanon, xvii, 38
Liberty Bell, 210
Lincoln Center, 57, 78, 258
Lindquist, Warren, 61
Lindsay, John, 57, 58–59, 62, 64, 80
locality studies, xv, xviii, 241
Loop, The, 133, 134
Los Angeles, xiii, xiv, xviii, 4, 5, 10,
    11, 12, 16, 21, 22, 27, 32, 33–
    34, 35, 36, 43, 87–122, 187,
    239, 243–273; aerospace indus-
    try, 93, 96; annexation, 91;
    banks, 112; built environment,
    92; deindustrialization, 103–
    107; economic activities, 91;
    employment, 93; financial con-
    trol functions, 112–117; high
    technology, 96, 97–103, 115;
    immigrants, 107–112; manufac-
    turing employment, 87, 92, 94–
    97; office buildings, 87, 114; of-
    fice construction, 114–117;
    population, 91; residential seg-
    regation, 108; service sector,
    110; undocumented workers,
    110–112; unionization, 103
Louisville, 10

Mahwah (New Jersey), 32
Manhattan, 45, 47, 50, 55, 58, 69,
    70, 73, 88, 114, 264
manufacturing sector, 9, 12–14, 25,
    28, 30, 33, 89; see individual
    cities
manufacturing-service shift, xiv, xv–
    xvi, 40–41
Marshall, George C., 14
Marshall Plan, 14–15, 26
Marx, Karl, 87
maquiladoras, 108
mediating agents, xiv, 257–268
Mellons, 79
Memphis, 21
metropolitanization, 4, 20–21, 33
Mexico, 29, 111, 164
Miami, 93
Middle East, 28
Midwest, xiii, xvii, 11, 32, 33, 185
Milwaukee, 20
military excursions, 38
military spending (see federal ex-
    penditures)
Minneapolis, 264
Mitchell-Lama, 60, 66
Model Cities program, 59, 81, 180
mortgage insurance, federal, 16,
    185, 200
Moses, Robert, 22, 54–58, 78, 80, 82
multinational corporations, xvii
Municipal Assistance Corporation,
    65
municipal utility districts, 178
Munoz, George, 139

National Aeronautics and Space Ad-
    ministration (NASA), xix, 166,
    169, 177, 185–186, 259
Negroes, 16, 26; see blacks
Negro removal, 57
Nehemiah Plan, 74
Neighborhood Housing Services, 74,
    175

New Brunswick (NJ), 264
New Deal, 8–9, 159, 185
New England, xvi, xviii, 32
New Haven, xv, 22, 24
New Orleans, xv, 39, 153
New York, xiii, xiv, xv, xviii, xix, 4,
19, 21, 22, 24, 36, 39, 43, 45–
85, 112, 187, 204, 222, 239,
243–273; architectural firms,
77; built environment, 49, 53–
54, 69–75; community groups,
83–84; construction investment,
47, 66; corporations, 75; developers, 76; development agencies, 71–73, 78; development
policy, 50; economic base, 76;
employment, 47–50, 63–64, 69,
70; ethnic groups, 48, 52–53;
fiscal crisis, 63–65; government,
80–82; housing, 49, 50, 66–67,
73–75, 77–78; immigrants, 68;
income, 64; infrastructure, 65–
66, 73; jobs, 48–49; labor
unions, 82; Manhattan business
district, 45, 60–62; manufacturing, 52; mayors (see actual
names); office construction, 47,
48; outer boroughs, 45, 68–69;
population, 46; public housing,
59–60; real estate development,
71–73; real estate values, 69, 71;
service industry, 68, 77; tax
abatements, 67, 72–73, 78;
transportation, 51, 54–55; urban renewal, 55–59
Newark, xvii, 180, 256
New York State Urban Development
Corporation, 62, 64, 66, 71
Newport News, 10
Nixon, Richard, 60
nodal development, 174–177, 179,
180, 192, 249, 250, 268, 271;
see outer cities
North, 7, 8

North Philadelphia, 26, 211–212,
229, 234
Northeast, xiii, 11, 32, 33, 35, 38–
39, 185
Northfield (Illinois), 20

Oakland, 22
office development, 41, 42, 250–
252, 262, 269–270; see individual cities
O'Hare International Airport, 42,
128, 131, 148, 250
oil companies, xix, 114, 158
oil exploration, xiii, 39
Olympia and York, 72
OPEC, 28, 29, 36
outer boroughs, 71
outer cities, 100
Ozarks, 7

Pawtucket (Rhode Island), xiv
particularities of place, xiv, xviii, 271
Penn, William, 195
Penn's hat, 195–197, 235–236
peripheralization, 97, 107–108
Persian Gulf, 38
Philadelphia, xiii, xviii, xix, 4, 7, 8,
10, 18, 19, 21, 22, 24, 34, 36,
40, 43, 177, 195–238, 239, 243-
273; built environment, 197,
198, 208, 209; construction,
200–202; demolition, 211; employment, 200–204, 213, 220,
226–227; ethnic groups, 197;
gentrification, 210, 224–225,
227, 230, 231; housing, 199,
207; industrial development,
212–213; infrastructure, 203;
local government, 222–223; local politics, 204–207, 223; manufacturing, 200; mayors, see actual names; office development,
214, 225–227, 230; peripheral
development, 216–219, 227–

229; physical deterioration, 199–204, 219–220, 229–230; population, 220; property values, 204; public housing, 211–212, 230; retail development, 213–214, 219–220, 221–222; restaurant renaissance, 225; social distress, 229–230; suburban growth, 200, 208; transportation development, 214–216, 222; urban redevelopment, 205–207, 209–214, 221–224; urban renewal, 210–211; waterfront development, 222

Phoenix, xvii, 33, 35

Pittsburgh, xviii, 4, 22, 32, 34, 35, 39, 40, 78, 79

plant closings, xvi, 32, 89, 104–106, 121f., 140

polarization, 252, 268, 270–272

population, 3, 5; migration, 10, 163; shifts, 10, 34; trends, 17; see individual cities

Portland (Oregon), xviii, 172

Port Authority of New York and New Jersey, 53, 54, 62, 78

Portman, John, 72

Post Oaks (Texas), 175, 177, 179

post-industrial; cities, 248; society, 35

postwar period, 3

priority areas, 18

product cycles, xvi

property values, 10, 21; see individual cities

Providence (RI), xviii

Puerto Rico, 29

Queens (New York), 47, 51, 53

Reagan, Ronald, 32, 36, 38, 56, 97, 221

real estate values; see property values

recession of 1973–1975, 28, 30, 63, 93, 224, 230

redevelopment, urban, 21–24; see also urban renewal, and individual cities

regional development, 2; resurgence, 38–40; shifts, xvii, 33–35, 163

Regional Plan Association, 79

Research Triangle, 40

residential polarization, 270

restructuring; economic, xiv, xviii, 35, 42, 75–76, 234, 241, 268–273; industrial, xvi, 33, 106, 233, 242–248; international, xvi; sectoral, xiv, 3, 28; spatial, 1; urban, xv, 89–91, 117

retail development, 42, 213–214, 253, 254, 262–263; see individual cities

River Oaks (Texas), 158, 160, 179–180

Rizzo, Frank, 214

Rockefellers, 54, 57, 60, 79; David, 61, 74, 79; Nelson, 60, 62

Roosevelt administration, 8, 167

Rouse, James, 72, 223, 262

rural areas, 7, 8, 11

Rural Resettlement Administration, 9

Rustbelt, xviii, 33, 163

Salisbury, Robert, 80

San Antonio, 33

San Diego, 10, 12, 27, 33, 35

San Francisco, xv, xvi, 21, 22, 78, 79, 114, 187, 222

St. Louis, 4, 8

Saudi Arabia, 164

Sawyer, Eugene, 138, 147

Scarsdale (New York), 19

Schaumberg (Illinois), 19

Scranton (Pennsylvania), 25

Seattle, 10, 11, 12, 27

service economy, 41, 76–77, 90, 234; see individual cities
shipping, 14, 34, 53–54, 155, 158, 164, 244
shipbuilding, 5, 7, 12
Silicon Valley, xv, 40, 96, 106
Singapore, 88, 97
skyscraper, 5
slums, viii, 18, 22, 23
Snowbelt, 33–34, 88, 257
Society Hill, 22, 210, 224, 232, 258
Soho, 66–67, 253
South, xiii, 1, 7, 8, 11, 33, 35, 39
South Korea, 29
South Side, 26
South Street Seaport, 72, 222, 252
Southwest, 36
Soviet Union, 27, 29
space, xiv, xvi, xvii, 153–155, 190–192
spatial scale, 2; switching, 231–232; transformations, xiv, 6, 248–257, 268–273
sprawl, 11, 180, 192, 249, 268, 271–272
stagflation, 30
Standard Metropolitan Statistical Areas, 20
state-managed capitalism, 92
Staten Island (New York), 20, 47, 53, 55, 70
steel industry, 18, 28, 39, 140–141
stock market crash, 7
Strategic Defense Initiative, 38, 166
suburbanization, 3, 4, 5, 15–20, 21, 34, 92, 250, 256, 269; ideology, 18, 19; see individual cities
Sunbelt, xviii, 33–34, 35, 88, 96, 257

Tacoma, 10
Taiwan, xviii, 29
Tampa, 34, 36
Tate, James H. J., 214
Texas Medical Center, 169, 186

textile industry, xiii, xvi, 12, 29, 32, 39
Third World, 88, 107, 110, 117
Tilly, Charles, 240
time, 153, 190–192
Times Square, 72
tourism, 34
Trammell Crow, 262
Triborough Bridge and Tunnel Authority, 55, 56
Truman, Harry, 14

uneven development, xiii
urban decline, 3, 21–24
Urban Development Action Grant, 72, 214, 221, 222
urban hierarchy, xviii, 1, 4, 8, 20–21, 35, 43, 45, 195, 239, 243, 251, 273
urban renewal, 22, 210–211; revitalization, 40–43; spatial impacts, 23; see individual cities

Vietnam, 2, 21, 28, 29, 30, 32

Wagner, Robert, 58, 56, 83
Walker, Richard A., 3
war, 21, 26–27, 28, 30
war economy, 4, 10
War on Poverty, 143
Washington, Harold, 128, 137–139, 144, 147, 151, 267
Washington, D.C., 4, 21, 22
Washington Heights (New York), 53
waterfront development, 42, 252–253
Watts, 26, 93
West, xiii, 1, 11, 12, 33, 36
West Germany, 28, 29
Wheeling (West Virginia), 25
Whitmire, Kathryn, 184
Wichita, 10
Willow Grove (Michigan), 10
Wilmington (Delaware), 7, 264
World Trade Center, 62, 78
World War I, 3, 4, 129, 131, 158

World War II, 2, 3, 9–10, 21, 27, 89,
    129, 159, 185, 198, 231, 251,
    254, 256

Youngstown (Ohio), 32

Zeckendorf, William, 61
zone of reinvestment, 254–256
zone of transition, 126, 249, 253–
    256

Contributors

Robert A. Beauregard is Associate Professor of Urban Planning and Policy Development, Rutgers University, editor of *Economic Restructuring and Political Response* (1988), and coauthor of *Revitalizing Cities* (1981).

Norman I. Fainstein is Dean of Liberal Arts and Sciences and Professor of Sociology, Baruch College, City University of New York, and coauthor of *Restructuring the City* (1986).

Susan S. Fainstein is Professor of Urban Planning and Policy Development, Rutgers University, and coauthor of *Restructuring the City* (1986).

Joe R. Feagin is Professor of Sociology, University of Texas at Austin, coeditor of *The Capitalist City* (1987), and author of *The Urban Real Estate Game* (1983).

John T. Metzger is on the staff of the Oakland Planning and Development Corporation in Pittsburgh.

Rebecca Morales is Assistant Professor of Urban Planning, University of California at Los Angeles.

Alex Schwartz is a Ph.D. candidate in the Department of Urban Planning and Policy Development, Rutgers University.

Edward Soja is Professor of Urban Planning and Geography, College of Architecture and Planning, University of California at Los Angeles and author of *Post-Modern Geographies* (1988).

Marc A. Weiss is a Research Fellow in the Center for Real Estate Development at the Massachusetts Institute of Technology, Cambridge, Massachusetts, and author of *The Rise of the Community Builders* (1987).

Geotz Wolff is a consultant to the Economic Roundtable of Los Angeles County.